DIGITAL BUSINESS

Also by Ray Hammond

The On-Line Handbook
Computers and Your Child
The Writer and the Word-Processor
The Musician and the Micro

Digital Business

Surviving and Thriving in an On-Line World

Ray Hammond

CORONET BOOKS
Hodder and Stoughton

To David Evans

Copyright © Ray Hammond 1996

The right of Ray Hammond to be identified as the Author of the Work has been asserted by him in accordance with the Copyright, Designs and Patents Act 1988.

First published in Great Britain in 1996 by Hodder & Stoughton
First published in paperback in 1997 by Hodder & Stoughton
A division of Hodder Headline PLC

A Coronet paperback

10 9 8 7 6 5 4 3 2 1

All rights reserved. No part of this publication may be reproduced, stored in a retrieval system, or transmitted, in any form or by any means without the prior written permission of the publisher, nor be otherwise circulated in any form of binding or cover other than that in which it is published and without similar condition being imposed on the subsequent purchaser.

A CIP catalogue record for this title is
available from the British Library

ISBN 0 340 66660 9

Typeset by Hewer Text Composition Services, Edinburgh
Printed and bound in Great Britain by
Caledonian International Book Manufacturing Ltd, Glasgow

Hodder and Stoughton
A Division of Hodder Headline PLC
338 Euston Road
London NW1 3BH

ACKNOWLEDGEMENTS

This book was conceived in Mendocino, born in San Francisco and raised in London. Many readers were kind enough to provide guidance and advice but in particular I must thank Professor David Brialsford for his criticisms, Liz Hammond for her careful correction of my manuscript and Simon Prosser for his knowledgeable editing. I also thank Maria whose patience, encouragement and love reduced the pain of the process.

CONTENTS

Preface	ix
Introduction	1
1 Something happened	5
2 Becoming digital	28
3 It took us by surprise	42
4 Publishing pioneers	60
5 Retailing pioneers	71
6 Adapt or die	91
7 The information economy	105
8 Advertising, selling and sponsorship on the net	126
9 Management is communication	136
10 Money goes digital	147
11 Does business need privacy?	163
12 Anonymous digital cash	180
13 Life on the Net	189
14 Net futures	207
15 Companions on Earth	223

Appendix 1: What is the Internet?	243
Appendix 2: Frequently asked questions about business on the Internet	255
Appendix 3: The demographics of today's net users	261
Afterword	284
Index	291

PREFACE: ABOUT THIS BOOK

This is a new type of book. It is complete in itself, but there is a companion edition available to you on the Internet. The on-line version provides updates to ensure that the very latest information about this rapidly developing subject is always available. The electronic version will also link you directly to the people, companies, organisations and resources to which I refer in this book.

Digital Business is a book for business people, not computer experts, and although you may not yet have an Internet connection, I think it probable that you will want one in the near future.

The address of this book's companion edition on the World-Wide Web is 'http://www.hammond.co.uk'. (This term and others like it are explained in plain language in the book.)

As well as a constantly up-dated and revised main text, the site also offers new stories, observations and comments which I have made since this book was printed.

A 'feedback loop' exists on the Internet which has already put me in touch with many readers who have made suggestions, pointed out errors and are helping me develop this work as business on the Net matures. If you 'visit' the site, you will also be able to see what others have had to say about this book and the ideas it contains. Above all, I would like to hear your reactions and ideas about how the Net will affect business.

The *Digital Business* site has been developed by Kevin Kolb and John Nugent of the Web design consultancy HyperMedia (www.hypermedia.co.uk) and I am grateful for their creative flair and skilled Internet marketing efforts.

INTRODUCTION

> The linking of computers around the world is going to have far reaching effects, and the spread of knowledge, the interchange of ideas and the dissemination of information are going to produce a revolution in our society.
>
> This statement has been trotted out so often that most readers are, understandably, immune to the import of the words, but the moment you go on-line you feel as though the revolution has sprung down the telephone line and invaded your own room.
>
> You will know what the wired world is like and you will begin to understand the implications! You become a pioneer of the information age, experiencing with awe the power of linked computers which the next generation will take for granted.
>
> The On-Line Handbook, Ray Hammond, 1984

It is now over 15 years since I fell in love with the power of on-line communication. I became obsessed with the potential of public computer networks and persuaded my agent and publishers that a mass-market paperback was needed on the subject.

For the jacket of *The On-Line Handbook* Fontana asked me to prepare some copy for bullet-points. It appeared as follows:

Going on-line is the best thing you can do with your computer. You can:

- *go shopping on line*
- *book plane flights, order books, play games, join education projects*
- *scan the world's magazines for articles of interest*
- *meet new friends through computer message boards*
- *do your banking from home*
- *read the latest theatre and cinema reviews*
- *search the world's libraries for books on any subject*
- *get free programs for downloading*

Sounds familiar, doesn't it? In the book I described the world's data networks and their potential for commercial exploitation, and I explained how to get dial-up access to computers all around the world for the cost of a local telephone call.

Twelve years on, the subject has not only come of age but we are in the midst of what has become a network revolution. It is proving to be so profound, so much more powerful than I imagined, that after a break of ten years from writing books, I have been drawn back to the discipline to see whether the implications for business turned out to be as I imagined in 1984, or if the future has arrived and presented quite a different set of circumstances and opportunities.

Although it took longer than I thought for on-line communication to reach critical mass I now realise that the implications are going to be far more profound than even I suggested. The old axiom was proved: 'change always takes longer to arrive than predicted but it is almost always more profound'.

We are entering a new era in which our economies and social fabric will be shaped by the world's public and private data networks. Three events combine to create this massive change: the first is the proliferation of personal computers in the office and in the home and their arrival in TVs and telephones; the second is the collapse in the real cost of making an international phone call (and in data communications generally); the third is an almost-global desire by governments to deregulate and privatise the telecommunications companies.

National economic boundaries, already blurred by the use of private financial dealing networks, will cease to exist in a few years and companies (and countries), large and small, will have to rethink how they conduct their business. This presents an astonishing challenge for managers and is the principal reason behind the flurry of mergers, acquisitions and take-overs in the entertainment, media and telecommunications industries over the last few years.

In addition, and perhaps most importantly, this new on-line economy will offer myriad new opportunities for small entrepreneurs and large companies that are nimble enough to think in an entrepreneurial way.

I have enjoyed being around long enough to see how my predictions from a long-ago age have turned out and, because there is an on-line companion to this book, I am able to look forward to acknowledging my successes and my failures for you the moment we have the answers.

Ray Hammond,
London/San Francisco
January 1996

SOMETHING HAPPENED

1

This lack of time in which to deal with a huge change occurring simultaneously across the face of the globe is a problem that will occur again and again as successive waves of new technology arrive.

The time gap between sensing a need for change and society's ability to implement it, is a subject to which I will return later.

Computers and Your Child, Ray Hammond, 1982

Something has happened that will change every aspect of business life. It had been developing quietly and unobtrusively for nearly 30 years, but at the peak of the blistering summer of 1995, an event occurred which will come to be regarded as symbolising the moment when the personal computer age ended and the network revolution began.

The event was an initial public offering of stock in Netscape Communications, Inc., a Californian start-up company making software for the Internet.* It was 16 months old and had never made a profit. The story has already been told countless times and has passed into business folklore: shares that were originally planned to open on the electronic *NASDAQ* market (The US stock exchange) at £8/$13 dollars hit £50/$75 in one day and, as if a schism in time occurred, Microsoft's grip on the future of world computing was instantly loosened and we suddenly understood that the future belongs to the network, not to the desktop PC.

We are only now beginning to realise the full implications of such a change. For *everybody* in business, not just those in technology companies or in the media, it marks a turning point in the way our economies will work which cannot be ignored. We have to change the way we *think* about doing business.

On its own a personal computer is fairly dumb, but place it on a network where it joins a community of millions of other machines, give the network distributed software to create a collaborative environment, and the solitary PC becomes part of a neural network of intelligence which, collectively, has stunning power. As we are now discovering, and as I attempt to illustrate and penetrate in this book, such networks will change almost every aspect of business and the societies within which it creates wealth.

---

* If you're not really sure what the Internet is, or if some of the terms used here are new to you, you'll find a plain language description and an explanation of how to get connected in Appendix 1. You'll find answers to a number of frequently asked questions about business on the Net in Appendix 2.

WHAT I MEAN BY 'THE NET'

This book is about all forms of on-line computer communication, but most people will think first of the Internet. I think this collective noun provides a good model for the concept of a 'low-cost, public access network' and from here on I will use the term 'the Net' to include the Internet and all other concepts of public network including America On-Line, Europe On-Line, Prodigy, The Microsoft Network, and so on. It makes no difference whether you go on-line with your PC, your TV, your PDA (Personal Digital Assistant), your cell-phone or your wrist communicator. All these will connect you in time and you won't give the means of access a thought.

And what of the much-vaunted 'information superhighway?' Well, an early version of it is here now and it's called the Internet. Politicians around the world love to talk of concepts such as highway building, but the fact is that our existing telecoms infrastructure will rapidly evolve and over the next few years high-capacity lines will reach most offices, schools, hospitals, libraries, factories and homes. The metaphor of 'a highway' is poor because we can increase the capacity of an existing line without replacing it whilst at the same time we can reduce the size (without affecting the content) of the 'vehicles'.

NO PASSING FAD

The first thing to realise is that the Net and on-line communication is no passing fad or craze. It is not like the hula-hoop, CB radio, skateboard or Rubik's Cube. It is something that will be a permanent and growing part of our lives, both at work and at home. The quotations from *The On-Line Handbook* and some of my other books which appear are intended to underline just how long the 'overnight success' of the Net has taken. It is in fact an ongoing, irresistible process with a substantial history.

By now you will have become tired of the 'hype' surrounding the Internet and its supposed blessings, evils and astonishing growth. Journalists have already started to exploit our fear of the unknown by inventing Internet-backlash and horror stories suggesting that the planet's population will suddenly turn its back on the world's first global computer network.

When I started to write books about the (then) new phenomenon of personal computers, interviewers, friends and the audiences I met at my lectures would challenge my enthusiasm for this low-cost slice of machine intelligence. Their arguments would usually suggest that I was the slavish victim of fad or fashion. They were wrong – all of them. More wrong than even I could have imagined at the time, and I was a convinced believer. The personal computer has changed every aspect of business and educational life and it is now (finally) starting to have the impact on home and leisure lifestyles that I mistakenly predicted for the mid-1980s.

The importance of the Net, including all its so-called sub-sections such as the World-Wide Web (the network formed by computers which communicate in multimedia form) has, if anything, been under-hyped.

It is impossible to over-estimate how much the Net (and its descendants and variants, whatever they are or will be called) will alter life in the developed countries of the world. Many people believe that the pace of change which has developed since low-cost computing arrived in the late 1970s is already too great, too frightening and too difficult for humans to cope with. This may be true, as suggested in the quotation at the start of this chapter, but it is unstoppable. Every aspect of life will change for all but the most severely socially disadvantaged in the industrialised countries and within a decade, they too will start to feel its effect.

It is not enough to think about individuals or individual computers linking via the networks. Humans don't have to be involved. Building will talk to building, conurbation to conurbation, dairy farm to milk silo, and video camera to police database.

All such communications – which can include commands, requests, exchanges, controls, profit, loss, love and death – occur at close to the speed of light. The full ramifications cannot yet be discerned. Those who witnessed the birth of electricity could not imagine that the technology would lead to the development of the skyscraper – it was only electric lifts which made such architectural dreams possible. As I shall discuss later, the digital networks will, in their turn, change our architecture and our cities and much more besides.

I am certain that the development of global computer networks will be the governing factor which shapes life on this planet in the first half of the twenty-first century. It will prove to be more important than any advance in a single scientific pursuit such as space travel, medicine or flight because it links and enhances *all* technologies. Perhaps only the achievement of a new energy supply – for example, the realisation of practical and safe cold fusion or a breakthrough in battery technology – could be more important.

I suspect that later in the century our attention will focus on the convergence of the bio-technologies and machine intelligence, but that is a subject to be kept for another book. For the moment, we are concerned with two things: how existing businesses can survive and thrive in the on-line economy, and how entrepreneurs can take advantage of the many new opportunities in cyberspace.

A NEW ECONOMIC MODEL ARRIVES

The Netscape share offering on 9 August 1995 had an importance greater than can be attributed solely to the company's innovative software. Through the insight and understanding of its 24-year-old co-founder, Marc Andreessen, Netscape had used the Internet to distribute millions of free copies of its software, the Netscape Navigator, and thus grab the dominant market position in Internet clients, originally called 'browsers'. (A client is the 'base' from which users 'point-and-click' their way around the World-Wide Web, the multimedia publishing sites on the Internet.) Netscape may have consolidated this position by the time you read this or it may have yielded ground to others, but it makes no difference to the scale of what has happened or the scope of change which follows in its wake.

What was particularly important about the feeding frenzy for Netscape stock was that the market suddenly grasped the concept of the Internet as a permanent new communications channel, one which will be bigger than all the others put together, a channel which will be, at one and the same time, *global*, *personal*, *interactive*, *low cost* and *forever-growing*. However, even these words undersell what the Internet and its successors will become and the impact it will have on business and social structures.

The market's astonishing reaction to Netscape symbolises a fundamental shift in understanding (and acceptance of) the future. This change in thinking occurred in what might be called a 'group-collaborative' way. Observers of the high-tech markets seemed to act in unison, as if with shared knowledge but without observable consultation – rather in the way a shoal of fish seems to change direction by automatic group consent. This notion of a group consciousness arising out of many independent parts is a subject which has been most eloquently expressed by Kevin Kelly in his seminal 1994 book, *Out of Control*. This has direct relevance to the sudden rise in popularity of the Internet and the semi-compulsive hold it has for most users. There seems almost to be a state of group consciousness growing within the Net.

In short, something extraordinary has happened and it will prove to be very significant.

BETTER THAN A GOLD RUSH?

The opportunities presented by the sudden explosion of the Internet and other information networks are often described as a modern-day gold rush. This is reasonably appropriate as I imagine feelings were as high in San Francisco in 1849 as they are today – and as they were in the early days of commercial television broadcasting.

But I firmly believe the Internet and all other networks

pouring information into our lives through PC, TV, cell-phone and cable offer an even better opportunity than the gold rush, or an early licence in commercial TV. I think the Net offers the best opportunity that most business people are likely to find in a working lifetime. In later chapters I will provide examples of some successful new businesses which have been founded on-line and suggest some ideas which haven't been tried yet.

For existing corporations, however, the emergence of digital, low-cost, global networks presents extreme challenges as well as significant opportunities. Many companies exist solely in order to exploit a physical means of communications or distribution – record companies, newspaper distributors and TV stations, for example – and the coming years will present immense problems. Many other types of 'content-based' activities – movies, books, music, even art – have a cost-base and pricing structure from a pre-network age and managers must turn existing ideas on their head in order to survive. The new opportunities far outweigh the problems, however, and it is clear that managers now more than ever have a clear reason to follow management guru Tom Peters's advice that they destroy and reconstruct their corporations, in this case specifically to accommodate and exploit the new medium.

A BUSINESS PLAN FOR THE FUTURE

This book is intended to be a business plan for the future. If you are not thoroughly familiar with the Net, I urge you to go on-line *yourself* and spend real time looking at the immense amount of marketing, sales and communication material that already exists there. Start with the World-Wide Web.

Do not delegate this task to an IT department, do not peer at somebody else's screen for a few minutes and think you have got the flavour of it. Do this personally *and for hours on end*, at home, however busy your schedule. Your investment will be repaid. All economic growth is fuelled by technological development and the growth created by the networking of the world's millions of computers will be staggering. The more you understand the Net, the more you will be able to participate in the growth.

Because you have been motivated to pick up this book I can assume you are aware that something extraordinary is happening. You are right, but if this book had a million pages instead of a few hundred, I would still be unable to convince you as effectively as will a few hours on-line. **Please make the call to get connected now**. Any of the many Internet magazines will give you the right local numbers and if you can get a connection in the next couple of weeks you can see for yourself how fast the ideas in this book are developing. I've inserted this paragraph after much of this book was finished and I have had to revise my text constantly as ideas I only imagined popped up as realities in a matter of days, weeks or months later. Let's explore the ideas for business opportunities on the Internet together, as you are beginning to get a taste of the things I describe.

THE ON-LINE COMPANION TO THIS BOOK

Unipalm/Pipex plc Netscape Communications has been kind enough to allow my publishers to include a disk inside the back cover of this book which carries an evaluation copy of Netscape Navigator with which to access the World-Wide Web. This piece of software is configured to take you straight to the Web site for this book and I have added all of my most important 'bookmarks' (pre-stored Web addresses) so that you are able to visit related sites of interest just by selecting site names from a pull-down menu. To avoid tedium when I discuss a topic in this book such as 'car rentals' or 'hotel reservations,' I will not list all of the resources I have discovered, but I have included them in my bookmarks file. This will allow you to explore many more on-line sites than I have been able to mention in print. Details of how to load and use the software are contained in a 'read me' file on the disk.

If you prefer to use an alternative piece of software (or if you already have a copy of Navigator loaded on your machine) type < http://www.hammond.co.uk > into the 'open location' window in your platform for the World-Wide Web (as it appears between the < > brackets) and you will arrive at the 'Digital Business' site on the Net.

You will have noticed already that quite a few references in this book are underlined. This is not to emphasise the importance of such text, it indicates that in the on-line version of this book these are 'hyperlinks' on which you will be able to click and be transported around the Net directly to the company, person or resource to which I refer for the very latest information. (For reading ease, the words which contain links on-line appear with a lightly-dotted underline, instead of a solid underline.)

This book is intended to be complete in itself, but where once a book could only offer footnotes and printed references about sources, I am delighted to be the author of the first business book in the world to provide an on-line companion version with references, up-dates and explanations in hyperlink form. What's more, you'll find the on-line sections relatively small and easy to read and use on-line, or to down-load on to your own computer disk for later use in the office or at home.

I think this book is a primitive version of what all factual books will become in the future. If you are reading a travel book and wish to know more about Sicily, you will merely touch the word to be transported to a site offering videos, maps, visitor information, fares and, perhaps, even Mediterranean breezes (I'm not mad, see chapter 13.). We will get an electronic version of paper which will be light, easily-transportable, durable and readable. My guess is that this technology will become practical and affordable between 2005 and 2010.

You will also find that the on-line version of *Digital Business* is constantly up-dated and the hyperlinks checked and refreshed. There will also be a substantial amount of new material added each month, while out-dated material is culled. On the Net, this book becomes a live and growing information resource for on-line business, and one to which I hope you will contribute. As it grows it will contain far more than could any single book and future editions of the printed book will act as a point of reference for the on-line resource.

After you have spent a little time on-line yourself, you will understand why it is important that your business should have a fast Internet connection. Domestic-type dial-up connections for

£10/$15 a month are currently slow and most businesses in the future will put in fast connections (usually called 'leased lines') to the Internet as automatically as they now install telephone or fax lines. Don't hesitate to connect your entire office networks to the Net via your leased line. It is easy to make your internal computer networks secure and completely safe from those much-written-about 'hackers' and viruses supposedly lurking all over the public networks waiting to trash your records or steal your commercial secrets. There are many books about on-line security available and there is now a reasonable supply of experienced security consultants available to help.

Even to consider not connecting your internal computer networks to the Internet is as crazy as installing a telephone switchboard and not allowing it to make or receive external calls.

Every member of staff who qualifies for a PC (and I presume and hope that that's almost everybody) also needs full Internet connection. Please accept that your colleagues and staff will surf the Internet and the World-Wide Web at first, apparently wasting many hours seeing what they can find and how it works. Don't complain. They're training themselves so they will be of much more use to you and your organisation in the future. The use of email, Web commerce, Internet video-conferencing and communication will slash the cost of doing business in the future and the companies that train their staff to use these powerful low-cost technologies will gain enormous competitive advantage.

In particular, managers *must* understand that organisations have to train themselves and their staff so they can eliminate all physical departments and activities which can be more effectively rendered *virtually*. Because humans can be incredibly resistant to change, this will take real effort and the speed with which your organisation adapts to change will serve as a success indicator for the future. If I was your company's bank manager or financial advisor, this benchmark would be high on my check-list.

New companies which will compete with your business will not be founded in office buildings or business parks. They will require little expensive real-estate, no particular geographic location and, over time, this trend will weaken the gravity pull of large cities (another reason why the global property markets will continue to suffer slow growth). Their directors, managers and staff will reduce their commuting time and travel costs, and they will hire information-processing staff (accounts clerks, order-processing departments, marketing staff and so on) in areas (or countries) where wages are lowest. They will meet in virtual boardrooms, sell products and services in virtual markets and confer across all national and time-zone boundaries. They will meet physically for social and team-building exercises, but the epidemic of today's endless company meetings will be converted into video-conferencing and semi-social relationship-building exercises. I don't underestimate the strong desire people share to be together, in a social group. This will not diminish. What will happen is that we will become even more conscious about what is quality time and what is not and we will increasingly restrict our social interaction to the former.

If you think competition is tougher today than it was in the 1970s or 1980s, you'll be in shock when we enter the hyper-competitive twenty-first century. How is your existing business, with its legacy of property leases, company cars, staff restaurants and inner-city wages going to compete with tomorrow's virtual organisation?

Well, first you can make some immediate use of the Net to

begin to cut operating costs, most importantly in the area of corporate communications. Another way in which you can gain immediate benefit is by reaching tiny niche markets which have previously been uneconomic to target (see chapter 4).

An additional factor that will affect many businesses, and which is the direct result of the move to the network economy, will be the emerging concept of 'perfect information' being available to buyers. Using 'software robots' on the Net (primitive forms are already travelling the Internet today), consumers and business purchasers will be able to ensure that for any given product or service, the specifications, price and terms at which they are buying will be the best available in the world (see chapter 5). The competitive pressures are going to be immense.

FINDING THE NEW WORLD

I practise what I preach and, as I am writing this book, I am changing my own businesses into semi-virtual organisations, while also developing several new business ventures in cyberspace. In addition I advise existing international businesses, institutions and labour unions in their struggle to come to terms with the need to reshape their organisations.

For entrepreneurs and companies who are considering new ventures on the Net, the opportunities are so numerous that another analogy which occurs is to imagine a country like North America being discovered, and a fully developed and rich population agreeing to emigrate to the new land over the space of a decade. Every store has to be built again, every service reinvented, every idea has to be retailored and millions of new ideas and twists will work.

Ideas imported directly from 'the old country' will not work without adaptation. New ideas and new ways of selling, trading and creating will be far more effective.

But to return to the gold rush analogy: about 50 million people currently use the Net. By the year 2000 I suggest this will be close to 400 million. This is my estimate based on my understanding of the potential of on-line communication and the way I see its growth developing.

(If you want to have some fun visit The Great Internet Population Predictor on-line. This tongue-in-cheek Net site has been put up by a Los Angeles computer programmer and is based on the 1995 growth figures which showed that the size of the World-Wide Web was doubling every 53 days. When I last visited in December 1995, I tapped in the date '31 December 1999' and the little program came back with the suggestion that on this day there will be 470,000,000 users.)

I repeat that by the Net I mean all forms of low-cost national or global public digital networks accessible through a variety of terminals, including the wireless networks which are now sending packets of data to our TVs, cell-phones and cars. As long as these networks are compatible and we can send information seamlessly across them, they are an expansion of the Net. Most estimates from official sources (for example, governments, Internet agencies, market commentators) suggest that Internet users will number around 200 million at the turn of the century. I think this is a serious underestimate.

All forms of computer network providers are reporting spectacular growth. America On-Line saw its revenues triple from £263/$394 million in 1995 to £660/$1 billion in

1996. The Internet Society has been reporting growth on the World-Wide Web of 120 per cent a year and Forrester Research of Cambridge, Massachusetts – one of the most respected consultancies on new media – has forecast that from a figure of around £200/$300 million in 1995, the value of the Internet-specific market will be £20/$30 billion by the year 2000.

One particularly illustrious commentator on the digital age is even more bullish than I am about the growth of Internet usage. Professor Nicholas Negroponte, Director of the Media Lab at the Massachusetts Institute of Technology says: 'I am convinced that by the year 2005 Americans will spend more hours on the Internet (or whatever it is called) than watching network television.'

Whichever forecast of network growth turns out to be accurate, there is, indeed, a new super-power in formation. It is called 'cyberspace' and this term describes the electronic territory inside computer memories and in the data networks which connect them.

What do we know about the settlers of cyberspace? Well, first of all they're young: the latest demographic is 17–45 with an average income of above £33,000/$50,000 (25 per cent over £53,000/$80,000). So they're a wonderful target group for any entrepreneur. The bad news (today) is that they're 66 per cent male, although this figure is expected to reduce to 60 per cent by the year 2000.

In 1849, excitement about gold in the Sierra Nevada was so intense that dozens of ships would arrive in San Francisco harbour each day. As soon as they had anchored, the hordes of immigrant prospectors would vanish into the hinterland (after pausing for their necessary supplies) and, in many cases, they would be quickly followed by the ships' crews, the officers and, in the later months, by the captains. The ships were left to rot and by 1850 the harbour was crowded with hulks.

So who got rich? A few prospectors made it, William Randolph Hearst's father for one. There were several hundred people who made fortunes, thousands more who made something and hundreds of thousands more who made nothing and died along the trails. Because gold mining was a finite, *physical*, opportunity it soon became exhausted.

This is not the case with cyberspace. The opportunity is infinite or as large as the population of the wired planet.*

One of the main activities during the gold rush was to stake out claims, and this is what is now happening in cyberspace. Companies are rushing to create an Internet presence before their businesses are really ready to start trading or publishing, anxious lest someone else should claim the territory or the idea. I believe this is a mistaken view. The 'land' available in cyberspace is infinite and it is important you don't go on-line with your business until your concept is well-developed.

I find it informative and fun to consider who, apart from the few lucky or super-tough prospectors, made money from the gold rush. Well, Levi-Strauss didn't do too badly, nor did the companies who sold the picks, pots, pans and mules to those who were buying a dream; likewise those who set up boarding houses (and the rooms above them!).

(An interesting sidebar to the Gold Rush/Hearst allusion is provided by William Randolph Hearst III's decision to quit as editor/publisher of the San Francisco Examiner in the middle of 1995. Will Hearst is the great-grandson of George Hearst who,

* (The growth opportunities in telecommunications are staggering. Four billion people in the world do not have a telephone. Fifty per cent of the world's population have never made a phone call. Fifty million people are currently on waiting lists for telephones.)

as a 30-year-old bachelor, arrived in San Francisco in May 1850 from a small plantation in Missouri to try his luck with the other prospectors. It took George nine years to strike it rich – and then it was silver, not gold, at first – before he was able to return home a rich man to marry the woman who would bear him William Randolph Hearst.

The grandson of the yellow press publishing magnate (and heir to the fortune) has now joined Kleiner, Perkins Caulfield & Byers, a venture capital firm in Menlo Park, Silicon Valley, where he is responsible for investing in high-technology companies providing software, services and information on the Internet. The firm was the first and only venture capital organisation to provide funds for a stake in Netscape's start-up (their block of shares has a paper value of over £400/$600 million at the time of writing) and one of the first investments he managed was a private placement of shares in Netscape Communications in late spring 1995. In this placement companies including The Hearst Corporation, Knight-Ridder, Times Mirror and Adobe Systems together acquired 11 per cent of Netscape's equity in the form of preferred stock. Will Hearst has also become the founding CEO of @home, a company I will discuss in chapter 7.)

I was living in San Francisco in the 1970s and I was caught up in the excitement surrounding the birth of the personal computer and the astonishing growth of Apple Computer. 'Something' happened *then* and it became the fastest growing company ever when it made its first public offering in 1980. As the primary enabling force of the personal computer revolution, that was entirely appropriate.

At the time, the synergy and enthusiasm shared by Steve Jobs and Steve Wozniak, Apple Computer's founders, reminded me of the golden period for The Beatles when 'something happened' and Lennon and McCartney reached an unrivalled creative zenith in popular music. (I was a frequent visitor to Apple Corps at the time.)

Nearly 20 years later visitors could sense a similar excitement in the air at the derivatively named computer company's offices on Bandley Drive in Cupertino – it could almost be tasted. In both varieties of Apple very young, incredibly gifted men were driven to a pinnacle of creative achievement. In both cases the combination of global popularity, huge amounts of money and a burning desire to achieve something worthy of an already achieved fame, created hothouse conditions for the achievement of almost superhuman performance.

I suggest a straight event dateline can be drawn between the 'happenings' of 1966 ('Sergeant Pepper'), 1984 (the Apple Macintosh) and 1995 (the World-Wide Web and the Netscape Navigator).

In 1966 the first post-Second-World-War generation asserted its demographic superiority and reoriented Western society towards the young. The Beatles weren't responsible for this, but their music was a catalyst and they became the symbol of the revolution.

In 1984 personal computers became powerful enough to start to work the way we wanted (instead of the other way round). Jobs and Wozniak didn't invent user-friendly computers but they understood the need and their achievement in providing the Macintosh set the standard for all computers which followed.

In 1995 the global networks reached critical mass and the Netscape Navigator provided the means for us to use it. Marc Andreessen didn't invent the Internet, nor the protocols which enabled 'point and click' navigation, but had imagined and created the first ever 'browser' for the World-Wide Web in 1993 whilst a 22-year-old student working for £4/$6 an hour at the National Center for Supercomputing Applications. Two years later he, and five out of six of his original programming team at NCSA, followed this with a superb piece of commercial software called Netscape Navigator. Now called a platform, rather than a browser, this software allows users to look at and access text, pictures, movies and sound on the networks.

In the future our platforms will become virtual versions of ourselves, travelling through the electronic networks. They are already our eyes and ears in cyberspace and they carry our address books and post-boxes. In the future we will attach representations of other important parts of our beings to them: they will carry our wallets, our watches, our diaries and calendars, our desks, our filing and phones, just as our PCs handle many of these functions today.

They may have to carry compulsory identity cards (although I suspect not) and they will include special modules, or agents, which will carry out specific tasks such as watching a range of stock prices around the world or looking for goods which become available below a certain price.

In the fullness of time these vehicles will gain more physical senses and will provide simulations of touch and taste. They will also carry several three-dimensional representations of our physical self: one will be a model of our actual body (for trying on virtual representations of clothes, jewellery, make-up, and so on), others may be representations of ourselves as we would like others to see us – psychologists will adore this feature and I suspect virtual-self modelling will become a hugely valuable therapeutic tool in the future. I shall leave the discussion of automated psychotherapy sites on the Internet until chapter 15.

You will see why the humble platform has such importance: its descendants will become our virtual selves!

(During the personal computer revolution one of the most frequently asked questions was: which computer platform should I use? It may seem as if the equivalent question during the network revolution is 'which software platform should I use?' but it has now become clear that we, the human beings, can be seen as the ultimate platform.)

The creative forces which led Marc Andreessen to create the Netscape Navigator were as powerful as those surrounding Lennon and McCartney, and Jobs and Wozniak. As fast as Andreesen hacked out new code, hundreds of thousands of devoted disciples down-loaded his work and the Internet exploded. The computers that publish multimedia information which can be read by browsers and platforms are said to form a network called the World-Wide Web (a term explained in Appendix 1) although they sit on the same Internet networks as ordinary computers which publish only in text.

The speed of growth of the number of computers on the World-Wide Web as Andreessen created his successive versions of browser software illustrates the explosive hot-house conditions in which he was working. The following data were compiled in mid-1995 by Network Wizards, a respected authority on Internet usage and growth. Today's data can be found at their site.

Date	Number of 'host' computers publishing on the Internet
Apr 93	1,486,000
Jul 93	1,776,000
Oct 93	2,056,000

Jan 94	2,217,000
Jul 94	3,212,000
Oct 94	3,864,000
Jan 95	4,852,000
Jul 95	6,642,000

The events of August 1985 marked a consensual agreement that a second watershed in the information revolution had occurred and Netscape took over the mantle of being the fastest-growing company ever from Apple Computer. If you're interested you can monitor the paper wealth of the Netscape billionaires and millionaires at a mischievous site on the Web called InterMania where the movement of Netscape shares (and those of many other Net companies) is tracked and the results converted into the personal holdings of the main shareholders.

On one day in December 1995 Netscape's shares were at £91.50/$137.25 and the result was as follows:

Shareholder	No of shares	Paper value
Jim Clark, Chairman	9,720,000	$1,334,070,000
Jim Barksdale, CEO	4,200,000	$576,450,000
Kleiner Perkins/Doerr, VC	4,400,000	$603,900,000
Marc Andreessen, CTO	1,000,000	$137,250,000
John Warnock	888,890	$122,000,152
Adobe Systems	888,890	$122,000,152
TCI Netscape Holdings	888,890	$122,000,152
Times Mirror	888,890	$122,000,152
Jim Sha, VP Apps	600,000	$82,350,000
Knight-Ridder	444,446	$61,000,213
The Hearst Corporation	444,446	$61,000,213
IDG, Holdings	444,438	$60,999,115

Conway Rulon, VP Sales	400,000	$54,900,000
Richard Schell, VP Eng.	400,000	$54,900,000

Within four months Netscape company had been valued at £4/$64 billion, overtaking the total value placed on Apple Computer, Inc. after 19 years of product development growth. Everybody accepts that such a valuation is likely to be a temporary abberation. The word from within Netscape is that the directors are extremely uncomfortable with such wild valuation because of the expectations which follow. But such a dramatic vote with the commodity which matters most of all, money, tells us that something has happened and we must rethink what we do and how we go about it.

BECOMING DIGITAL 2

You may need information for any number of reasons: for fun, for an examination, for profit, for a book, for personal advantage or to give to someone else. Whatever the reason, once you've discovered on-line searching you'll realize that we've finally solved the problem that has been weighing us down for most of this century: how to access information.

Now, information, so long static and locked up in old papers, books, magazines and broadcast tapes, can be sorted, ordered, filed and retrieved so as to produce the right information, at the right time, in an instant.

Out of selective information comes knowledge and out of knowledge comes fulfilment and joy.'

The On-Line Handbook, Ray Hammond, 1984

The explosion of the Net as our new communications medium has to be seen in a wider context for its importance to be fully understood. Our global civilisations are in transition from an information age that was physical to an information age that is digital. I shall provide two examples to illustrate that the leap between these ages is bigger than the leap from the hunter-gatherer age to the agricultural age, from the agricultural to the industrial and from the industrial to the physical information age. Some people consider it is the greatest leap so far in the development of civilisation on the planet but I think the development of machine intelligence itself deserves that award.

Physically presented information exists in the printed, spoken or displayed work (thought, idea, picture, sound, graphic, music, and so on, sometimes expressed as an electric analogue). When we pick up an airline timetable at the airport or the bookstore, we have physical (or atomic) information in our hands. We can do nothing but consume it.

At some central point, humans have gathered the information and written it down. They have then asked a company to smear that information in the form of ink on to a product made from dead trees and then pay for trucks to carry the many tons of static, unalterable information in the form of atoms (ink on paper), to its many different points of distribution.

In the digital age, the information stays as computer bits, and only becomes physical when a consumer wants to carry that information around in the organic world. Thus an airline timetable will be published in *bits* (as computer information on the Net) and users can get their information on-line without the need to haul dead trees around the world's roads. Information published in this way can be updated minute by minute and users may print local hard copy (converting the information to atoms) when they wish. The traditional information publishing paradigm has been reversed: until now we have printed then distributed; in the future we will distribute then print. This book exploits both techniques, as many will do in the future.

My second example uses a book in a library as a metaphor, 'borrowed' from Nicholas Negroponte. If you have borrowed this book from a library, nobody else will be able to read it until you return it. But if you have accessed parts of this book electronically, the copy you are reading on-line, or the copy you have 'borrowed' by downloading it to your computer, leaves the original intact on the library's 'shelves'. An infinite additional number of people may borrow the same book without depriving anybody else of the chance to read it. In fact, if you are accessing this on-line, several other people may be visiting this site now reading the same section as you. This difference is profound and will affect every aspect of business life.

This change is so important that we must all ask how our businesses can start to deal in bits rather than atoms. Only those companies that can start to deal in bits, will be able to stay competitive in the rapidly approaching digital age.

Let me provide three examples.

It may seem obvious that food, the most basic human commodity of all, cannot be converted into 'bits'. Of course it can't, but the way it is *sold* can and this has already started to happen. As I write, a number of new companies are starting to experiment with creating 'virtual supermarkets' on the World-Wide Web. These are not to be confused with the 'shop window' type sites which existing supermarket chains such as Sainsbury, Tesco and Safeway have published. In the new virtual supermarkets, shoppers can view pictures of the items for sale, compare prices and order on-line. Using a World-Wide Web browser with 3D capability (which will be given away) visitors can 'walk' around the store, look at products on the shelves and add them to their 'shopping basket.' A 'till' display in a small window records the running total spent. The company delivers the products the same day. I can't publish the Net addresses at the time of this printing as they are still experimental but I will include them in the on-line version of this book.

While I think these virtual reality stores are a novelty, I doubt whether they represent the future of shopping. It really isn't necessary to walk through virtual aisles to select goods. I'm sure we will select what we want to buy from lists and we will only want to see a picture of a product when we're unsure. This is the approach taken by the first supermarket to come up on the Web, the Smart-Food Coop. This virtual supermarket was developed by former students of the Massachusetts Institute of Technology and it delivers orders in the Greater Boston area.

The cost structure of the transaction changes profoundly. The two largest costs for the major supermarkets are distribution and the retail outlets. As buyers start to order electronically so supermarkets can lower the cost of distribution and retailing. A warehouse for goods on an industrial estate is far less expensive than prestige premises in a good residential area and this more than pays for home-delivery charges.

You would be right to think that most shoppers prefer to select fresh food personally, but an analysis of the way most people shop reveals that fresh food accounts for less than 10 per cent of purchases from supermarkets. We may well see boutique shops reappearing to provide fresh food to personal shoppers with virtual supermarkets delivering all other necessities.

The Smart-Coop delivers all types of supermarket produce, fresh meat and vegetables included, for prices well below those of traditional supermarkets in North America. If I were living in Boston I could buy pre-seasoned fillet steak au poivre for £4.30/$6.50 a pound and Colombian ground coffee for £6.59/$9.89 per 36oz (as I write).

This is wonderful news for the consumer – the time saved on the big weekly supermarket trip could be reallocated to leisure, family time or work – and it is great news for the environment. A van making 20 home deliveries in an afternoon is infinitely preferable to 20 shoppers getting in their cars to visit supermarkets.

But the giant supermarket chains of the physical world do not believe on-line supermarkets constitute a significant threat to their future. They suggest that home-deliveries would require an extra 10 per cent on prices and say that few shoppers will pay this. They remind us that when the delivery van calls at the allotted time 30 per cent of customers are out or unavailable and that frozen or perishable goods can't, therefore, be included. I understand that from their viewpoint both these objections seem valid. Large supermarket chains already buy food much more cheaply than any other organisation could and they find it hard to imagine that a new structure could get prices lower or persuade customers to provide some sort of suitable accommodation for deliveries.

I also fully accept that for a section of the population, shopping is as much a social interaction as a pure provision-gathering activity. Despite these objections, I still contend that a significant proportion of supermarket-type provisions will be sold via the Net within the next five years and it will probably not be the legacy corporations behind the existing supermarket chains who take this new market. In chapter 5, I provide an outline business plan for such a project.

My second example of a physical business being transformed into a virtual operation is drawn from one of my own activities. Presenting and organising conferences may also seem, at first sight, to be an essentially physical activity, during which a few hundred human beings gather to learn from each other's experiences. In developing my business I have placed great emphasis on allowing time for people to network (I now use the word in its human sense) with other like-minded people although I know that my delegates will only come if the speakers have got a valuable message or the information on offer is very timely.

But for many delegates, conversations held in the bar after a conference day are often the element that, in the end, makes attendance worth while. A conference is a modern 'market square' where a group (not forged together by geographic location around a town but brought together by an industry or a discipline) come to learn, to do deals, exchange gossip, meet each other and so develop their place within the group. This may seem like the most intensely human of activities and one that will not change because of the digital revolution. Yet it will, and if I do not alter my business model to accommodate this, my conferences will lose ground to others.

So I now deliver my conferences in bits as well as atoms. We present 'virtual conferences' alongside our physical conferences and virtual delegates are able to access and take part in our events through audio and video conferencing over the Internet. For the communications cost of a local phone call, delegates all over the world can 'attend', and see and hear the speakers. This takes a very fast connection to the Net and cannot yet provide high-quality pictures, but for important speakers or sessions, this does allow delegates to attend without having to move their atoms around the planet. Virtual delegates don't get to chat personally to other delegates in the bar after the event, but they are able to contribute both to the conference via a live on-line 'chat' session and, of course, possess an instant electronic recording of the event.

I think that despite the experience being less sociable when conducted virtually, this aspect of conferencing will grow. One reason for it is the apparent lack of development in the world's aeroplane industry since the late 1960s. The astonishingly rapid developments in information technology have led us to expect that technology as a whole should develop at a similar pace. But because aeroplanes are solely concerned with transporting atoms, physical constraints marginalize the technological improvements which are cost-effective. (Having made this point, I remain surprised that a viable supersonic aircraft has still not been developed. The British/French Concorde is an unacceptable form of supersonic transport for reasons of noise and pollution, but engine and airframe technology has improved so much that a vastly improved form of supersonic transport could now be flying.

My third example of being digital will seem more exotic and futuristic. Clothes are a very personal item. Despite this, people are already buying clothes on-line from electronic catalogues, but designer clothes will still require a fitting and this demands a bringing together of the necessary atoms. However, I suggest that within a decade virtual clothes shopping environments will be common as will virtual garments. We will have accurate virtual representations of our bodies in cyberspace where we will be able to 'try on' garments and have a good look to see if they fit. For the first time we'll be able to see round the back!

These few examples of what it means to be digital cannot provide you with a real primer. If you are finding my attempt at a plain-language guide to the network revolution heavy going, or if you know someone who has yet to grasp the concept of physical vs. digital, I recommend Being Digital by Nicholas Negroponte who has earned world-fame through his work at MIT. His book is also published by Hodder & Stoughton and, apart from providing me with a hard act to follow, his short, accessible book is the best introduction to the subject ever written. Why not order it on-line from The Internet Book Shop and see how much cheaper it is when a bookseller doesn't have physical overheads?

A COMBINATION OF CIRCUMSTANCES

Whenever something spectacularly good or bad occurs, whenever the dynamic is vast, way outside normal levels, it is always caused by an unusual combination of events or circumstances. The developments I have described so far would, on their own, be capable of bringing about enormous change in our society and our economies, but something else is happening which, in combination, will ensure the effects of this particular wave of technological development sweep over us all. This is the collapse in telecommunications costs.

Today it costs only a small amount to use the Net. Tomorrow it will cost virtually nothing. The underlying costs of telecommunications are collapsing at exactly the moment the

Net is experiencing exponential growth. As if part of a master plan, there is global consensus to deregulate national networks, to open up nations and territories to competition, to forge alliances between former competitors and to 'wire' up the three-quarters of the world still unconnected. *Connection* is the key to economic growth and this wave of understanding is sweeping across the planet.

The trend towards telecommunications deregulation and privatisation started in the USA in 1984 with the break up of AT&T and is now unstoppable. Even the new AT&T and the 'baby Bells' (the regional telephone companies created by the 1984 enforced break-up of the national Bell Telephone Co.) are now allowed to compete in each other's market. At the same time, the media mergers such as that between Bell Atlantic Corp. and Nynex, which was being contemplated at press time, are creating companies with enormous financial muscle and vision. In particular, Ray Smith, the CEO of Bell Atlantic has a vision of our networked future which makes the description 'bullish' seem inadequate.

Huge corporate alliances have also been formed in the jostle to be a European 'super carrier'. These include DeutscheTelecom and France Telecom (with their US partner Sprint). These two huge national carriers are bogged down by restrictive practices springing from outdated union attitudes and huge social commitments within their markets. Other alliances such as British Telecommunications and MCI and the WorldPartners alliance led by AT&T seem to have a freer hand and they hope to compete effectively across Europe.

Almost every government in the developed world (and some in the less-developed) is selling off state-owned telecommunications companies and ending monopolies. The result is that when setting customer tariffs newly formed competitors do not ask 'how much can our customers tolerate?' ('cream skimming' in the trade jargon) they ask 'what is our base cost in providing a telephone call?' They are asking this question at the very moment when digital switching and transmission are causing a collapse in the real base-price of both voice and data communications. As a result the public has now discovered that the base cost of a call, both international and local, is minuscule and bears no relationship to what we have been used to paying. This has already caused a reduction in phone charges and by the time we get to the end of the century I doubt whether international calls will even be 10 per cent of today's cost. Local calls will be free in most territories.

But if the cost of a telephone call has been discovered to be tiny (including all the contributions necessary for maintenance and development of the network and system), we have found out that the cost of a data call is so low it can hardly be measured. Telephone calls require a dedicated connection between the parties. Data calls send packets of data across the networks on any route that is free. It utilises the gaps and the spaces and thousands of users can use the bandwidth dedicated to a voice call – it is like one giant party line. Further, computers and software are getting so fast that even voice calls can utilise the super-efficient packet-switched transmission method. This was visible from quite far off. In *The Writer and the Word-Processor*, published in 1983 (when telecoms companies were still government 'authorities') I wrote:

> *The reason international data communication is so cheap is that many users can share the same telephone line. The telephone authorities use computers to control the flow of data as it is sent at*

> *high speed along lines in 'packets' which are individually identified.*
>
> *Voices require a dedicated line, of course, and the words sent and received by humans can't (at the moment) be coded and bundled in any different way. In the future human speech may be sent in a similar way, but that is a different topic . . .*

Well, that future has now arrived and several Internet telephony packages that enable very low-cost voice telephone calls across the Net are becoming available. (Incidentally, for those who need it, they are very good at thwarting all attempts at phone tapping, even before scrambling is applied. If you are totally paranoid you can even encrypt the data packets containing sections of the voice call. Nautilus encryption software for voice calls is available now on-line.

For those of us brought up to worry about the cost of placing a phone call, we shall have to adapt or miss out. The Net will continue to explode as users compare the benefits of being connected on-line to the almost negligible or non-existent cost of the call. In most developed countries we will pay our Net provider a low monthly fee and we will leave the connection permanently open.

Under advice from their economists, governments have been driven to make the development of telecoms infrastructure a political issue. Led by the USA, the creation of the so-called 'super information highway' is high on many political agendas. In the USA this has led to AT&T wiring every school to the Net free of charge (110,000 of them at a cost of £100/$150 million), while in the UK both major political parties have said they will strike similar deals with British Telecom.

The European Union has been very aggressive in its pursuit

of an open telecoms market. The Union's member countries have set the date of 1 January 1998 for full EU telecommunications liberalisation and although a few countries (Ireland, Greece, Spain and Portugal) have been granted an additional five years to comply, Brussels is using its considerable powers to ensure that the major markets of Germany and France overcome their reluctance and are fully opened up to competition and lowest prices on schedule. The UK is closer to the US model and is ahead of the rest of Europe by nearly 15 years.

Some countries are taking additional initiatives. The Italian bureaucracy (I hesitate to say government) has committed Italia, a holding company for the five local Italian phone companies created in 1994, to wire the country so that every home will have a fibre-optic connection by the year 2000. Japan's partly deregulated NTT is building a £303/$454 billion fibre-optic network expected to be finished a few years later (although this currently seems to be a 'bone' being offered to the Japanese government to stave off further attempts at eroding the company's effective monopoly in Japan).

In future, the costs of on-line communication will be a major factor in setting a state's business competitiveness. This is despite the collapse of telecommunications costs in most parts of the world. A corporation or organisation of any size is likely to have all of its staff on-line *all* the time. That is how they will conduct their business, how they will hold meetings and how they will communicate with each other. The cost of the aggregated on-line charges is therefore of considerable importance and the ability of a telecommunications provider (or alliance of providers) to get the costs down to the lowest level will have a significant impact on a region's economy.

I believe that the fullest use of communications systems in

general and data networks in particular is so important that it will become the difference between the survival and collapse of every type of organisation in the future. This has been apparent for some time. I contemplated its effect a decade ago in a book called *Forward 100: A New Way of Learning* which Penguin/Viking published in 1985:

> *It is this astonishing spread of personal computing power that is causing the greatest separation of the West from the Soviet block. The imbalance of nuclear arms is the usual factor considered in the context of the balance of power, but either the Soviet Union has not seen the computer revolution coming or, more likely, the rulers have realised that the spread of personal computing power will make their territory ungovernable in the traditional sense. Whatever the reason, while the majority of Westerners buy computers and go 'on-line,' creating an electronic matrix around the world, the majority of Soviet citizens have never seen a computer.*
>
> *In the West a major thrust of the computer revolution has taken place in tiny free-enterprise ventures, and this massive head start is likely to have very profound effects on the future balance between the world's main ideologies.*

Today, many commentators believe that the USSR's economy collapsed primarily because the totalitarian regime was ideologically unable to contemplate the deployment of personal computers and public (or commercial) data networks. The imperative is clear: *communicate or die.*

In those territories without telephone systems, or with an old-fashioned or poorly maintained telecoms infrastructure, there is immense activity to create new networks.

Despite its claim of heroic success in electrifying the USSR, the Soviet Union failed to keep its telecommunications network in good shape. The country has one of the lowest telephone-to-population ratios in the industrialised world and the network is so antiquated that today's liberated Muscovite will find that her access to the Net is more likely to be curtailed by water seeping into a broken cable than by software bugs or traffic jams on the information superhighway. To solve this problem, Russia's government has sold a 25 per cent stake in a newly formed national telecoms consortium to Western investors and today's 25.5 million telephones in the country will double over the next ten years.

In territories where there are no wires at all – and in countries where the domestic connections, 'the local loop', are in the hands of a monopolist – telecoms providers are planning to provide access by wireless. AT&T has announced plans to launch 12 satellites in the year 2000 to create a network called VoiceSpan. The new network would be part of the Net, handling broadband data as well as voice and mail, and would bypass the 'final mile' of the local networks now controlled by Baby Bells, BT, DT, & NTT. In remote areas of the world the network would provide wireless 'phone booths and data ports' for the local population.

To sum up, we are in a time of management confusion and price collapse but the opportunities are so large they are almost limitless. As industry wags say, 'POTS' (plain old telephone services) are changing into 'PANS' (pretty awesome new stuff).

IT TOOK US BY SURPRISE

3

Computers and telephones have joined hands and, with a little knowledge, a very little money, and an idea of what is out there, you can discover the real use of a personal computer.

The On-Line Handbook, Ray Hammond, 1984

Most commentators on the digital age and the established computer industry were caught off-balance by the timing of the explosion of the Internet and its commercial activities on the World-Wide Web. Despite my observations on the power of networking over a decade previously I was completely unprepared for the moment when the point of critical mass actually occurred.

It also caught Bill Gates and Microsoft by surprise. In the same month as Netscape offered its shares to the public,

Microsoft released its first proper attempt at a windows-type operating system for PCs, Windows 95, and launched its own proprietary global on-line network, the Microsoft Network (MSN) which was intended to replace the 'uncontrolled' Internet with a properly regulated commercial service.

For months before these launches the press had been braying about the likelihood of Microsoft increasing its already overwhelming dominance of the PC market by finally giving PCs a Macintosh-type ease of use. In addition, many of the long-established proprietary on-line service providers such as America On-Line and Compuserve were bitterly afraid that the built-in link to MSN from Windows 95 would be unfair competition and a huge market would automatically be created for the new Microsoft service.

I was so concerned that for some months I had been toying with the idea of writing a new book to be called *Why Bill Gates Must Not Succeed*. The argument I wanted to develop concerned the importance of global networks to our future and why it is vital that they should not be under the control of any one company. I was also planning to discuss the inevitability of Microsoft becoming a bank and issuing its own currency, despite Bill Gates's public statements to the contrary. It can now be seen, however, that two weeks before Windows 95 was released and the Microsoft Network launched, the future of computing moved from the desktop PC to the Net (and a generic, uncontrolled Net in distributed ownership at that).

It was easy to miss the wider implications, but these became clear when three months after the launch of MSN, Microsoft announced that it was abandoning its plans for MSN to be a proprietary on-line service: it would, instead, be an Internet-based service; just another Web site, albeit a very rich one.

Perhaps Bill Gates saw the implications just as MSN was

being launched. A month later Jim Clark, the president and co-founder of Netscape told me that Microsoft had tried to buy the company shortly before the public offering and had even demanded 20 per cent of the start-up company's equity in return for access to codes to make Netscape products work efficiently with Windows 95. This might have been just Bill Gates's famous hyper-predatory ambition at work, but his internationally syndicated newspaper column published during the year revealed that during the run-up to the launch of the Microsoft Network he was becoming increasingly aware that the Internet had become an unconquerable entity and his massive investment in MSN – the American telecommunications giant, TCI, invested £83/$125 million for just 20 per cent of MSN earlier in the year – might fail to achieve dominance.

In his newspaper column the week after the Netscape flotation Gates wrote:

The surging popularity of the Internet is the most important single development in the computer industry since the IBM PC was launched in 1981. Like the PC, the Internet is a tidal wave. It will wash over the computer industry and many others, drowning those who don't learn to swim in its waves.

Four months later he owned up fully. Speaking at a conference in Boston organised by the Forrester Consultancy he said:

We all knew that the future of the PC industry was in communications, but we missed the incarnation of it. We didn't realise just how fast it would reach its critical mass. I certainly didn't expect everyone to be talking about the Internet the way they are now.

ALL-OUT-WAR

As you read this, we are in the middle of the most important war ever waged in the computer and information industry. Netscape, Sun, Silicon Graphics, Oracle and a host of smaller network-oriented companies have control of the Net, and Microsoft and Intel have committed their billions of dollars and the personal attention of Bill Gates to wresting back their former dominance of the industry.

We are now entering the fourth phase of computer development, the Network Age.

The mainframe period was followed by the mini-computer era which was followed by the personal computer age. Each of these ages had its ethos: the Mainframe Age was white-coated, the Mini-computer Age was corporate, the Personal Computer Age was 'nerdish' and the Network Age is cool. As *Wired* magazine testifies, being digital is suddenly fashionable.

Unfortunately for Bill Gates, all of the money in his personal and corporate coffers can make him neither cool nor fashionable. This may seem trivial, but I'm trying to illustrate an important point: Bill and Microsoft have become what IBM was and they now face having to reinvent themselves completely for the Network Age. In short, the upstarts became the establishment, providing yet another proof that the future always belongs to the young.

In his book *The Road Ahead*, Bill Gates naturally attempts to reassure his investors, partners, employees and the market generally that the race to control the information superhighway hasn't even begun and he suggests that the Internet will not evolve to become it. Being very smart he attempts to pre-empt negative comment by acknowledging how things might be perceived. In the book he writes:

> *It's a little scary that as computer technology has moved ahead there's never been a leader from one era who was also a leader in the next. Microsoft has been a leader in the PC era. So, from a historical perspective, I guess Microsoft is disqualified from leading in the highway era of the Information Age. But I want to defy historical tradition. Somewhere ahead is the threshold dividing the PC era from the highway era. I want to be among the first to cross over when the moment comes.*

Gates is also sensitive to the comparisons drawn between the much-publicised billion dollar 'home of the future' he is constructing on the shores of Lake Washington and the ultimate folly of William Randolph Hearst in building his palatial home San Simeon: 'I am certainly in no way comparing my house with San Simeon, one of the West Coast's monuments to excess. The only connection I'm making is that the technological innovations I have in mind for my house are not really different in spirit from those Hearst wanted in his. He wanted news and entertainment, all at a touch. So do I.' But others are making the comparison. If on-line readers would like to see how Bill Gates's house is progressing, you may see pictures of it taken at regular intervals (from a boat on the lake) at a site called 'Walls '96, The House That Windows Built'. The site has been put up by a local environmental group called the Coalition for Public Trust.

THE NET EFFECT ON THE COMPUTER INDUSTRY

As I am writing this chapter Microsoft is making its first tentative move towards delivering software applications on-line. It is obvious that the computer market itself presents the first and most obvious sector to benefit from the move to the on-line economy, but it was fascinating to see the world's premier high-tech company get caught out by a legacy structure.

On-line delivery is the obvious medium for software but it radically changes existing economic models. Netscape Communications had never delivered a line of code any other way in the first explosive year of its growth; it gave everything away free. But Microsoft was and is stuck with an international chain of dealers, resellers and stockists who give acres of shelf space to its products and take margins of between 15 per cent and 40 per cent for selling them. Few resellers provide any additional value to the package other than their stocking capacity.

In order to avoiding upsetting the large national chains of computer resellers who are responsible for a large percentage of Microsoft's retail sales, when the company started to offer on-line delivery of software, they asked its computer dealers to operate the service. Illogical, but perhaps unavoidable, as Microsoft grappled with its own legacy.

The emerging network economy will cause widespread 'disintermediation' (the elimination of middle distribution channels) and it is clear that only those companies which move quickly to the new model will survive and thrive. Microsoft has the market position, money and power to buck this trend for a while, but the legacy of a middle distribution tier which it must not offend, opens up a competitive opportunity which hasn't existed before.

If the street price of a copy of Microsoft Office is £330/$495, what percentage of that has been spent on the manufacture, quality control, packaging, manual printing, sales distribution administration, trucking, stocking and re-selling? About 20 per cent. This is probably the most extreme example of the difference on-line distribution is going to make to our economy. How many additional registered users would there be of Microsoft's products if they were sold for 20 per cent of their current price? Microsoft's profits would soar with their sales.

Worldwide there are about 100 million users of Microsoft products. If it were to continue its existing growth patterns for the next few years, the company would have 20 million new users each year and about 20 million would purchase up-grades of existing software. Of the new users, it is estimated about 60 per cent receive their software already installed when they buy a PC. This leaves around 32 million people as individual buyers per year.

Those with a modem and Internet connection could theoretically log on to a Microsoft site, pay for the required software by credit card (with automatic on-line clearance) or digital cash, register their ownership details (something which only 50 per cent of Microsoft customers currently bother to do) and then down-load compressed versions of the software and manuals to their computer disk. Even on a slow domestic modem I regularly down-load compressed software many megabytes in size and the 'time factor' is going to cease to be an issue (rather as PC users moved from loading software from audio cassette players, to floppy disk to hard disk).

For Microsoft (and every other software company) this

represents a change so profound it will completely alter the market perception of the value of software. It will also change the economics of software production as many marginal items that are currently too uneconomic to create may now be produced.

Some companies such as Adobe, Macromedia and Meta-Tools have been quick to adapt to the new model and now provide both software and support on-line, but the bulk of the computer industry is still stuck with old models.

The change is also catapulting small software developers back into the market and it has been doing this quietly for some time. Internet hackers have been putting 'freeware' and 'shareware' on the Net for years. Some have done so because they wish to illustrate how clever their ideas are, some because they want to help the Internet community, some because they have understood that a new economic model makes such an apparently crazy business practice viable and some for a combination of all of these ideas.

Back in 1984 when I was writing *The On-Line Handbook* there were thousands of free 'programs' on the Net. Today we divide software into 'applications', 'utilities', and other programs, and the number of free items is now in its millions. *Freeware* is what it says it is: you may take and use it free of charge. *Shareware* is a distribution model which allows someone to take the program for free and, if they find it useful, they are asked to send a small payment to the author – typically £10/$20 or £20/$30. Those who take the program and who use it frequently are 'honour bound' to send some money.

Often the author or publisher of shareware will provide upgrades, improved versions and supplementary products to users who elect to send payment. It is very hard to know what percentage of users pay for shareware software they use. I have some I have paid for and some which I haven't, but mean to. My guess is that it's a very small percentage, but a small percentage of a very large distribution (which has not cost the author or publisher any incremental costs per distribution) can be larger than net income received after a small or specialist piece of software has been marketed through traditional channels. The cost of software manufacture, quality control (disk checking), manual preparation, design and printing, packaging, marketing, shipping and selling is enormous. Shareware is a great idea and new ways of generating income to authors (so they are encouraged to create more useful stuff) are constantly being devised.

The young Turks at Netscape understood that the Net provides a powerful feedback loop in a way that eluded the old timers in Redmond, even while they were preparing to launch the Microsoft Network. If Microsoft had originally produced its Blackbird browser (now called Internet Studio) for the Web and given it away free, the company would have owned the networking future. But can you imagine how such an idea would have gone down in *Seattle* in 1994? Microsoft has now followed suit and is giving away its Internet products, but it may be too late.

Jim Clark told me that when he started Netscape Communications with Marc Andreessen he asked the young programmer how much the company should charge for the Navigator browser. 'Nothing,' said Marc. 'We should give it away, people will pay later.'

It is to Jim's credit that he gave Marc his head, although he admits he had serious doubts. The programmer was steeped in the Internet shareware ethos which is often mistakenly thought to be based on altruism. It is nothing of the kind. The idea of giving away ten million beta copies (test versions) of Netscape

Navigator was only possible because there were no manufacturing or distribution costs. In an incredibly short space of time, the company could seed a new medium with products and grasp the pole position. They encouraged Internet users to download the beta software and copy it to their friends.

With millions of Navigator clients, there was suddenly an immense market for server software which could interact with the Netscape platform in specific ways. These functions included the ability to accept secure credit-card payments over the Internet (the browsers and the server software could talk to each other in secure 'encrypted mode') and special features to facilitate Internet publishing. Netscape made the price of its server software low enough to be affordable and as soon as the company went into trading profit, it halved the price of the software. This will be a continuing trend.

The Netscape phenomenon is not unique and it will now be repeated over and over again. The company is now migrating users of its free version of Navigator to one which costs £32/$49 and I, and most other users, have gladly paid. The reasons are that new versions allow much more to be done (better graphics, more features, and so on) and if I stick with my old version, I will increasingly find that I am not getting the best out of the World-Wide Web.

New sites are very quick to implement new extensions to design and functionality made possible by the clever Netscape programmers and if I stick to my old software I will soon arrive at sites which will warn me that 'to view this site properly, I should be using version so and so or higher'. It won't just be cool designs I miss out on. I will also miss out on important functionality, such as the ability to spend and receive digital money or visit 3D worlds.

Netscape Communications could, in fact, force all users of free software to upgrade to a paid-for version at any given moment, although I doubt very much whether they will. Every piece of Navigator software downloaded from one of the many sites serving new versions of Navigator software records the e-mail address embedded in my platform. The company could, theoretically, block me from using my software by supplying server software which recognises the e-mail addresses in the platforms arriving and not allowing in those who are not specifically authorised. (This is a good basic technique for a closed or private site which does not require a high degree of security.) A much more likely scenario is that new server software issued by the company will start to block platform software which has serial numbers below a certain sequence. However, I don't believe any such action will be necessary to force users to pay £32/$49. I think market forces alone will do that.

(As an aside: four days before writing this sentence I was authoritatively told that the number of 'hits' recorded each day at the Netscape home site at Mountain View, California, had reached 17 million. A 'hit' is a click which requests action – asking for a graphic, a section of text, a move to another page, a move out of the site, and so on. Therefore it wasn't 17 million people a day who were accessing the Netscape home site, but a number of people who made 17 million clicks. The normal Web wisdom is to divide the number of clicks by 10 as a rough median of the time someone stays on a site. This would produce a figure of 1.7 million. As Navigator is delivered with its home page set as < w.w.w.netscape.com > the default setting, many users don't bother to change this and arrive at the Netscape site the moment they log on to the Web. They will usually then move on to their desired destination after one or two hits at the Netscape site. I would therefore estimate the number of visitors which make up the 17 million daily hits from a lower ratio than 10. I would guess it is six or seven, which suggests that between two and a half and three million people were connecting to the Netscape home site each day in the middle of November 1995. These visitors were served by seven Silicon Graphics high-end workstations connected via a high speed bps Internet connection.

If you are interested in watching the development of this phenomenon, come back here < www.hammond.co.uk > now or in the future and I will have updated the figure. Netscape is planning to split their home sites with new sites in Europe and the Far East, so I'll try to aggregate these figures for you. I also know that some serious Netscape user groups are being formed and I'll also try to keep these usage figures current for as long as Netscape remains a synonym for the World-Wide Web.)

I mentioned above that Netscape platforms have a default setting which points them to the Netscape home site whenever they are fired up. This is easy to change and most experienced users will select a more useful home site for their platform (just as the copy of Navigator supplied with this book is pre-configured to use the Digital Business Web site as 'home').

I also mentioned that the platforms have serial numbers and that the e-mail address of the person downloading the software is recorded. This type of 'concealed' network communication has a very sinister side.

When Microsoft released the first beta versions of Windows 95 which included software for the forthcoming Microsoft Network (MSN), the Internet lit up with discussions about a hidden feature. Net heads claimed that when installed on a user's hard disk, Microsoft's software would automatically carry out an audit of all of the software on the local and attached hard disks and, when the user logged on to the MSN, the software would automatically send back this audit information to Microsoft's headquarters! This would allow the company to discover all the potentially illegal (or unregistered) copies of its software in use and provide marketplace statistics on other's software of unparalleled accuracy.

Net users were up in arms and Microsoft quickly provided reassurance. It said that the software audit function was optional and under the control of the user. But the alarm points to a disturbing and little understood facet of on-line communication. You don't always know what software is up to on your machine. For now, the Net heads are our guardians and as soon as they smell misuse, we know about it. This cannot be the case for long. As the Net grows and grows we must be our own custodians and use both software and hardware protection to avoid such abuses.

Another feature in Windows 95 also attracted attention. Four months after Microsoft sought equity in Netscape in exchange for information about Windows 95 code, the US Justice Department issued a new round of civil subpoenas in their on-going anti-trust (anti-monopolies) investigation into Microsoft. The recipients were Netscape, CompuServe and Netcom (a major US Internet provider). The focus of the investigation was to find out whether Microsoft's Windows 95 operating system improperly disabled rival programs that allow users to access the Internet. In Netscape's case, Navigator will work under Windows 95, but only when the user avoids Microsoft's built-in 'easy option' path to the Internet. If a user does click on the simple 'connect button' in Windows 95, Microsoft's software 'overwrites' all of the preferences and settings which have been set up in the Netscape Navigator software. To resume using Navigator, a user must re-enter all of the specifications for connections and display and risk having the Microsoft software wipe them out yet again.

It is impossible to know how aggressive Microsoft is being, but Bill Gates says that 80 per cent of his company's resources are committed to snatching back the initiative from Netscape. It can't have pleased him that *Wired* ran an interview with Marc Andreessen in December 1995 headed 'Why Bill Gates Wants To Be The Next Marc Andreessen'. (If you're on-line, you'll find an update on the battle here.)

TESTWARE

The Net is also creating another type of distribution pattern I call 'Testware'. Since the first lines of code to control a computer were written, the most difficult part of the operation has been eliminating the bugs, the lines of faulty code, or the design flaws which fail to anticipate a particular situation or operational routine and either fail to work properly or cause the routine to cease (crash).

The thorough testing of alpha, and then beta, software prior to commercial release is a vital and lengthy part of all software production. As software applications have grown ever larger and more complex, so it has become more and more difficult to find all the possible faults. Microsoft sent out 100,000 copies of Windows 95 to enthusiastic early adopters all over the world who used the software for months, reporting back to Microsoft the errors which showed up. But it has now become accepted that the testing process has to be so lengthy, and conducted by so many users, that early commercial releases of software aren't bug free and the saying 'Never buy a Version 1.0 of anything' has gained wide currency.

The Net has turned this on its head. The 'beta' distribution of Netscape Navigator gave the company over 12 million free beta testers. In another brilliant move, the company started to offer £660/$1,000 prizes to users who could find and report significant bugs not previously found (a list of all bugs found is published immediately they are confirmed). Netscape has given users a real incentive to test whilst distributing the software free. Even now that Netscape is charging for its platform, beta software will still be distributed and tested this way either directly by Netscape or through its user groups (reachable on-line at <www.netuser.com>).

For years, digital age commentators have worried about the increasing sophistication of software and our inability to debug such complex codes. For certain applications, the Net will provide an answer. Super-distribution and incentives such as free software and bug-funding rewards, will produce an army of beta testers who in a few months will achieve stable software which would otherwise take years to develop. This is very encouraging. It has been clear for a long time that software design must be changed so that we use specific software modules or 'objects' (for example, a spell checker, a spreadsheet, a word processor) rather than sets of over-blown applications with duplicated features – but a much more efficient method of testing software will also be of significant help.

As I contemplate this, there is an argument going on about whether the emergence of the Net spells the death of the desktop computer. In essence, the argument that it will is promoted by companies whose expertise is in networking and networked products aimed at Microsoft which dominates desktop computing. The argument goes like this: 'We no longer need to have independently capable desk-top computers. The world needs inexpensive connection devices to the Net. Once on-line they will find the storage, application, memory and processing power they need constantly available to them. The stand-alone, or independent PC is dead. We function when we're part of the network, we don't need to when we're not.'

The ideas of the networkers (notably Oracle, Sun and Novell – Netscape has remained silent) are too simplistic, however. We will not migrate from one information processing model to the other; we will use *both*. In chapter 1 I wrote that a massive change has suddenly occurred which has loosened Microsoft's grip on computing and focused it on the networks, but there are many reasons why we will continue to need independent processing power and functionality away from the networks. In fact, that ability is vital for the successful development of the networks. Their use and acceptance by all of us is conditional upon our ability not to rely on the Net and our ability to be both anonymous and private in this super-open community.

But powerful technologies for the Net are emerging to provide new capabilities when we are on-line. Sun Microsystems has developed a programming language called Java which delivers small programs as and when required on the Net. As I navigate my way around cyberspace they provide me with whatever functionality I need while I am at a given site. If I am visiting a site which sells life insurance, a small program written in the Java language automatically makes itself available to me to carry out the spreadsheet calculations so I can establish the premiums and benefits of a highly customised policy. I don't have to have my own large spreadsheet program running. These Java 'applets,' as they are called, provide almost any functionality from offering cartoon-type animation to editing music. In short, the software Net users require is found at individual sites, used for the duration of the visit and then left behind. This turns the model of today's bloated software applications (many of which are produced by Microsoft and which reside on our desktop PCs) on its head.

Microsoft does understand that a new model of computing is emerging and with the Windows 95 Internet Add-on has provided a way of looking at the applications loading on to a PC disk as if they were Web resources. It is clear that despite our need to keep some computing power within our own machine, we will increasingly take the view that it is just another resource on a much larger network.

For many years the industry has been calling for an 'object-oriented' approach to programming to replace the current monstrous overblown applications with all of their redundant parts (I have got six different spell checkers on my machine, all incompatible, each working with a different application). The problem has been that all competitors have been frightened that a modular approach would deprive them of their market position. As a result, the Microsoft camp has developed its Olé language for creating object-oriented software while the Apple group (which includes many who are anti-Microsoft rather than pro-Apple) have developed a competing 'standard' called 'OpenDoc'. The concept behind both is that the user opens a 'document' which has no inherent functionality and then attaches modules, for spreadsheet working, graph-making, word-processing, as required and functions common to all applications, for example, font sizing, spell checking or colouring, would be handled by common modules. Years of discussion and millions of dollars have been spent pursuing these worthy aims. It now seems as though the model may have abruptly changed and the modules may, in time, originate and reside on the Net. I suspect we will retrieve them, pay a micro charge for them, use them and discard them, as we go. It now seems as if this future could belong to Java, rather than either Olé or OpenDoc.

To meet this new model we have already seen the emergence of a new type of terminal dedicated to network access. These 'stripped down' PCs are now on sale but I don't see them replacing desktop PCs, which have their own memory and storage, for a few years. What is happening is that they are forcing manufacturers of conventional PCs to cut their prices in response. PCs, both Wintel and Macintosh have been overpriced for some years, largely because of the duopoly enjoyed by the main microprocessor manufacturers Intel and Motorola. There has been very little pressure on these two manufacturers to cut the cost of the main microprocessors used at the heart of all PCs. This is changing and the cost of terminals will now start to fall, further fuelling the growth of the Net.

Desktop PCs will not entirely disappear in favour of Network terminals. We will use both, according to our needs, just as we will also access the Net from TVs, from PDAs and from cellphones.

PUBLISHING PIONEERS

4

> *In the future an increasing number of publications will be available in both electronic and printed forms. The advantage the on-line version offers is that it can usually be accessed without taking a subscription to the publication, it can be accessed from the other side of the world, all back issues held on file can be searched for a particular topic instantly and the researcher doesn't have to leave the comfort of the home or office.*
>
> The On-Line Handbook, Ray Hammond, 1984

Unsurprisingly, the early attempts at making money on the Net were mostly adaptations of business concepts imported from the physical world. Such translations do not work very well in the network economy and few such efforts turn a profit. Newspaper and magazines were quick to leap on to the Web but, equally quickly, their publishers started to ask 'How can we make any money at this?' Most of the publications which came up on the Web were merely electronic counterparts to their physical entities and little thought was given to the very different nature of the medium. Examples of poorly thought out early attempts include *Time Out*, the *San Francisco Chronicle*, *the San Jose Mercury* and the *Financial Times* but I hope (and expect) they will have improved their content by the time you look. (For on-line readers a good listing of on-line newspapers can be found here.)

It has long been clear that advances in computing power will personalise our world increasingly and thus change the viability of older business models. This has occurred in stages. When desktop publishing arrived, for example, magazine publishers were given tools which radically altered the economic model of short-run special-interest magazine publishing in which the cost of pre-press preparation (typesetting, artwork preparation, colour origination, and so on) was a significant proportion of the production cost.

Every major new technological development goes through an initial phase of self-referral. I think this reflects on the nature of how human beings debate the importance and relevance of a new technology. In desktop publishing, the technology initiators and primary beneficiaries were Apple Computer, Adobe and Aldus (the developers of PageMaker, now taken over by Adobe Systems), but the pioneer businesses which followed fed upon the new technology itself for their inspiration. The first products, publications and services to grow from DTP were either to enhance DTP or were about DTP. A good example was the magazine I launched in 1987 called *Apple Business*. This monthly glossy magazine was produced as soon as reasonably decent typography became possible with the new technology. During a visit to Apple two years earlier the then president John Scully had shown me a beta copy of PageMaker running on a Macintosh 512k (with its little nine-inch screen) and it seemed as if the room lit up. A few years before I had written:

> Working with a system which handles pictures and text will allow electronic art work to be created. This is 'screen paste-up' and it will mean that publishers and writers who take on that role will be able to create a finished page on screen and either print it from a printer/plotter or pass it to a typesetting machine.
>
> At the time of writing, such a system is still just around the corner, but its arrival will further serve to place control in the hands of the writer and shift it away from the publisher and printer.
>
> There is still sufficient paper-based copy generated to keep the majority of typesetters employed. By the end of the eighties this will not be so, and typesetters will face the choice of re-training to learn another skill, or giving up work. (The Writer and the Word-Processor, Coronet, 1983)

I came back to the UK, borrowed a Mac from Apple and started raising the money to launch *Apple Business*, a monthly magazine about the use of desktop publishing technology. The magazine was a great success and after 11 issues we sold it to EMAP, a large British publishing conglomerate, for an excellent profit.

During the preliminary period of desktop publishing technology, the most successful businesses were those which were about the technology itself and it was some time before the technology was applied for broader economic advantage.

For publishers, the most powerful benefit of DTP was that production costs were reduced to the point where more carefully targeted magazines and newspapers were possible. After selling *Apple Business*, I founded a systems-integration house to supply software and systems to publishers (EMAP became my first large client), and I used to joke that it would soon be economically feasible to launch a magazine called *Thursday Afternoon Trout Fisherman* and still make money. (What actually happened was that the worst recession for 50 years killed off all such ideas and EMAP and one or two other publishers with foresight invested heavily in DTP and slashed production costs of existing titles in order to survive.)

PHASE TWO:
SUPER-VERTICAL MARKETS

By comparison, the opportunities promised at the start of the desktop publishing revolution were nothing to those now presenting themselves in the emerging network economy. World-Wide Web technology is currently emerging from its initial phase of self-referral during which time magazines (on-line and printed), conferences and software were about the Net, for the Net and concerned nothing but the Net.

The change in the economic model that desktop publishing produced was relatively minor compared to the changes being caused by network communications. DTP was merely a better way to achieve the same end. Now, the end has been changed by the nature of the medium.

The Net is global, personal, low-cost, interactive and forever-growing. This is worth repeating, over and over. Are you interested in cars? How about a 1958 Corvette or a 1963 Austin Healy 3,000 Marque III? Shall I publish a printed magazine for aficionados of these marques? I think not: there may be thousands of them, and although they're likely to be a rich group, how would I find them? How could I mail to them? How could I make money from them (or from advertisers who would only wish to reach them at a viable cost)?

The answer is to publish on the Net. If I can publish 'coolcorvette.com' – a Web resource which has everything on and about fifties and sixties Corvettes – I am likely to have a modest success on my hands. Provided I know my topic and I market the site's presence well around the Internet, people searching for information about Corvettes will find my site. It will cost me the time and expense of putting the site together, putting it on the Net and marketing it, but after that my 'readers' find me.

The key to understanding is to realise that most users search something out rather than having it placed in front of them. There are dozens of 'search engines' (or indexes) on the Net and users always search in one or more of these using specific key words or ideas. The better they understand how to search databases, the quicker they will find relevant material. No single search engine can be comprehensive because the Net is growing so quickly but there is more than one search engine which searches other search engines on your behalf. In the immediate future we will use software agents who will search on our behalf and database technology will improve to the point that it can handle the sort of 'fuzzy logic' in which humans seem to specialise.

The reason my imaginary Corvette site will work so well is that I have concentrated on a topic that is ultra-specific. Corvette enthusiasts on the Web will not search for sports cars. Because they have the ability to be precise, they will be. *Thursday Afternoon Trout Fisherman* is now a possibility. An extreme level of specialisation (or personalisation) is now not just possible, it is required. I call this a 'super-vertical' economy and it is important that publishers and others who plan to do business on the Net understand this fully.

Before providing some ideas about how to tailor products for this market it is worth exploring the problems facing traditional publishers.

Although I said earlier that a reduction in the pre-press costs of magazine production allows for greater specialisation, the underlying economic model of newspaper and magazine publishing is dictated by the costs of printing, distributing and displaying sheets of paper within a specific geographical territory. Until the mid-1980s the dominant economic model demanded that magazines cater for broad areas of special interest rather than tiny niches. The territory over which it was economical to distribute such a publication was, at best, a nation or a state. Improvements in production efficiency (in both pre-press and printing) enabled publishers to down-size publishing concepts at the end of the decade to the point where local magazines could be contemplated, but the main assets remain the national or international magazine and newspaper titles.

As a result of this publishing legacy, most traditional publishers, of both newspapers and magazines, will want to extend their existing 'franchises' to the network medium. Many of them have expressed the fear to me that if they do not migrate titles to the Net, someone else may do something similar on-line and steal a territory they believe to be theirs. If they own 'Sports Car Driver' in the physical world, they will naturally attempt to secure an extension of that brand in cyberspace. The problem is that this is an old idea for a new medium. The fictitious title 'Sports Car Driver' is far too generalist for network publishing.

Condé Nast, publishers of *Vogue*, *GQ* and other style bibles, launched themselves on the Web during the period I was writing this book. The new medium presented the company's London office with several problems. The first was that the tools for presenting graphic material on the Net were relatively unsophisticated, the second was the limited nature of graphics supported by general 'browser' software, and the third was the relatively slow on-line delivery times.

For reasons which will be obvious, *Vogue* people see themselves as the embodiment of style and panache and they flatly refused to compromise their 'standards' because they were going to publish on the Net. Instead of rethinking what it was they wished to publish on this new medium, the company attempted to bend the Net to meet the requirements of Condé Nast. To achieve that 'high standard' of presentation the company sets itself, it commissioned special software to be written which improves graphics performance and allowed *Vogue* and the other magazines to keep their unique 'brand' identity. Visitors to the Condé Nast site have to down-load the special browser (a 'helper' application for Netscape Navigator) before their are able to view the company's offerings. This special browser is of no use at other sites on the Net. (Readers interested in the thinking behind Condé Nast's approach will find an 8,000-word transcript of a presentation made by Colin Landsley, Condé Nast's Special Projects Director, on the topic here.)

On the face of it, the approach taken by Condé Nast London might seem eminently sensible. At the time of their research the colour and typographic features available on the World-Wide Web were very limited and it seems understandable that the publishers of *Vogue* should decide to produce their own software and computer architecture to maintain standards.

I hope I am wrong, but by now I expect Condé Nast to have announced that the Web and the Internet in general is an over-hyped medium and is a waste of time for 'serious' publishers. At the very least, I expect the site to have changed dramatically in its approach and the custom software to have been dumped.

I believe Condé Nast's approach completely misunderstood both the way the Internet works and the new economics it produces. The company's magazines were initially published on the Web as electronic versions of the print originals to be viewed via the special software. In our networked future only common platforms will work and Web graphic standards and access speeds are improving exponentially. The need for specialist software will not last long and Net users will not keep an application which is of use at only one site. In addition, Condé Nast opted to provide a Windows-only version of the 'helper' application barring the 30 per cent of Net users who use a Macintosh. As the Macintosh is the 'designer computer' for the style conscious, this may prove to have been an error. Finally, the style embodied by a glamorous print magazine such as *Vogue* is very much a component of its glossy medium, and the tactile element of the product and its physical possession, as a visible statement of style consciousness, forms a considerable part of its unique selling proposition.

On the Web, the key is super-vertical specialisation and

attempting to migrate the doyen titles of print to the networks in an unchanged form – in a form so close to the print originals that a proprietary browser must be used to see them – is not the answer.

One pioneer publisher on the Web which has reported great success (and a growing income) is the Electronic Telegraph, the *Daily Telegraph*'s on-line companion. This is staffed by a different team (with a different editor) to the newsprint version and although the ET – as it is universally called – has access to all of the news, information and archives of the *Daily Telegraph*, its composition is very different. The rapid success of ET was described during the keynote session at Interactive Newspapers, a conference my company presented seven months after the on-line publication first appeared. The session was called 'How To Make Money Publishing On-Line' and this is how Hugo Drayton, Marketing Manager of ET described their success:

> *Fortunately we are being lauded as Europe's best on-line newspaper. Some say the world's best on-line newspaper but I think that in the seven or eight months that we have been going, we have produced a product which has certainly become one of the front-runners in electronic publishing.*
>
> *ET is produced by a separate team with Ben Rooney as editor. Obviously most days you will find that the splash that we run on Electronic Telegraph is the same as the Daily Telegraph, but that is not always the case. If you follow it carefully there have been days when we have decided to run something different. The editor has a free hand in putting in whatever he wants. He weighs up the fact that his audience is more international, it's younger, it's male-dominated. Sometimes he chooses not to run a political story from the UK because he doesn't think that will*

> *be of such interest. The news sources that we get in are obviously wide-ranging and in any newspaper a huge amount of information comes in which doesn't make it to the page and is then dumped. There will be times when we will carry much more information in Electronic Telegraph than the Daily Telegraph.*

The Electronic Telegraph rapidly became Europe's busiest Web site. The on-line paper has almost 90,000 registered users and the publishers know who they are and what their interests are. Approximately 10,000 people a day access approximately 100,000 pages of the paper and this is a real and tangible on-line success. Just over 30 per cent of the Electronic Telegraph's readers are over 35. About 60 per cent of them are between 20 and 35 and the readership is over 85 per cent male.

The paper attracts a global audience, with 35 per cent of readers coming from outside of the UK. The territories from which readers access the paper most frequently are the USA and Canada but other countries which feature significantly are Scandinavia, Germany and to a lesser extent France, South Africa and Australia.

(On-line readers interested in the story of the Electronic Telegraph will find the 5,000 word transcript of Hugo Drayton's presentation here.)

One of the first sites put up by any publication ought to have clearly shown the way for other, less imaginative publishers. The site is HotWired, the on-line companion product to *Wired*, the publishing success story of the 1990s and the magazine that has now became a *Vogue* for the digerati – those who understand that digital embodiment and the Net is central to everything. If you have read *Wired* you will know that it is design-led, has indepth linear content and is discursive in style. In short, it is a great read in the traditional sense of a printed product.

HotWired isn't like this at all: most importantly, it is an on-line community. It is fun to visit and it changes regularly. The site was instantly successful and makes serious money. When I visited *Wired*'s offices in May 1995 Louis Rosetto, the founder told me that while it took the printed magazine over a year to move into positive cash flow, it took HotWired only six weeks. The income is from advertising and HotWired currently charges clients £20,000/$30,000 per quarter for a graphic and hot-link (to the client's own site) on the HotWired home page (see the analysis of top ad revenue owners in chapter 8). Louis introduced me to HotWired's newly appointed president, Andrew Anker. I asked him where he had been before he joined HotWired. 'I was the company's bank manager,' he told me.

(In another interesting irony, S. I. Newhouse, Jnr., the legendary President of Condé Nast, committed his company to be the second-stage venture capital suppliers to *Wired*. Newhouse, famed for his tough dealing, surprised *Wired*'s founders by committing his company's money without trying to improve on the terms they offered. He secured Condé Nast's stake in the *Vogue* of the twenty-first-century.

If you're interested in the full story of how *Wired* was founded on-line readers will find my interview with the co-founder and executive editor Louis Rosetto here.)

RETAILING PIONEERS

5

Armchair shopping has long been one of the fantasy catch phrases of the futurists who enjoy telling us what tomorrow will be like. Now they're going to have to find another concept to expound as Compunet has already made this one a reality.

The type of shopping available is likely to be limited to goods which don't have to be examined – books, records and videotapes are good examples – but in time you should expect to find national supermarket chains offering food shopping, etc. on-line.

The On-Line Handbook, Ray Hammond, 1984

Chen Jian is 23. He lives in an outer suburb of Shanghai and he has two material possessions: a bicycle and a lap-top computer. He also has access to the Internet at the university where he studied English. Until recently the most he could hope to earn in China was £50/$80 a month.

Michael Wolff is a 52-year-old entrepreneur who, after founding and developing a £30/$50 million telecommunications business, sold his company to DHL and 'retired' to his homeland to live in a village near Inverness in the north of Scotland. Because he understood the implications of the network revolution he decided to prove that he could earn a new living from that remote corner by founding a 'virtual organisation' in cyberspace. In early 1995 he set up a retailing site on the World-Wide Web called 'The Highland Trail', a vertical marketing site to sell Scotch salmon, whisky and all things Scottish to expatriate Scots and Gaelophiles world-wide.

Chen stumbled across the site on the Internet and 'met' Michael via e-mail. Today he is the 'cyberspace publicist' for The Highland Trail with the responsibility for ensuring that whenever a Web wanderer stops to search for 'Scotland', 'salmon', 'whisky' or 'shortbread' at one of the many search engines on the Web, a link to The Highland Trail pops up high on the returned list of 'hits'. He also has the responsibility for negotiating cross-links with other retailing and travel sites around the world. Chen now earns £100/$160 a day and Michael has cost-effective PR representation on the Net. They have never met and they probably never will. Chen has now set up his own Web site selling Chinese goods (at Chinese prices) to the world. You can visit him at Chen's Home Page.

'One thing you must understand is that you cannot 'own' relationships on the Internet,' explains Michael Wolff. 'Everybody can reach everybody else.'

In the early twenty-first century a far greater proportion of energetic, thinking people will be running their own enterprises than do so now, most of them in cyberspace. Many of them will be part-time, many of them will make considerable use of anonymous, untraceable digital cash and an alarming number of them will exist outside of taxed economies.

The global networks will create completely new entrepreneurial possibilities within an entirely new economy, one aspect of which is my 'economy of super-vertical specialisation' which will develop in parallel to today's dominant 'economy of scale'. For the first time this change will allow individuals and small organisations to compete with major corporations in a cost-effective way.

JUST FOR ENTREPRENEURS

During the early years of Net commerce, buyers have been prepared to pay for items which are difficult to buy physically, which can be bought more efficiently on-line, and products and services which are much cheaper from an on-line source. They have also paid on-line for convenience items which they are already used to buying over the telephone. As Net commerce gets into full swing, the focus will shift to completely new 'super-vertical markets' and this will offer significant opportunities to new entrepreneurs while causing legacy corporations very great difficulties.

Examples of items which are hard (or impossible) to buy physically include boutique wines which are not normally exported from their country of origin, locally published books and music, ethnic and cultural items which would be uneconomic to export traditionally, international magazine subscriptions, and so on. Also included in this category must be sex-related products, pornography and gambling.

Wine may, at first, seem an unlikely commodity to benefit from on-line marketing. The reason that many wineries, vineyards, merchants and supermarkets have been successful with this product is that it matches the demographics of the early user in what I call 'Phase 2' of Net growth, that is, the first phase of commercial exploitation.

In the first few years the users were mostly male with incomes above £33,000/$50,000 a year and aged between 30 and 45. This is the premium wine-buying group and offering them wines which are hard to find, at direct delivery prices, is very appealing. I like certain Californian wines which are not imported into the UK and although I *could* have made a private import arrangement using traditional communications, it is very much easier (and cheaper) to visit a site on the Web, order a few cases of my favourite 'Raymond' chardonnay and wait for delivery. Even with shipping and duty (calculated instantly) the savings the winery is able to make by selling to me directly (they don't even have to make a phone call – I do that) enable it to offer me prices which make it worth while for me.

This type of purchase falls into two of the categories I identified above: I buy wine I couldn't otherwise get *and* I do so at 20 per cent less than the cost of an equivalent wine sold by the case at my local wine merchant. I pay all tax and duty, I insure the shipment, pay for packaging and buy three or four cases at a time. I pay by credit card on a Netscape secure site and I have also begun to buy wine from Italy where I send my credit card details encrypted using the site's PGP 'public key' encryption (see chapter 11). Some people I know buy for groups of friends and many Web wine merchants supply mixed cases.

Another reason (apart from availability and price) that wine selling was an early success on the Web is that US citizens suffer a much more fractured regulatory environment for alcohol than do their EU cousins. Alcohol regulations are fixed at state level, not federal, and this allows regional democracies to apply local value judgements. Many states levy tax on wine while others only allow the sale of alcohol through state-authorised agencies.

The only states in which free inter-state personal alcohol shipment is permissible are California, Colorado, Idaho, Illinois, Iowa, Maine, Minnesota, Missouri, New Mexico, Oregon, Washington, West Virginia and Wisconsin. The other 37 states all provide a partial or complete barrier to personal importation although I suspect these restrictions to be liberalised in the near future.

In the first few years of commerce on the Web many of the wine retailers simply shipped wine to any state once they had received payment, flouting the law. This has now largely ceased because commerce on the Web is becoming mainstream and the growing businesses now wish to comply with the law. Today, it is difficult to buy wine for shipping into a US state which prohibits such importation, and wineries, merchants and retailers content themselves with in-state trade, trade between states where there are no barriers and export to other countries. They do not attempt to ship to countries where all alcohol is banned.

In physical terms wine is probably one of the worst examples of products which can benefit from on-line marketing because of its weight, fragility and the international duty and taxes it attracts. But such operations were among the first to make money on the Web and wine now 'travels' like never before. If you're interested start at Wines of America.

Book sales have proved another early success on the Web.

Virtual book stores such as Amazon in the USA and The Internet Book Shop and Blackwell's in the UK have reported substantial profits flowing from on-line buyers.

In these instances, and for the many more operations joining them on the Web, the real keys to their success are their search engines. Both Web sites allow visitors to search for a book by title, author or topic and they have worked hard to make their databases as comprehensive as possible. As someone who has spent a life-time buying and looking for books, I find these sites magical and, when a particular book is needed for research, they are unbeatable. In particular they offer me a service I cannot get any other way. Like wine, some books are considered unsuitable (which usually means unprofitable) for export and, as an example, I can order books such as *Adultery* by Alexander Theroux (surely one of the saddest books written by a twentieth-century novelist) which are unpublished or out of print outside the writer's home territory. These virtual bookshops, and the many other book search engines on the Web, offer access to millions of titles equalling many miles of 'virtual' shelf space.

Some of the book sites on the Web are virtual extensions of existing book re-sellers who hold stock in their own warehouses, while others are ordering centres which pass the orders on to publishers or to a fulfilment house for dispatch. What is now becoming clear, is that the ability to buy books on the Internet will change book selling (and publishing) completely (as it will change what books are and how they are used).

The first problem for established publishing and distribution structures is that a virtual bookshop on a server located in Denver, Edinburgh or Melbourne is equally accessible from anywhere in the world. If I am in London and I want a book shipped to me from Chicago, this will cost me more and take longer than if I order it from a UK source. But if the price of an expensive book is much lower from a US-based virtual bookshop, then I may well purchase it there and wait a few extra days for its arrival. More importantly to me, I am able with ease to buy books not published in the UK.

THE VIRTUAL SHOPPING MALL

In the first couple of years of commercial activity on the World-Wide Web one of the most popular entrepreneurial activities was setting up virtual shopping malls where on-line shoppers could visit one Web site and 'wander' from store to store as they would in a real shopping centre. Some of the early mall managers even set up 'meeting points' and 'virtual coffee shops' within their malls to foster the idea of community. Examples may be found at The London Mall, The Milestone Superstore, WebMall, San Diego Mall, and The Internet Mall.

By the time you read this, some of those links may have been deleted from the on-line companion to this book as I believe there will be very few malls left on the Web. Those which have survived will have specialised or will be concentrating on related product areas. The very concept of a virtual mall is crazy. The only reason for shops clustering together in the real world is for our physical convenience. When a CD store in New York is only a click away from a bookshop in Boston, where is the value in electronic proximity? I fully accept the argument that most of us prefer to buy goods within our own country or state from retailing names we already trust, but there seems no advantage to create an electronic echo of our physical environment. This phenomenon came about because, in their rush to make money on the Web, the pioneer entrepreneurs didn't have the time to consider the implications of digital information on global networks.

In the autumn of 1995 this was already becoming apparent and delegates to my conference *Retailing On The Internet* were treated to some very frank presentations about the business realities of the early virtual malls. One UK mall operator was particularly blunt. He said that his company had suffered significant problems because of the inability of suppliers to deliver to a global audience on a 24-hour basis. They were not ready for the challenge presented by the Net market. The mall found that low-cost impulse buys worked – flowers, for example – but that although many visitors to his site requested product information and insurance quotes, very few enquires translated into actual sales.

Another major problem for the UK-based operator turned out to be import tariffs outside of the UK. These were so varied and changed so frequently that the company decided to turn non-EU orders away. (On-line readers with a particular interest in the problems facing a 'general-purpose' shopping mall on the Net will find the full text of the presentation here.)

UNDERSTANDING A SUPERVERTICAL ECONOMY

At the risk of repeating myself, the five most important things to fully understand are that the Internet is:

1 Global,
2 Personal,
3 Interactive,
4 Low-cost,
5 Forever-growing. (Each time it grows it becomes more valuable to users and so it grows some more. This is a form of self-replication and is a very powerful concept.)

These five factors turn conventional business models on their head because until now they have been mutually exclusive. How can something be both global and personal? How can such a concept be low-cost? How can growth be sustained automatically? The Internet achieves these goals effortlessly and adds the bonus of interactivity. We have a completely new economic model.

The first result of such a model is that economies of super-vertical specialisation replace such ideas as economy of scale. This should be a point worthy of consideration by those readers charged with responsibility for sizable corporations.

It may seem as if supermarkets have already achieved super-vertical marketing in the physical world. Everything to feed us and for our homes is gathered in one place. But the Net will pose an extreme challenge even for these ultra-efficient retail machines.

In Chapter 2 I referred to the Smart-Coop Virtual Supermarket. I don't know if you have looked at the site yet, but I'll bet it has expanded since it first came on-line in November 1995. Then the company made deliveries only to the Massachusetts Institute of Technology campus and the immediate area, but said it was hoping to expand operations to include Greater Boston soon.

By the time you read the printed version of this work the major supermarkets may have moved heavily into on-line trading. As I write they have been gaining experience by 'testing' the market with on-line wine ordering. If a giant Safeway, Tesco, Asda or Sainsburys has started to allow Net ordering and providing local deliveries, it might seem there is little opportunity for smaller organisations to succeed in this most basic but dependable of all markets. That would be a mistake. Every one of the major retailing corporations has two negative inheritances from the pre-Net age. The first is their overhead in terms of people, real-estate and IT systems. The second is their relationship with the suppliers of 'branded' goods, for example, Heinz, Lever Brothers, Nabisco, Gallagher. (This latter relationship has been under strain for some years as commoditisation has eroded brand equity.)

The opportunity is for someone to form a *network* of suppliers to service orders taken over the Net. It is a neat idea to respond to the opportunities of the virtual community formed by distributed networking with a virtual physical organization. It will work.

Let's play an MBA student-type game and assume I decide to found a corporation. Let's call it 'Lowest Local Foods' which, in time, I will brand as 'LowestLocal.' Step one is to raise some serious venture capital and recruit senior retailing executives from the well-known supermarket chains (for their supplier contacts and knowledge) to join me on the board.

We put up a Web site with this name for your country, for example, LowestLocal Ireland (not necessarily *in* your country, although it will be presented in your local language(s)).

At this site shoppers will see a map of their country with the cities where LowestLocal operates highlighted (most, we hope, on Day One). After clicking on their city (and in some cases, defining their neighbourhood) shoppers will fill out a membership form (name and address) and will be given their password so that on future visits they can go straight to ordering.

Shoppers will then see a list of the goods on sale by brand name, or by type, or by category. These will include fresh meat and vegetables. They can browse or search and they can scan lists of goods for things they might have forgotten to jot down on their shopping list. I doubt whether my new company will bother to render any of the store as a virtual world, but we might. This depends on how popular non-necessary virtual worlds are proving on the Web at the time of our launch.

What I will do is give the site a strong sense of personality. Shoppers who want to 'see' the manager will be able to do so and each department will have an individual buyer who will provide explanations about the food and goods. These will be the real people who are actually doing the buying and shoppers will be able to learn a lot about them. There will be recipes and serving suggestions contained in links to certain items and there will be 'cross link' price promotions between items in various departments not easy to show in the physical world.

Above all, the site will offer the LowestLocal prices available. 'Lowest local price', means the lowest price available from an ordinary supermarket or from an organization able to deliver your order to your door between 6 a.m. and 10 p.m. You may order at any time, day or night.

The price is gauged on a 'typical' shopping basket which contains £25/$40 worth of mixed items. As you shop, your shopping basket icon will display the total of what you are spending. You may put back items you have added to your basket and after 'going to the till' and logging off, you may still go back and amend your order up to 30 minutes later. (This is to allow for those items we all forget to put on our shopping lists.)

The prices really will be the lowest and, without the buying power and distribution of the giant supermarkets, how will we achieve these prices and delivery for our customers? The answer is to build a virtual organisation of distributed franchises.

LowestLocal, Inc. will sell local franchises for the fulfilment of orders in each town and city. In the larger conurbations there might be several. These franchises might be trucking companies, or existing independent food retailers. They might be new corporations set up specifically for the opportunity. What is certain, LowestLocal will have no trouble selling these franchises during the run-up to testing and going live. Here are the reasons:

- All stock (except fresh food) is bought centrally by LowestLocal, Inc. on behalf of its franchises, with orders delivered directly to local franchises by the suppliers.
- The corporation and its franchisees have no retail premises, no long-distance delivery infrastructure, no shelf stocking or till staff, no display staff, no store managers, no mainframe computer systems and dedicated networks, and so on. No percentage of the 'available margin', the raw difference between purchase and sale price, will be needed for these items.
- Franchisees will be in charge of their warehousing and delivery infrastructure. These will be quality-controlled by LowestLocal.
- Margin splits between LowestLocal and franchisees are laid down in the franchise agreements and the consumer's price is directly dictated by the purchase price.
- Customer orders are sent directly to the franchisee over the Net for fulfilment. Error checking techniques are used to ensure accurate e-mail reception.
- Stock ordering is driven directly from the instant EPOS information available from the LowestLocal Web site(s) and this provides superb 'just-in-time' manufacture and ordering pro-

cesses to suppliers. Communicating with franchisees' stock systems, LowestLocal will maintain each franchisee's stock at the optimum level in a 12-hour window.
- LowestLocal, Inc. will carry out regular spot checks on fresh food quality and franchisee performance through local spot purchases.
- LowestLocal will advertise nationally (on TV, in newspapers, and so on) and franchisees will promote within their own geographical area. Net marketing will be carried out by LowestLocal.

I hope you'll agree that this mini-business plan is starting to look interesting. Someone may already have done it by now. But how many countries are there and how many such operations can any one territory support? What about such operations for cultural sections of a community (the Chinese or Japanese equivalent of LowestLocal) and what about specialist versions (health foods, gourmet, vegetarian)?

Let's push the ideas further: how much do you care about packaging? Does Maxwell House coffee have to come in a glass jar of a certain quality with a particular label? At the moment it does because it has to look good on the shelf and compete with the other jars in the physical world. It has to have the right 'look and feel' as we hold it and transfer it to our physical basket.

But none of this occurs in a virtual supermarket. If Maxwell House was put in a plain jar with a non-fancy label we would all trust its quality because of its manufacturer. Will they allow LowestLocal to stock non-packaged versions of their brands? Apart from costing less, think of the ecological benefit. Packaging manufacture consumes enormous amounts of unrecoverable natural resources and it is mostly to do with the physical sale. (I'm aware that some people also like products to 'look good' at home, but refills provide the answer to this need.)

LowestLocal could also offer non-branded equivalents, the 'own label' variation of products at very low prices and these would certainly not have expensive packaging. The prices will be wonderful and I'm sure our customers will try them. What impact will this have on branding?

LowestLocal will also offer discounts for bulk buying without expecting you to have the storage problem. Buy 400 lb of potatoes or 60 kilos of dog food today and we'll deliver it to your door in weekly or monthly quantities, as you require.

We can do many tricks with money, of course, and there are wonderful promotional opportunities. We will give a discount for shoppers who use digital cash and we'll also provide discounts for satisfied customers who choose to set-up prepaid accounts. We can do bulk discounts and you can imagine how we can market special promotions.

Think about our advertising opportunities. In each area we've got an identified local membership. Would other local suppliers like to reach them?

LowestLocal could also become a 'smart' supermarket. If you shop with us regularly we could have a semi-prepared basket of goods available for you when you arrive and, if we've got it wrong this week you can trash it, or throw out a few items you don't want. We could watch your buying patterns and suggest savings you could make by bulk buying (with a single delivery or staged deliveries – by popping the pre-purchased items in your basket when you arrive).

We would promote LowestLocal as the store driven by its members, as a modern-day version of the UK's oldest labour movement food-buying co-operative, the Co-Operative Stores. Our slogan is 'The more *we* buy, the cheaper it gets!'

From this imaginary example we can extrapolate where all retailing is heading. 'Perfect price and quality information' will defeat all existing retail structures and present wonderful opportunities to new entrepreneurs.

The way has already been shown in the physical world. In the last few years 'discount shopping clubs' have been hugely successful in the USA and have now been launched in Europe. One of the largest US clubs, CUC International, has launched an on-line shopping service called Shopping Advantage which offers 250,000 branded goods at between 10 per cent to 50 per cent off the manufacturer's suggested selling price.

PERFECT INFORMATION

In chapter 1 I referred to the concept of 'perfect information' and suggested it was going to have a profound effect on the way business is conducted in the on-line age. I used dramatic language to illustrate the idea suggesting that 'software robots will roam the globe' looking for the best deals. This is where I must substantiate such a bold claim.

The inexorable rise in the importance of price in most consumer and commercial buying decisions has come about solely because of the improvement in communications. Twenty years ago a driver shopping for a new car would base a purchase decision on the best information which could be collected at an *acceptable cost or level of difficulty*. The customer would look at newspaper advertisements and visit those showrooms which could be reached relatively easily. He or she might make a few telephone calls to showrooms further away, but the time necessary for each exchange of information and description of the fine details of the intended purchase made this a time-consuming affair. The amount of information which could be gathered about cost (or added-value features) would be very limited and if a dealer 400 miles away was clearing stock for 15 per cent less than the best price available locally, the consumer would be unlikely to know.

Ten years ago customers started to type up their requirements and fax requests for quotes to a much larger number of dealers and the consumer's ability to gather information about a car — or about any other commodity products from a computer system to an airline seat — improved enormously. The same was true for business-to-business purchases. In response, some marketeers started to introduce convoluted pricing and added-value schemes to obfuscate and confuse buyers and prevent them finding either the real price or the best price/added-value combination. The seller was trying to make the information the buyer could gather imperfect or, make it non-cost-effective to take the time necessary to get at the best information about price. Spending three days to find the best price on an airline seat across the Atlantic or Pacific is uneconomical for everybody except the very young, the retired and the very poor (for whom such a quest would probably be irrelevant).

But the improvement in communications and their lowering cost also allowed some marketeers to sell solely on low prices, getting the information about low prices directly to customers. If you are over 40 and have ever wondered why all of our shops seem to have descended to a permanent state of 'sale now on' when once sales were genuine twice-yearly stock clearances, you'll now understand why. Shops can only communicate through their shop windows (and shop windows on the Net) and for commodity retailers the communication of price information has taken over from all other factors.

Other marketeers such as the large supermarket chains switch between periods of offering (and aggressively communicating) genuinely low prices and periods when prices are increased in the hope that the main body of consumers have habitualised their buying patterns and have ceased to be vigilant or caring about price.

Equally, companies exploit distance and national and continental boundaries across which information has been difficult or expensive to obtain to avoid customers getting at the best prices. The best example of this is the wide disparity in the cost of most American and Japanese goods when sold in the USA compared to similar offerings in Europe. The areas where this is most noticeable are in software, computers, peripherals, CDs, books, videos, clothes and automobiles. At this time of writing I can (and do) buy 28.8 bps modems for £65/$98 in the USA on the Net which I bring into the UK at around £88/$132. The cheapest I can buy the same modem for in the UK is £170/$272.

It is clear that the economy of scale possible in the US market, contrasted with the difficulty of doing business on a continent with many different language and exchange rates, can explain part of this discrepancy. But internationally distributed goods are typically between 50 per cent and 100 per cent more expensive in Europe than in the USA.

The network economy will make this difficult to sustain.

Increasingly, on-line buyers will use software over the Net which will act as a 'buying robot'. Slightly less dramatic terms for these simple pieces of software are 'smart agents' or 'representatives' and, in truth, it is the Net itself which brings the element of drama, not the small and very simple pieces of software.

The international consultancy firm, Anderson Consulting, was one of the first major organisations to make experimental use of such a software agent (the term I prefer). They have developed a small program called 'BargainFinder' which a user could call to a PC screen and then type in the name of a particular music CD required. The user then connects the PC to the Net and the software travels across the net, querying search engines in CD-stores co-operating in the experiment. At these stores, automated software is ready for the software agent query and provides the information automatically. After completing the task the software agent returns to its base with information about the best price on offer.

The first commercially available robots for indexing information on the World-Wide Web were offered by Verity, Inc in late 1995. The Topic Websearcher allows users to build a searchable text index of any Web site over the Internet. This is a 'search engine for search engines' and solves the problem of how to find something on the Net.

Software agents are going to become a central element in our Networked society. They will roam the world seeking out the very lowest price for a particular product and order it there. If that product can be delivered to the buyer economically, that will be the fixed 'perfect price' of the item and it will be difficult for others to sell the same product at a higher pricer without adding recognisable value to it.

Software agents will also have the time, patience and mobility to compare terms and options as well as price and the use of such agents produces a concept called buying with 'perfect information'. Currently our retail and services economy relies upon the buyer being unable to get perfect information. The development of multiple choice, of variations in regional price policy, in the way financial products are constructed and presented, of spot product reductions and promotions, are designed not to offer the consumer greater choice, but to befuddle the buyer and obfuscate the true terms and conditions. This approach is endemic in the West and it is loathsome and fraudulent. The consumer finds it uneconomic or too difficult to understand the small print, to drive to extra locations, to ring round more shops, to check 'the extras'.

Over the next decade we will develop better and better software agents which will be our inexhaustible shoppers. We will still have to determine and decide what is right for us, but the tasks of finding the lowest price, establishing the price of the extras and invisibles will drive down prices. In addition to the fundamental change in the underlying cost structures of corporations, profits will soon have to be made in an economy in which the consumer has considerably more power.

There will be a large part of society (I estimate 50 per cent–60 per cent in the developed nations) who will be the 'information have-nots', people who can't, or don't, make efficient and regular use of the Net. Marketeers will still be able to use confusion techniques for pricing to this group, but this community will form the poorest demographic group. This does, however, suggest that companies targeting this group will have more marketing freedom than companies selling to the digerati (just as this same sector is more vulnerable to traditional advertising).

Most governments dimly realise that Net access (and experience) is akin to literacy in the population and is, therefore, economically vital. There are various schemes in place to provide Net access in public places and in poorer areas, but although I support all such efforts, it has to be understood that as our society develops from being almost entirely physical to one which is increasingly information-based, this must favour those who have been lucky enough to be born with higher IQs and who receive appropriate education. Until very recently size and strength were the key markers for human survival. As we become more digital, evolution favours other qualities.

ADAPT OR DIE 6

> *Many large corporations are realizing that there are ten million personal computer owners in the Western world and that they're all going to want to break out of their prisons of isolation and tap into the electronic matrix which girdles the planet.*
>
> The On-Line Handbook, Ray Hammond, 1984

Many well-established service sectors and industries will find that their very existence is threatened as business users rush to connect to the Net. The process of disintermediation will accelerate and, if your company falls into the intermediate service sector typified by travel agents, insurance brokers, estate agents or employment agencies NOW is the time to be considering changing what your company does, or changing what you do.

A superb example of a service industry under threat is the

estate agency. By their nature, estate agents exist to connect sellers with buyers and landlords with tenants because these parties are unable to reach each other economically or effectively. But what real value do estate agents offer a vendor for the percentage they charge? I know that in theory agents are supposed to offer professional advice about marketing property, supply local information and act as a useful 'cut-out' in negotiations but in scores of property transactions over the years I have never found such supposed 'added-value' to be worth very much. Until now, an estate agent's principal value has been provided by the agent's shop window in the High Street or in a newspaper advertisement.

If you want to move to a new area and rent or buy a new home, you may start by having the local newspapers sent to you, but you are almost certainly going to have to make a large number of reconnaissance trips to the area in order to get a feel for prices and locales. Posting available properties on the Net saves an enormous amount of time and offers significant entrepreneurial opportunities, but not necessarily to real-estate agents.

If my company wants to relocate me and my family to a city 800 miles away, or to another country, how shall I go about finding somewhere to live? The Net beats every other conceivable medium.

Many estate agents are already feeling their way onto the Net, but I haven't yet seen a Web property site which has got it right. They're still trying to make old ideas work in a new medium. The first people to get it right in each major city or city area will develop a valuable resource.

I want two things from an on-line real estate service. The first is to be able to use powerful search features, the second is to get detailed information about the properties I select and the area in which they are located. I may wish to search by price/rent, size, age, location, plot size or south-facing, for example. Probably I will wish to search by several or all of these. The Web site I visit for London or Sydney has to be comprehensive, with a wide range of properties available.

Having narrowed down my search to a shortlist, I want to see as much information as I can. At a minimum I want to see several colour pictures of the property, floor plans (and where appropriate plot/garden plans). I want all dimensions and I want location maps at three different scales showing me where the house is located in relation to schools, shops, freeway ramps, bus routes, airports, rivers, and so on. I want to see pictures of the views in all directions. (There could a security risk for vacant properties and this is something to be borne in mind.) For an inner-city property I would like to see listings of nearby restaurants, shops and cultural amenities.

Such a resource would quickly gain a reputation and become very valuable. Why hasn't it happened yet? I suppose it's partly lack of understanding and partly competitive pressures. In each town or city there are usually many different estate agents and if these companies have grown, they've done so horizontally, spreading out across a country. Their shop windows in each town may represent no more than 5 per cent of the properties available in the area. On the Web, the dimension is vertical and all of the properties need to be drawn together and offered at a single site.

There are many embryo estate agent sites on the World-Wide Web and by the time you read this there will be many more (see them here). One of the first was World Property Real Estate Index but this seems over-ambitious as it tries to cover the globe and has very few properties in each country, let alone each city. Because of the specialised nature of the Net very local and specific directories will work the best, but I haven't been able to find many sites which understood this. The sites which will be successfull will be 'Hampstead Homes' or 'New York Lofts'. It won't take long.

One of the first real estate sites which seems to have grasped the idea is from the London firm of Goldenberg. This up-market realtor specialises in properties in Mayfair, one of London's most exclusive areas and because many Mayfair buyers are from overseas, the Net provides a perfect shop window. (Incidentally, for those who are trying to understand the arcane techniques of marketing a site to the search engines on the Web, a look at the bottom of Goldenberg's home page will give you some useful clues.)

Estate agents aren't simply going to shut down, of course, because the vast majority of buyers and sellers will be ignorant of the Net and its uses for a few more years, but what will happen is that the top echelon of buyers and sellers (as well as the sector which is digitally literate) will start to use the Net to find property. If I were an estate agent I would want to be sure that it was my company which operated a well-stocked Web site for my area and I could then offer my clients some real added-value as well as securing a stake in the future.

Property is going to be a very important aspect of Net marketing and we can expect to see every type of vertical specialisation covered as entrepreneurs come to understand the new medium. The property resources that have come up so far include Property Line, Property Find, the Internet Real Estate Directory and Estates but, as I mentioned above, I don't feel these sites have got it right at the time of writing.

Home rentals are also covered on the Net with local, national and international services including Simply Rent, which is a UK-wide register of houses and flats to rent which is free of charge to both tenants and landlords, Rent Net which offers US apartments in 250 cities and Around Town Flats which specialises in flats in Manchester, UK for students.

The property sector will boom on the Net and I expect to find my 'dream site' – with property photos, floor plans, views and local information – appearing shortly. What most of the sites fail to do is specialise and only those which target a narrow area or property type will succeed.

Other property resources on the Net include Nationwide Property Selections (properties in the UK, Spain, France, and Portugal), Edwin Hill Chartered Surveyors (a comprehensive UK commercial property site, showing properties and services available), Estates Today (a resource for commercial real estate. Based in UK, with worldwide directory and hundreds of property and business links), Nelson Bakewell (UK real estate agents – purchasing, selling, portfolio, retail, public sector valuations, rent reviews, building surveying, Rates, planning), Citycorp (a guide to property investment in the UK), First Virtual Estates (US real estate), InternetWeb Property Centre (for commercial or residential property from UK estate agents, or advertise your own), Property Line (on-line listings, with pictures, of UK and European real estate), UK Property Pages, Virtual Estate (UK property listings), International Real Estate Directory and News.

THE TRAVEL TRADE

Travel agents, particularly business travel agents, will also find themselves increasingly vulnerable as new and competing services appear on the Net. My company presented a conference called 'Travel on the Internet' in June 1995 specifically to address such issues and our audience was a cross-section of travel suppliers keen to find out how they could exploit the Net and agents who were worried in case they might.

At that time, the big issue was whether airlines would start to sell seats directly to the public from their own Web sites. A handful of airlines including Cathay Pacific, Aeroflot, Qantas, Canadian Airlines, Air South, Austrian Airlines, Lufthansa and Virgin Atlantic had established experimental 'shop window' type sites but were not actually offering direct bookings over the Net. (Six months later Virgin Atlantic became the first company ever to be fined by a US court for publishing misleading material on the Web. They were fined £6,000/$9,000 for advertising low fares to the UK which were no longer available.)

After the conference was announced and before the actual event, the UK travel press, *Travel Trades Gazette* and *Travel Weekly* in particular, filled their column inches with speculation about when or if an airline would dare to make such a move. I was monitoring the market and a few days before the conference was due to take place I saw that a new site called PCTravel in Raleigh, North Carolina had come up which was offering on-line customers the chance to book airline seats on the Web. I tested the service and found that this entrepreneurial and well-established travel agent had created a real-time link to SABRE, one of the centralised computer reservations systems used by all major airlines. There were no discount fares on offer, but an on-line customer could check out flights and schedules, be taken through a step-by-step booking form and pay with a credit card. This was a first and I informed the press and our delegates that I would be showing the site for the first time in Europe during our conference.

The evening before the conference I visited the site and went through the booking procedure to be sure I was sufficiently familar with the process to be able to demonstrate it easily in front of our delegates. At eight the following morning I decided to log on again to be sure all was working properly and I found that the site had disappeared! I tried to find it repeatedly, using every trick I know, but it had simply ceased to be on the Net. It was three a.m. Raleigh time and all I could do was to leave a voice mail at the Marketing Director's number.

Those travel agents and members of the press who were concerned about the threat of the Net were delighted when I had to announce that we were unable to show live airline seat bookings on the Net as promised. The flakiness of the Internet had been clearly and publicly demonstrated and I am sure that more than a few of them breathed more easily because of my embarrassment that morning.

Shortly after mid-day we found out what had happened. North Carolina had suffered its worst electrical storm of the century overnight and the lightning had knocked out the local Internet provider's systems. The entire Nando Net network which serves the area was out of action. PCTravel were all-too-aware of the audience sitting in London waiting to see the demo and two hours of frantic recabling allowed me to access the site via a point-to-point phone at 2.30 p.m., London time.

The site worked perfectly, a reservation was duly made, I paid with my credit card (the site is Netscape secure) and the delegates were left to ponder the implications.

The Net is going to change the way we plan and excute our travel a lot more than simply by offering us the chance to make on-line ticket reservations. Using the old indirect systems of buying we have become used to buying many services 'blind' – hotel rooms, rental cars, holidays, restaurant tables and so on. Those of us with the time and inclination can research such things, but the media we have used – guide books, TV programmes – have inevitably been both passive and dated. The business traveller has no time (or inclination) for such research and thus a 'homogenised' type of market approach has developed in which large corporations work hard to ensure that we will know exactly what to expect when we book a Marriot, Ramada or Holiday Inn room anywhere in the world. The same is true, to a lesser extent for car rentals.

Now, everything has changed. Unsurprisingly, San Francisco, my favourite city and sometimes physical home, leads the world. If you want to find a hotel in San Francisco you go to San Francisco Reservations on the Web, click on the city map in the area where you wish to stay and you'll be offered a range of hotels in different styles and price ranges. Click on the hotel and you will see a picture of its lobby and of a typical room. Click again and the images are enlarged. You can check out the restaurant menu, the hotel facilities, its exact map location and room availability. You can make your reservations on-line.

At one of my favourites, The Fairmont on Nob Hill, you can even go up to the roof and get a view out over the bay from a video camera. (If you'd like to see the Bay today on-line readers can click here.) And if Alcatraz is visible through the fog you can take a virtual tour at Alcatraz. For a guide to all of the San Francisco Web sites see Z-PUB.

In the near future we will see videos of the hotel, you will be able to 'walk through' 3D virtual worlds of the hotel and its rooms, you will get to meet the staff and gain an impression of the establishment impossible by any other means.

For somebody in my business (conference organising) access to floor plans, logistical information and virtual walk-throughs of facilities will be an incredible boon. Those hotels which are first to offer me information in this way will be at the head of the line for my business.

Another example of buying blind is car rental. Americans don't know European cars and Europeans don't know US autos (although the Japanese will always find something familiar). How many times have you agreed to a certain type of car at a rental desk (or on the phone) without having the slightest idea of what you will end up driving? The Web solves this. You can now look at the types of car on offer (see Alamo, Budget, Eurodollar, Hertz, Rent-a-Wreck), view their interiors and see any statistics you need.

Most sites will be offering virtual cars in which you can 'sit' and videos of the vehicles in action. You can also make your reservation on line, of course (which is also causing some marketing confusion as an American booking a Budget rental car for the UK, for example, will pay a much lower rate than a UK citizen booking the same car for the same period).

For the first time, arrival in an unknown city does not have to be a nightmare. In one of my early businesses I used to drive all over the USA and Europe selling and marketing the magazines I published. I didn't know the cities, I didn't know the hotels, I didn't know the cars, the restaurants, the road layouts: nothing. Although it was exciting, it was desperately inefficient. Now I can 'visit' the city in detail before I travel. Digital City (Amsterdam) was the first city comprehensively represented on-line and I can choose my hotel from good information and down-load the maps. Other cities represented include London, Paris, Cape Town and New York City and we can expect every city in the world to provide information to visitors and locals alike over the coming decade. What an opportunity for entrepreneurs who wish to design, create and maintain such sites! In due course almost every area in the world will publish information about itself on the Web and whether we're driving, flying or taking public transport to a destination for the first time we will access information on the Net about the place as naturally as we now look at a map.

Already I can see nearly all of the world's subway maps and this Web site will work out my tube journey, telling me how long the journey will take me, where to change and which stations I will pass through

The wired-world is littered with new opportunities. I will bet that as you read this, the proportion of the world's hotels resident on the World-Wide Web is still less than 5 per cent. Within a decade no sizable hotel will be without a Web presence and most small hotels – even the B&Bs – which depend on long-distance customers will be touting their accommodation in cyberspace.

Who is going to develop these sites? Who will host them? What is the commercial logic which will create successful business opportunities out of this? Obviously hotels will pay suppliers to create the pages, the videos, the 3D virtual representations and to provide server space, as will thousands of other types of company and organisation. By the year 2002 or thereabouts almost every business organisation will have a site and individual professionals and small businesses will not be able to function without at least having a home page.

Travel is going to be heavily Net-based. If you want to get a taste of what is happening take a look at London Calling, which is a delightful visual tour around London allowing you to navigate east, west, south or north through views of the city, or Nepal, a beautifully illustrated diary of a private trip through the country, or Bangaldesh. There are many others which I have included in my bookmarks.

DEATH FOR SOME MEANS OPPORTUNITY FOR OTHERS

The disintermediation which will occur in the traditional service industries does not mean there are no new opportunities in these fields. For entrepreneurs who learn the mechanics and ethos of the Net there will be myriad possibilities.

How about using the super-vertical power of the Net to sell travel in a more targeted way than has ever been possible before? The cost of putting up a site which specialises in South American adventure tours compared to conventional costs of reaching such a specialist market will be minute. This will allow you to offer quality tours at much lower prices than those which are traditionally marketed and the degree of customisation possible will also be far greater. Or you could organise rambles through England's Lake District or tours through the wineries of Nappa or the vineyards of Bordeaux. Such super-vertical specialisation makes excellent sense on the Web and, if well-executed, would certainly be attractive to the hotels, restaurants, car rental companies and airlines which would act as suppliers.

With no brochure to print, mail or distribute and with instantly up-dated information and on-line reservations the economics of package vacations will change completely. Automated availability information and on-line reservation for all elements within a virtually planned vacation package will increase utilisation and lead to further economies. A variety of economic models will be used for such sites and the entrepreneur may be paid by the suppliers, by the holiday-makers, by regional tourist authorities or by all three (or none of these). Many different models will work.

The obvious ideas are to present Web sites with themes – for example, 'Hotels for Lovers in Vermont', or 'The Bass Fishing Trail of Ireland'. Just think of the golf possibilities!

Another site might just offer last-minute vacation bargains as in: 'Last-Minute Holidays in France' at which you can view package holidays available for departure within seven days. Here the element of extreme specialisation is in reaching those who are able to take a vacation at very short notice. Without leaving his or her desk the holiday-maker can see the hotel, apartment or château, its rooms, floor plan, views from the balcony, and street location as well as get a current and future weather report from the area. The customer could book on-line with a credit card and find the tickets waiting at the airport.

If I lived in a tourist spot, or if I was interested in a certain sport, or historical period, I'd be busy planning a Web resource. (I am, actually, but on an entirely different topic.)

The ideas for such cyberspace marketing enterprises are limited only by your imagination and knowledge of what is possible on public networks. I can imagine virtually planned vacations with religious, historic, cultural, cult, genealogical, musical, filmic, literary and artistic themes. That list could have been far longer, but you get the point. Specialisation is the key and the new networked 'economy of specialisation' makes all things possible.

One of my enduring interests has been Mary Shelley, her origins and family, the writing of *Frankenstein*, and the metaphor it provides for our future. I wrote a book, a radio play and a TV drama on the subject. But this is very much a minority interest. Until now I have had no efficient way to reach the thousands, or tens of thousands, who share my interest. Now I can capture all those who type '*Frankenstein*', 'Mary Shelley' or any of the related subjects into one of the search engines on the Web.

As well as the book itself, my imaginary *Frankenstein* site might contain all of the many Frankenstein movies to buy and down-load, sample text from the myriad books with the ability to order them on-line (or down-load them), information and digitised documents from Mary Shelley's life, William Godwin's life (her father), Mary Wollstonecraft's life (her mother), Percy Shelley's life, maps and photographs of Lake Como, Switzerland where she had the idea for the book, and Bath, where she actually wrote it. You might be able to book yourself on to a Frankenstein-theme vacation in Switzerland and England. The site would also provide links to other related sites such as 'Women's Liberation Movements' and 'English Romantic Poets'. Well, I'd like to develop that site, but my obsession with Mary Shelley has subsided in recent years.

(Of course, before this book was delivered, guess what I found: Frankenstein is a site which offers the full text of the book divided into three sections: Shelley's preface; letters from

Dr Frankenstein's listener, Captain Walton, to his sister in England; and the chapters that comprise Frankenstein's horror story proper. It is very nicely done.)

I hope you're getting the point, however. The emergence of super-vertical markets has opened a million possibilities. I have long realised that a large percentage of small entrepreneurs who build up successful businesses have invested in what was formerly a hobby or something for which they had a special enthusiasm. As a teenager I loved pop music so I set up a management and record production company. The business succeeded. Musicians were my favourite people at that time and I established a publishing company in 1974 to publish a magazine called *International Musician and Recording World*. It was a hit in the UK, the USA and Germany and I was able to sell my shareholding six years later for a good sum.

My point is that if you have a special interest or hobby, *that* is what you should develop on the Net. The medium was built for the enthusiast and that is why I love it.

THE INFORMATION ECONOMY

7

> How much should the author of the work receive each time someone 'down-loads' the words? Should it be the full price of the book, as though the researcher had bought it from a bookshop or should it correspond to a library lending right? These are questions that authors, authors' associations and publishers must address very soon.
>
> The Writer and the Word Processor, Ray Hammond, 1984

> Logic would appear to suggest that there is now no protection for any single published piece of creation which is stored electronically and total reward must be sought before publication.
>
> The Musician and the Micro, Ray Hammond, 1982

INFORMATION 'WANTS TO BE FREE'

Sections of this book are available free on the World-Wide Web. Because it contains so many live hyperlinks to business and information resources, the on-line version is probably closer to software than a book, but the distinction between the two will become increasingly blurred. Readers are free to use the book in its on-line form while on the Web, or they may down-load sections in either hyper-text format (HTML) or as standard text.

In chapter 1 I said I would explain why such an idea makes economic sense and why my publishers haven't lynched me. As a writer, naturally I want my ideas to reach the largest number of people and I want to be paid for my knowledge and my work. Unless it is a phenomenon, a printed best-selling business book typically sells in scores of thousands and, sometimes, hundreds of thousands. This takes a long time, reaches relatively few and there is enormous wastage in the process (manufacture, distribution, and so on).

On the Web, key parts of this book are now available to millions of people, only they will access and use it differently. I believe print will remain the best medium in which to read linear fiction and for sustaining lengthy arguments for some time. I hope by now you will want to stay with this 'read' but you will not want to use the Internet version in the same way. If you visit this book's site on the World-Wide Web, you can quickly check the up-dates I and my staff have posted, can use our hyperlinks to visit the sites and resources to which I refer to see how things are developing and can copy and save any of the bookmarks you please for your own use. This is using the on-line edition as software.

This concept for a book, with its on-line live companion waiting for you on the Net, is only a pale shadow of what books will become in the Network economy. Reading from perfect screens with the luminance and clarity of paper, we will peruse certain types of 'book' which contain many live hyperlinks. If it is a travel book, a click or a spoken command will take us to film, sound and smells of the destination, often through wireless links. Only fiction, that most private word in your ear, will remain on paper or its equivalent.

Not everybody agrees with me about fiction, however, and I may be revealing my prejudices or my ideas may be becoming fixed. Peter James, the best-selling Penguin author of *Host* and other horror titles explained his belief in interactive fiction at my conference *Publishing On-Line & CD-ROM '95*. He asked why novels should be on paper, and suggested that fiction writers ignore the new developments at their peril. In particular, he argued:

> *Where the electronic novel really scores is in the features that elevate it beyond the limitations of a traditional printed book: At the click of a key it will go into Large Print format, a boon for the poorly-sighted and for tired eyes. Ultimately the reader, not the publisher, will select the font and size with which he or she is comfortable reading. And with the book of the future, if you are lying on the beach feeling too lazy to read, at the click of a button it will read itself aloud to you.*
>
> *Electronic books are smart. They can remember where you got to, so no more dog-earing, or losing bookmarks. They have all the search and find facilities of a word processor – enter a*

word or a phrase and you will find the passage instantly, and should you want to make notes in the margin, you can do so. Because they have their own light source, you can curl up in bed and read them in the dark, and instead of the nerdy author photograph, in 'Host' you get a video in which I introduce the novel.

(The full eleven hundred word transcript of Peter James's presentation is available to on-line readers here.)

Another best-selling novelist has also announced his faith in interactive and on-line fiction and in the role of the Net as a distribution medium. Tom Clancy, author of *The Hunt for Red October*, *Patriot Games* and *Clear and Present Danger* is now writing a series of animated stories for Internet publication called *Net Force*. Set in 2025, *Net Force* is about FBI agents intent on catching Internet crooks and cyber-terrorists. Real-world spin-offs such as videos, films and books are likely.

I suppose I think of the more literary novel when I propose that certain types of fiction will remain on paper but within a generation or two I suspect the medium will have almost disappeared.

FEEDBACK, PLEASE!

Another reason for putting a companion product to this book on the Net is that I want to hear from my readers. Feedback is a vital ingredient in spotting factual mistakes, poorly thought-out ideas, or misconceptions. Regretfully, despite my best efforts and those of my editors, there may be many in these works, for which I take full responsibility. Traditionally, only the most motivated (or nutty) readers take time to put green ink to paper and write to authors (usually following a circuitous route via the publisher's office) and we treasure the occasional gems from busy people who offer some genuine correction, insight or argument.

On-line, interaction is instinctive. If you agree, disagree or want to tell me something, click here, and an e-mail message box will pop up with my address already in place. Get it off your chest and hit 'Send'. I'll receive it and I will answer. The amount of feedback I get and give via e-mail is magnitudes greater than I've experienced in the physical world, but it is very much easier to respond to.

This interaction helps me grow my ideas and weed out errors. Important topics have a habit of running continuously throughout our lives and the development process should be continuous. One aspect of being a professional writer which I have least enjoyed, is the need to 'freeze' a story, idea set or argument for the purposes of printing. The quotes reproduced in this book from *The On-Line Handbook* show how excited I was in the early eighties about the potential for commercial and social exploitation. Now I am able to publish these ideas in a form which I can effortlessly update as I learn (from my readers or otherwise) about errors, developments and new concepts. On the Web, a book remains alive and growing from the moment it is first published and, when the time comes for a second printed edition, most of my new material will be to hand.

YOU WON'T 'READ' THIS BOOK ON THE NET

Why have we made parts of this book available and easy to 'steal' on the Net? If you download this as a text file, you may read it on screen or print it out on your computer's printer. Either is highly unsatisfactory. Humans do not like reading long texts on today's computer screens and would not plough through 70,000 words and hyperlinks. If you print it on your laser printer, it will take a long time, it won't contain some of the background, it will cost you more than buying the book and it will be far less attractive, portable and durable. Further, there is something else that occurs which is unique to the book.

If you are reading this in its extended printed version, I hope some of the ideas are making your mind race. You will have entirely different skill sets, insights and business experience to me and, in the quiet and contemplative mode required for sustained reading, many ideas and implications will occur to you of which I haven't even dreamed. Intellectually, reading a book is far more creative than consuming electronic information. In a pure intellectual sense it is also more interactive because it engages not only conscious knowledge and experience but also *unconscious* knowledge and experience. The facility of accessing these deep and vital parts of your being occurs through deep and quiet consideration, such as is triggered by reading a book. For me, writing for print was the right place to start this work because it is the painful act of long-distance writing itself which coaxes ideas and understanding out of the unconscious. I have understood more about what is going on from writing this book than from a thousand live conference appearances, broadcasts, on-line interactions or journalistic endeavours. Writers don't know what it is they know (or need to learn) until they sit down to write. Readers don't know what they know until they are jogged to produce the ideas through the most personal of all forms of communication, reading a book. Therefore, the value of this book on the Web is for its hyperlinks, not its extended arguments.

But I (and my publishers) are at considerable risk of copyright theft. When you have down-loaded this text, you are physically (but not legally) free to copy it, duplicate it, include it as your own words in your own documents, and otherwise disseminate it. This could make profits for you on the back of my work and I and my publishers are theoretically protected against you doing this by the laws of copyright almost everywhere in the world.

It is impossible to stop digital copying. What's more, the digital copies are perfect replicas of the original. It is for this reason that many argue that the concept of copyright, for books, music, film, photographs and all other forms of intellectual and artistic property which can be digitised (try doing it to a sculpture!), is an outmoded concept which will not last for many more years.

In the 1982 quote reproduced at the head of this chapter I said that logic suggests that total reward must be sought before any publication can take place. But this is not practical because it makes no allowance for fostering new talent which would be unable to demand a sufficient advance to earn enough to create a further work. Traditionally, new writers (and musicians, poets, photographers, illustrators, and so on) receive minimal advances and their career is built through the painfully slow process of sales achieved through reviews and word-of-mouth. As publishers find themselves reprinting books or preparing new editions, so they are able to contemplate increasing advances.

It is hard to think of a substitute mechanism for the royalty process in the physical world although it is clear that the Net will offer many new artists exposure to the public in a much more efficient way. Another concern with scrapping a royalty system in exchange for a one-off payment is that it denies writers any long-term security (although I acknowledge they have no more right to this rapidly vanishing concept than the rest of the population).

Writers seeking publication who cannot interest a traditional publisher may be offered a viable alternative to vanity publishing (where an author pays a quasi-publisher to 'publish' a book) by the Net. Having started out primarily as self-help groups, there are now several resources on the World-Wide Web which will either publish complete works or will put up samples for publishers to review.

The Arachnoid Writers Alliance (which has its physical presence in Santa Cruz) provides writers with an electronic publishing forum where visitors to the site can read sample chapters, can order electronic versions of the books, and learn about the authors. The Online Writery provides a gallery where authors can publish their own work and provides links to writing resources on the Net.

Whether prompted by concepts such as the Net and new media or not, it has recently become clear that the traditional model of copyright protection and royalty-based reward is also under threat in the physical world. This is because the relentless downwards pressure on the price of all information and books in particular is resulting in some agents and publishers speculating that the royalty system will be scrapped in favour of a one-off 'purchase payment' by a publisher.

Books have long been discount items in the US but the recent scrapping of the Net Book Agreement in the UK (which allowed publishers to fix prices and resellers to observe them) has resulted in a fierce discount war. While sales of books have increased it is not yet clear what the effect will be on writers' royalties. Another clear indication of the trend has been the success of the 're-born' paperback. Just over 60 years ago Penguin turned the book publishing trade on its head by launching inexpensive editions of classic books bound in card instead of a stiff jacket. To mark their 60th anniversary the firm launched 60p (85 cents) editions of classic books as a promotional stunt meant to last only a few months. To their surprise these pocket editions were so successful the company sold out on the first day and went on to make significant money from the idea. They quickly made the list permanent and, as this rather more expensive book was going to press, eight other publishers were preparing to publish 'miniature editions' and an avalanche of inexpensive books (mostly, but not all, fiction) has now hit the UK streets. The idea is rapidly being exported and the price of many books will be forced down as a result.

TODAY'S COPYRIGHT MECHANISMS

In considering the concept and application of copyright in the digital age it is helpful to understand how our laws are applied and enforced today. Over the last twenty years or so we have become used to the idea of copying sound recordings on to audio cassettes, taping films on to video cassettes from TV broadcasts and reading photocopies of articles and journals. These abuses of strict copyright law have been (mostly) tolerated because infringement is impossible to detect and most copies have been made for private use rather than for financial gain through commercial pirating. Although regarded much more seriously, pirating and private use of software by individuals (not companies) has become a reality because it is so hard to police.

What has not been tolerated, and what is always ruthlessly tracked down and stamped out, is the pirating of intellectual works for resale and large-scale commercial gain. It is here we get to the real heart of what copyright law does, as compared to what its principles suggest. Copyright law exists to ensure that originators receive a 'fair' return for their intellectual and creative works, rather than to guarantee they get paid every time something is reproduced or broadcast. I believe this model will translate to the digital age.

On the Internet it is easy to steal a sound, an image, a graphic or text. If you re-use that privately, it is unlikely anybody will ever find out. If you publish the pirated material yourself on the Net you stand a chance of being found out, particularly if you market your efforts (although you are currently more likely to be asked to desist rather than be sued – depending on who you are and what the pirated material is). If you distribute the stolen item to friends, either over the Net or physically, you are still likely to escape detection, but if you attempt to sell that item publicly, in the harsh light of day, you will be likely to attract the attention of the 'copyright police' in whatever form they take in your locality.

To put it simply: the copyright law is used to prevent sizable commercial rip-offs and not private pirating or even petty exploitation. I think this model of copyright can transfer the on-line economy even allowing for the different attitudes to copyright theft around the world.

Despite this apparently reasonable approach to the enforcement of copyright principals, there is a risk (although I think it is an outside one) that the US government may cave in to vociferous lobbying from the Hollywood Studios, TV producers and print media owners to toughen up the existing copyright laws because of the threats posed by the transference of digital information over the Net.

Under Bruce Lehman, Bill Clinton's Assistant Secretary of Commerce, a white paper called 'Intellectual Property and the Information Infrastructure' is now being examined by Congress. If adopted as law, the proposals contained in this document would tighten up the laws of copyright to the extent that it would be illegal for American buyers of this book to lend it to a friend, illegal for reviewers to quote a short passage and illegal for electronic readers to make a private electronic copy. Most importantly it would mean an end to the whole US concept of 'fair use'.

A lot of Net publishing would fall under the old category of 'fair use' because it isn't done for profit – it is often done for fun. But copyright owners have been threatening those who have used copyright material in this way just because it is on the Net and is therefore so easily distributed. Dutton Children's Books recently forced an amateur site to remove 'Winnie the Pooh' images and many other publishers are pursuing similar policies.

Such draconian measures are being urged because the producers of expensive properties such as films and videos see digitisation and the Net as the Armageddon for their industry and, pointing to their £33/$50 billion annual export contribution to the American balance of payments, they are able to capture government attention. Within the proposals is a right for copyright owners to incorporate 'electronic copyright management systems' into their work which buyers must agree to use and a requirement that on-line service providers who deliver their work must act as copyright cops and account for all uses. Another proposal is that the use of encryption on copyright works should become illegal (whether applied by the person who has purchased the copyright work or not).

If such measures were to be passed in their entirety I suspect such a bill would hasten the end of the copyright system. In a democracy any law requires the general consent of a population to be effective and I hope the proponents of the bill will realise this and understand that the existing law is adequate to deal with commercial pirating. I will be updating this section on-line as the white paper continues its progress.

I doubt that any luddite readers will have got as far as this chapter, but I can imagine a technophobe with a little knowledge saying 'It's all a bit academic, isn't it? At the current speed of the Internet it would take an hour to transfer one minute's worth of CD-quality audio or one second of VHS quality video. It will be a long time before this is a real issue.'

Well, a small group of consumers is already able to access feature-films rapidly from the Internet. @home, the company founded by Will Hearst which I mentioned in Chapter 2, has just started to provide inexpensive 'cable modems' for offices and homes in Northern California which provide Net access over the cables used to deliver TV channels. @home modems allow CDs and movies to be down-loaded in a few minutes and this type of Net access will spread to every area which has been cabled. Most of metropolitan USA is cabled and the UK is now 'being wired' with over one million households already connected. In addition to the high-speed cable modems offered by @home, products with similar performance are being offered for those with cable by Motorola and AT&T.

Unsurprisingly, this has terrified film producers and record companies, not because they plan to offer their products over the Net, but because others will be quick to try and sell (or give away) pirated copies. The cries for a legal response are not confined to the USA. Across the Atlantic, the European Commission gave four million Ecus (£3.3/$5.3 million) in 1995 to a new study group called Imprimatur whose brief is 'to agree on a unified copyright management infrastructure for the electronic markets'. The body includes lawyers, publishers and trade organisations but it is not expected to produce a preliminary paper until 1996 and a full report in 1988.

An alternative approach to the problems posed by the ease of digital copying is to incorporate 'digital fingerprinting' or 'watermarking' into electronic products, particularly images (still and motion). This technology adds a signature to data which can be extracted from copies to prove their point of origin. The developers of the systems claim that the nature of the data is unaffected and that the recovery of the identifying mark is possible even from a very small section of information which has been incorporated into something else, – for example, a small part of an image or piece of music which has been collaged into something else. The difficulty for those who wish to adopt this method is in finding out where the parts of their original data have been used.

PLEASE STEAL THIS WORK

But I think the Net will produce other ways of providing originators with a 'fair return' for their effort. The new models may include some which recognise the power of super-distribution. For example, I would be flattered if you felt you wanted to steal this work – so flattered in fact that I hereby give you permission, including use for profit, wherever you are in the world, to do just that, strictly on the following conditions:

1) You take the electronic text from my Web site and do not attempt to re-typeset this book or capture it in electronic form by other means.

2) In any use of this text in any of your productions (e.g. report, essay, brochure, presentation, book, etc.) you MUST include the following wording (it may be behind a hyperlink in an electronic version) within the first two hundred words you use (or within the section if less than 200 words): 'This text, and 000 more words contained in this work, are extracted from 'DIGITAL BUSINESS: Surviving and Thriving in an On-Line World' by Ray Hammond. Available at < http://www.hammond.co.uk > .'

In any HTML reproduction (the mark-up language used to create Web documents), the hyperlink to my site must be live.

3) Any reproduction of text from this book must be used as a continuous stream, without alteration or editing. If sections are used in separate locations, conditions 2), 4) and 5) must be observed for each section used.

4) You may not reproduce more than 10,000 words and

hyperlinks, whether continuous or sectioned, in any single electronic or printed work.

5) Immediately after the last use of any piece of my text in your work, you must include the following:

'DIGITAL BUSINESS: Surviving and Thriving in an On-Line World' is published in book form by Hodder & Stoughton, ISBN 0340 66659 5.

That's it. There are no other conditions.

How can I make any money from such an approach?

First, putting this text on the Net achieves potential super-distribution. Whether or not anybody visits, looks, uses and down-loads depends on: a) how I market the presence of this book on the Net; and b) the quality of the ideas and hyperlinks contained here.

Marketing a product on the Web is a subject I cover in Appendix 2, but I will do my best to ensure that most of the main topics are thoroughly posted in the search engines on the Web so that queries concerning any of my topics are likely to find my Web address.

I will also market the on-line version of this book in traditional media and you will realise that is exactly what I am doing in this sentence. I hope that the printed version of this book will eventually lead you to look at the on-line version and to see the updates (updates will be available as separate sections, clearly marked). I hope you will like the updates you find and I would be very pleased if you would leave me an e-mail message with comments and thoughts.

The on-line product will contain links to new business resources as they come on-line. If I and my team do our job thoroughly the site should become a useful business resource. In addition, I will be providing links to information about my other business activities.

From this, you will realise that this printed book, and its subsequent editions, is feeding my Web site (and the links I choose to include there), and providing me (I hope) with feedback for later editions intended to reach people just coming on-line. With the Net I can establish a bio-feedback loop which feeds my work, allows me to improve what I do and have direct, on-going contact with my readers. I will ask you to register when you arrive (I won't extract your e-mail address from your platform without your permission) and, if I may, I will let you know when a significant percentage has been up-dated (more than 50 per cent) and when a new print edition is due. Suddenly I am connected to my readers (or at least those who wish to make a connection).

The printed version benefits from the input of the Web site and the Web site grows from the publication of the printed versions. The products are, in fact, complementary.

Will my publishers and I make money by doing this? That depends on the quality of my ideas and information and that is for you to judge. If it is any good, readers will want up-dates and will spread the word. The loop will feed both the printed version and the on-line version. You might wish to give a copy of this book to clients or friends who are not on-line and are struggling to understand its implications. Being on-line I can provide a facility for you to e-mail me if you would like my publishers to quote for supplying a number of copies of this book with your company's logo or a special message on the jacket. If my ideas and explanations are not any good, attempting to protect the sale of a printed version by not providing an on-line version is like protecting something you can't give away.

TRANSITION PROBLEMS

The arrival of the Net brings considerable problems of transition for information industries. You may have ordered this book from a virtual store on the Web. If so, it may have been mailed to you in a geographical territory where Hodder & Stoughton don't have the rights to publish it. My publisher in your territory would have every right to be upset. I have asked the management of several of the virtual book shops about this issue and, at the time of writing, they all reconfirmed their willingness to ship books to anywhere in the world if the on-line customer is prepared to pay.

The problem isn't so bad for authors, although royalty rates do vary from territory to territory, but it makes life difficult for publishers when it comes to the timing of editions, such as paperbacks. If a popular novel is only available in hardback in one territory, yet it is already out in paperback in another, we can guess where many on-line buyers will choose to make their purchase.

Of course, digital network delivery is going to change book publishing in a much more profound way than simply muddying the territorial borders. A large percentage of books produced are information-based — dictionaries, encyclopaedias, guide books, recipe books, 'how to' books, user manuals, and so on. These will be increasingly delivered on-line, with, for example, pictures, videos, graphics, and the publishing mix will change substantially.

Many of the 'out-of-copyright' classics are now available in full text on the Internet and for research purposes and providing they are required for research and not for leisure reading this is an infinitely superior method of gaining access. Down-loading plain text does not take very long now and will be very rapid in the future. I save the text to my hard disk where I can search it for characters and scenes I wish to review.

But it isn't simply that packaged information will be delivered in a new form, our networked future is likely to obviate the need for us to 'own' some types of information. We will, instead, access it. As I write I have a Webster's Dictionary open beside me. My copy of Microsoft Word on my PC naturally includes spell-checker and thesaurus modules, but I still need the Webster's to check etymology, extended meanings and redundant meanings. But my Webster's isn't a book, I can see it in a window on my computer screen beside my word-processing page. The dictionary is sitting on a Web server on an American university campus. As I can find no remarks regarding copyright on the server I won't print the location or provide a link, but it offers me a search box for words I wish to find and returns the meaning with all of the synonyms and descriptors hyper-linked so I can, in turn, click on them to see their meaning with their hyper-linked synonyms and descriptors. I don't need to buy a dictionary, either physical or electronic. My PC is nearly always connected to an open Internet line and I can search this dictionary, and many others, in a much more powerful way than is possible on paper.

I suspect that the provision of on-line resources such as the Webster's will undergo change. I have noticed that some of the reference works available on-line have disappeared recently and I think this marks the development of the Internet from an anarchic medium – 'let's just do it' – to one where lawyers are advising clients to pull things off the Net in the face of copyright complaints.

But my point stands and has wider meaning: when resources are available in a window on-line, at the click of a button, we don't need to own them and they may be located anywhere in the wired world. The nature of reference publishing and learned journal publishing, already decimated by CD-ROM, is still in a state of profound change. In the medium-term future – 10 to 15 years from now – the vast majority of information books will be delivered electronically over the networks. Many of our bookshops will have disappeared and our publishing houses will have completely changed their function.

As I hope to demonstrate with the *Digital Business* site, books will no longer be static collections of information frozen in time, they will be living, dynamic streams of information which are constantly updated and revised. The economics of publishing will change completely and micro-payments (see Chapter 10) to the author by people who access all or small parts of the information will provide the revenue stream for the up-dating and revisions. Most importantly, the general body of ideas and new knowledge produced each day is likely to be of much greater value than those produced today.

Not long ago, Nicholas Negroponte and his colleagues at MIT wrote an 'open' letter to Newt Gingritch and congress asking for a 'Bill of Writes' and urging them to make the Library of Congress a digital depository. The concept calls for the mandatory depositing of the original digital data behind any work (printed or otherwise) to be made at the Library before copyright could be awarded. Nick argues that such a requirement would turn a depository into a 'retrievatory' where everything can be searched and accessed locally and over the networks. As he points out, such a step would turn millions of books accessible only to a few, and then with great difficulty, into a resource of almost unimaginable power which everybody could access.

When I was researching for this book I turned to some of my earlier books to see how my thoughts had changed over the years. It took me days to re-read them (most of them were written on obsolete computer systems and the technical task to convert the huge floppy disks to run on modern systems was daunting) and I found quite a lot of relevant material. But nearly all of my time was spent scanning pages for appropriate passages and I was only working with six books which were conveniently to hand on my own bookshelf! Apart from newspapers and on-line sources, my other reading material consisted of new and recently published books on specifics such as copyright law. These were painfully and slowly gathered from bookshops all over the world.

What I could not do was search the hundreds of books written over the last decade which discuss the implications of the developing networks. I am sure there are thousands of ideas I have missed which are vital, useful or thought-provoking. Neither I nor any other writer can search through such dead information effectively. We can only get at those books which are well-known, totally specific in title and descriptor or found serendipitously.

As a result, new ideas and knowledge have developed at a snail's pace, all too often in ignorance of the work of others. In the future, writers (and by this term I mean all those who are attempting to communicate new ideas, find new solutions, provoke thought, and so on) will be able to make far more effective idea and information searches. The 'eco-system' on which the network economy is founded will ensure that ideas and information which attract readers and users in sufficient quantity will produce the finance required for development. Those which do not will 'die' (will remain static and eventually disappear, as do most of today's books).

Our legislators must follow Nicholas Negroponte's advice and ensure that the depositories (the libraries) gather digital data and provide electronic access. The cost is relatively low as storage requirements for digital data are minute – a point entirely missed by the designers and bunglers responsible for the new British Library in London whose construction is not only intolerably late, unconscionably over-budget and hideously ugly, but is also unnecessary.

ADVERTISING, SELLING AND SPONSORSHIP ON THE NET

8

> *On-line advertising has one advantage over all other media: it is very selective.*
>
> *It is wasteful to advertise a new movie to people interested in motorcycles, because the advertiser can't be sure whether or not the searcher watches films.*
>
> *But if the ads are shown only to those enquiring about film reviews (and equally motorcycle ads go only to those searching motorcycle topics) then the advertising is targeted directly to the correct group.*
>
> *This is cost-effective and powerful and most commercial databases in the future will carry some level of advertising.*
>
> The On-Line Handbook, Ray Hammond, 1984

There are sites on the Net today which deliver advertisements specifically tailored to your interest. If you arrive at a search engine and query 'American football' the results will be accompanied by an ad informing you of a future game in your area. This is the perfectly targeted advertising of which I dreamed in 1984 and, if there are still any sceptics remaining this far into the book, I hope you will agree this presents a wonderful opportunity to make money.

Perhaps the best example of early profits from such an approach is seen at one of the most popular Web indexes, YAHOO! This site was set up by two PhD students at Stanford University in April 1984 as a hobby. A year later the venture capitalists had arrived and David Filo and Jerry Yang started leaves of absence from their university. By the end of 1995 YAHOO! was welcoming 800,000 querying visitors a day. Advertising rates were £13,000/$20,000 a month for each of 46 prime slots with £660/$1,000 a week for small bottom-of-the-page positions. By now the company will have floated and, unless there is the much-feared general collapse in US high-technology stocks, I hope I will be an investor by the time you read this.

WebTrack, a company which specialises in monitoring Net advertising expenditure conducted the first ever survey of the market in the last quarter of 1995. The research assumed that all ads were paid for at rate card prices (which doesn't allow for the many contra, cross-link deals which are common) but it nevertheless gives us our first taste of a market gearing up to explode.

The top ten advertisers that WebTrack found were:

Advertiser	1995 Q4
AT&T	£378,000/$567,000
Netscape	£370,000/$556,000
Internet Shopping Network	£219,000/$329,000
NECX Direct	£214,000/$322,000
Mastercard	£185,000/$278,000
American Airlines	£169,000/$254,000
Microsoft	£160,000/$240,000
clnet	£158,000/$237,000
MCI	£154,000/$231,000
SportsLine	£145,000/$218,000

The ten publishers which received the most income were:

Publisher	1995 Q4£/$
Netscape	£1,177,000/$1,766,000
Lycos	£864,000/$1,296,000
InfoSeek	£810,000/$1,215,000
YAHOO!	£724,000/$1,086,000
Pathfinder	£540,000/$810,000
HotWired	£480,000/$720,000
WebCrawler	£440,000/$660,000
ESPNET SportZone	£400,000/$600,000
GNN	£396,000/$594,000
clnet	£360,000/$540,000

What's remarkable about this list is that Netscape tops even the most popular search engines – Lycos, YAHOO!, and so on. The company's current dominance as a software provider is also turning them into the most successful 'publisher', a development which should provide food for thought.

A year after YAHOO! was founded I chaired a London conference called 'Advertising, Selling and Sponsorship on the Internet'. It was the first meeting of its kind in the UK and it would have sold out twice over had we sufficient space. The people who came were from advertising agencies and corporate marketing departments and they were desperately trying to understand the implications of what they saw as simply 'another medium'.

Our speakers included Bill Thompson of Pipex, Jane Morgan of Eurodollar, Simon Phipps of IBM, Nigel Penn-Simpkins of ICL on behalf of the Innovations catalogue, Gerry Fielder of Legas Delaney, Stephen Groome of Lewis Silkin, Christopher Ogden of the Advertising Standards Authority, Kristi Nuelle of Leo Burnet, and Carl Foster of Future Publishing.

Few of the delegates had ever looked at the World-Wide Web and the message all the speakers tried to deliver was that traditional marketing techniques do not work on the Net and that a completely different approach is called for. As we discovered during the event, trying to explain the feeling of intimacy that exists in on-line communication to someone who has never used it personally (and by this I mean someone who is thoroughly familiar with on-line navigation) is rather like trying to explain the essence of sex to a virgin. You can discuss technique and technical detail for ever, you can write books and show film about it, but only through personal involvement is it possible to understand the power.

We had an ISDN (Integrated Systems Digital Network) connection to the Net and projected large images of various sites on to a large screen. Speaker after speaker emphasised the personal nature of on-line communication and warned advertising professionals that they would have to learn new techniques of presenting their messages to be successful. Unsurprisingly, a lot of advertising professionals were (and are) quite dismissive of the Net and the role it will play in their lives.

Advertising is an intensely creative business and one which, for a few years, I enjoyed enormously. Until recently, though, technology did not sit well in the creative world. The introduction of desktop publishing technology, which led in turn to desktop graphics technology, went some way towards changing this attitude but although Macs now sit in many advertising design studios, the creative department is usually intensely conservative and dismissive of technological wonders. I understand this. Their product is human creativity and anything which appears to lessen its importance appears an enemy.

However, because of the Net the advertising industry must re-invent itself, as must all of its clients. When it is as easy for a client to put its own site up on the Net as it is to buy space on other people's sites, what becomes of general advertising?

Almost every advertising agency has founded a 'new media' department and a few agencies understand the nature of the Net very well, but they are the exception. In a survey published at the beginning of 1996 by Forrester Research, it was revealed that traditional full-service agencies were involved in building only 26 per cent of World-Wide Web sites put up by major advertisers. Most of the sites were created either by newly formed Net marketing companies or by Internet service providers. I am not surprised; in countless other conferences (including a couple of my own) I have listened to senior advertising figures deliver absolute nonsense with all of the gravitas associated with those whose profession it is to make the trivial seem important.

Chiat Day, New York, now TBWA Chiat Day was the first

agency to publish a really creative site on the Web and the firm now describes itself as an 'idea factory' rather than an advertising agency. A glance at the company's site will tell you that Net fever has swept over this creative group and, from providing visitors with a tour of their virtual office, to publishing thoughtful and intellectually sound papers on the evolution of the Net as a communications medium, it is clear that most of their creative energy is directed towards the Net.

Four months after our initial conference for the advertising industry, we presented a conference called Interactive Newspapers Europe and in that short period a lot more information had become available about the effectiveness of advertising approaches on the Net. During the conference, Pippa Littler, Advertising Director of the award-winning Electronic Telegraph provided an insightful paper into her early experiences with advertisers and the new market.

She told the audience that ET's market is, as expected, male, upmarket and young but she said that they behave differently than they do with other media. She pointed out how much control on-line readers have over the interaction but she cheered the audience by confirming that ET's readers *do* want to see on-line advertising. In ET's survey, the readers generally thought advertising is the right way to pay for Net delivery.

Pippa said that her readers want the opportunity to purchase on-line and she said that the main advantage she can offer advertisers is the ability to know exactly how many people looked at an ad and, via ET's reader registration system, who the readers are.

On-line readers can down-load the full three thousand five hundred word transcript of Pippa Littler's presentation here.

THE SHIFTING DEMOGRAPHICS

Advertising people live and die by demographics and market research. One of the questions most frequently asked is about how this new market can be tested and categorised and, as you might imagine, companies like Nielson and ABC have sought to extend their physical franchise in audience measurement to the Net. However, cyberspace presents a unique set of advantages and problems.

The good news is that raw statistics are easy to come by. Computers are excellent at collecting and regurgitating such data. You can tell how much activity a Net site has by the day, by the hour and by the minute. You can tell which part of the site attracts the most attention and individual ads can be tested on-line and receive instant ratings. The bad news is that it is very hard to get definitive data about the number and nature of those accessing Web sites without resorting to physical means.

Publishers of sites on the World-Wide Web often speak about the number of 'hits' their site enjoys. In an earlier chapter I mentioned that the Netscape site located in Mountain View, California was getting 17 million hits per day at one point. A 'hit' is a request for information. If I click on a hyperlink to jump down the page, to copy an image, to save some text, to jump elsewhere on the same server, to jump to another server on the Net this 'request' counts as one hit. In order to translate the number of hits per day or per hour into the number of individual users of the site per day or per hour it is necessary to estimate or measure the average number of hits carried out at a site by each visitor. Even for a single site, this can be very difficult. There is no standard which may be applied across different Web sites as the number of hits carried out by each user will be dictated by the nature of the site: some sites will provide lists which take visitors to other sites and those gain only one hit per visitor. Other sites may be designed so that visitors have to click through information sentence by sentence which will generate an enormous number of hits. Only an experienced Web site designer will be able to make an educated guess about the number of hits and the length of time a typical visitor might stay at a site.

As you might imagine, a number of Net-oriented young companies sprang up with technological solutions to such technical difficulties and these include Site Trak, WebTrak, iAudit offered by the Internet Audit Bureau (which has now partnered with ABC) and the I/Pro system from Internet Profiles Corporation (which has now partnered with Nielsen Media research).

These companies got in before industry behemoths such as ABC & Nielsen, but because the international advertising industry is so conservative, I am sure the traditional media measurers will achieve dominance on the Net.

So what is the most recent demographic profile of Net users? At the time of writing Nielsen and Commercenet, a non-profit organisation for promoting business on the Net, had just published the first serious survey on the American and Canadian markets which had been gathered by traditional telephone interviewing techniques.

The survey shows that 17% of the population over 16 in North America are regular Net users and over two and a half million people have already made purchases on the Internet. The survey revealed that the time spent by the population on-line now exceeds the time people spend watching rented video tapes.

The executive summary of the survey is reproduced in Appendix 3 and I am grateful for Nielsen's and Commercenet's permission to reproduce it. On-line readers will find details of the latest survey here.

Many others companies, bodies and individuals conduct Net surveys but few have the resources of the large media measurement organisations. The best 'alternative' I have found which is prepared by the Net community is carried out by the Georgia Institute of Technology, Atlanta.

Unfortunately, no proper study of Net usage among the general population has yet been conducted or published outside of North America. There is a real need as massive investments are being made on instinct and limited private research.

MBA students at Dundee University in Scotland were preparing to publish the results of an on-line survey into Net business as this book was going to press and I will be providing up-dated links to demographic information at this book's companion site on the Net.

The limited research that has been undertaken in Europe includes a study by CNN International and Continental Research which shows that of the larger European countries the UK has by far the largest percentage of its business executives connected to the Internet. The percentages are:

Finland	34%
Norway	31%
Netherlands	26%
UK/Switzerland/Denmark	23%
Austria/Ireland	19%
Germany	15%

Greece	13%
Belgium-Luxembourg/Spain/Portugal	12%
France	10%
Italy	8%

MANAGEMENT IS COMMUNICATION

9

If you want to get serious about your on-line activity and apply it to your business, you can tap a wealth of hard information so vast that it is difficult to imagine: On-Liners have a hard time trying to tell their non-computing friends about what's out there; they're often greeted with scepticism.

The On-Line Handbook. Ray Hammond, 1984

A year or so ago I received an e-mail from a young man looking for work in Net marketing, by which he meant marketing in cyberspace. His e-mail query and the attached CV were interesting so I arranged a meeting. At the interview I asked the applicant how much he knew about my company. 'Quite a lot,' he said as he unfolded a paper copy of my CV and credits list on the desk along with some printed pages from our Web site. This tiny reversal of role illustrates the potency of the Net as a communications medium and the way it changes established norms. As an employer for over 20 years it wouldn't previously have occurred to me to send *my* CV out to prospective job applicants – but if they choose to research my company by visiting our Web site, I'm delighted if they read it.

I asked John Nugent why, at the age of 28, he hadn't yet settled on a single career path. 'I thought you'd understand,' he answered referring to my own zig-zag career progression.

Above all, the Net is about inexpensive, instant communication and it opens up completely new types of interaction within companies and between companies and their suppliers, potential employees and their marketplace. Communication is a vital but costly activity for almost every company and organisation, and many of the early and most successful exploitations of the Net were applications for this purpose. The White House quickly understood that this was a powerful, low-cost personal communications medium and other governments and political parties quickly followed suit and developed sites including Britain's Conservative, Labour and Liberal parties, Australia's Democrats, The Australian Labor Party and The Liberal Party of Australia.

The major activist charities like Friends of the Earth, Greenpeace and Amnesty International weren't far behind and all charities are beginning to discover that the Net presents an ideal low-cost way of fund-raising. When digital cash is available, or another form of micropayment scheme which allows us to make five penny donations without there being any transaction overhead, we will find charity appeal stations all over the Net. The Net user demographic is perfect for charities and we can expect to see many links between socially responsible organisations and the charities they choose to support (see chapter 13).

The Net gets an organisation closer to its audience than any other communications method. Visitors self-qualify to be (or stay) at the site and from that point onwards they are able to review the organisation's work, structure, aims and personnel in an intimate, zero-pressure environment.

SAVING MONEY WITH AN INTERNAL WEB

You may feel that some of the points I am making in this book are too futuristic and are therefore irrelevant to the needs of current business. I do understand that the pressing need for every manager and executive is to improve efficiency *today* as well as to plan for the future. Applying Net technology *inside* your company can save an organization substantial costs and improve efficiency within as little as twelve months. Using the technology in this way is described as building an 'Intranet.'

An Intranet is a private World-Wide Web network established within a company or organisation solely for its own use. Web technology and protocols are so simple to implement and use that, after years of promises about the potential of collaborative, work-flow computer networks to reduce the amount of paper in use and improve work group efficiency, the idea has suddenly caught on. During the latter part of 1995 just over half of Netscape's revenues came from sales of client and server software to corporations setting up private Web networks – Intranets.

The proposition is simple: if computer users in an organisation are provided with a Web platform or browser they are able to access sites on the World-Wide Web as well as sites on an internal private Web. Password security and other technological barriers to entry prevent general users on the Net gaining access to the organisation's private Web, but users of the private Web may leave their internal network and roam out across the world.

Earlier I described the experience of using the World-Wide Web as 'compulsive' and it is this factor which is ensuring the highly successful implementation of many Intranets around the world. If employees get pleasure from using an internal network it becomes a very powerful corporate tool.

Until now most medium-size and large corporations and organisations have communicated with their officers and employees with paper and e-mail. House journals, often the target of employee humour, have to be exceptional to communicate well and e-mail has the disadvantage of being text-only and one-to-one or one-to-many. A departmental Web site, on the other hand, can sit patiently on the network containing a wealth of information which may be accessed by anybody within the company. Password hierarchies may be used to restrict access to private or semi-sensitive information. Company information which is sensitive or highly sensitive should only be placed on any Net with strong encryption (see chapter 11), after which it is perfectly safe.

An excellent example of the power and use of an Intranet is provided by US West, the American airline. Of the company's 50,000 employees, 15,000 were originally connected and one site on the network was rapidly dubbed 'the virtual secretary'. This site contains a collection of useful tips about 'how to get things done' at US West from ordering catered lunches to sending paperwork to the right department. The Virtual Secretary is a growing entity and relies heavily on contributed ideas from the staff. (For on-line readers the full case history is here.)

Other early adopters of Intranet communications were Levi Strauss and Lockheed Martin Corporation, and over 150,000 employees of these two companies now communicate via internal Web networks using Netscape's ubiquitous technology. At first, Levi Strauss's employees were told that corporate information sites were available and here they were offered company information. They could also see videos of commercials in production, communicate in 'virtual conferences' with each other and have private 'chats' on-line. Today almost every department has its own Web site and thousands of the executives have their 'home pages' permanently available. If a sales executive in Berlin wants to get details of the latest product options, he does so by looking at a site in San Francisco located in the main sales office.

As is the nature of the Web, the idea caught fire at grassroots level, and in these organisations as well as a rapidly growing number of others, the Intranets are becoming mini-Webs with thousands of sites set up by departments and individuals within the company. Other companies now deploying sizeable Intranets using World-Wide Web technology include Eli Lily, Sandia National Labs, Chevron, Goodyear, Pfizer, Morgan Stanley, Turner Broadcasting and many computer companies including Hewlett-Packard, Silicon Graphics and Sun. (On-line readers will find an up-to-date list of corporate Intranet users here.)

Groups of workers all over the world are now working on collaborative projects using Web technology and the great hope for groupware of the early nineties now seems to have become a reality, but on inexpensive Intranets, not with expensive purpose-made software suites. The main loser in this development seems to have been Lotus Notes, the proprietary groupware product which was purchased by IBM in mid-1995 for a massive £3.4/$5.1 billion. At the time of writing, a Lotus Notes system is much more powerful and better organised than any Internal Web network can be, but users have to learn a dedicated application acquiring knowledge which can't be used anywhere else, and installing a Notes system for, say 2,000 staff members, costs ten times what an Intranet using Web technology would cost until the end of 1995. Lotus is currently trying to reinvent itself (it cut its prices by 50 per cent a few months before this book was published) and tack on Net-friendly capabilities to its products, but while it does this other companies are bringing Notes-type capability to Web-protocol servers. I think we've seen this type of battle before and we can predict the outcome. It looks like IBM has made yet another very serious and expensive mistake.

Most importantly an Intranet can be expanded out to a company's wider 'family' to include regular suppliers, customers and freelance workers – even shareholders – and with suitable levels of security it can be used for private publishing.

The Douglas Aircraft Company, the commercial airplane division of the £8.5/$13 billion McDonnell Douglas Corp is using an Intranet to deliver maintenance manuals for its aircraft. The MD-11 jet has 40,000 pages in its maintenance manuals, all frequently up-dated. Delivering these, or up-dating pages over a secure Intranet will save the company significant printing and distribution costs. Airline customers access McDonnell's servers over the public Internet, but encryption and digital signatures are used to confirm customer identification and to ship documents securely encoded. Crews on MD-11 jets now have Pentium PCs to access this private Web both in-flight and on the ground.

HUMAN RESOURCES AND RECRUITMENT ON THE NET

Within a couple of years I expect most major organisations to be running Intranets as well as public Web sites and one of the most important uses of these superb communications tools will be in the management of human resources and in recruitment. Most HR managers would agree that the single most important (and often most neglected) factor in successful people management is communication. Old-style bosses fear workers knowing too much, yet it has been proved definitively that a workforce is more loyal, more understanding and more hard-working when kept well informed.

Inside very small companies – 20 people or under – communication is not the problem it is in larger corporations. The problem in small companies is that everybody has to do a bit of everything. Once the numbers begin to swell into the hundreds and thousands, the task of communication between departments and individuals becomes the biggest single problem in keeping a company efficient and ensuring morale stays high.

A private Intranet solves this problem brilliantly, most of all because people love to publish on it and enjoy looking at it. In an organisation where most people have a PC it would be hard to imagine making a case for not setting up an Intranet as quickly as possible. Communication with staff via e-mail was a big step forward and this will continue, but when a staff member chooses to 'visit' the human resources department site to scan the employee list, or to check the social calendar or to look at the various new health insurance packages on offer, this is proactive and much more valuable than when the information is thrust at people on a leaflet, a memo or in the pages of a housejournal. The ethos of using a company-wide Web spreads quickly and I am sure that as we monitor the growth of Intranets we will see them become the standard method of inter-organisation communication. Human resource departments will be able to communicate much more effectively and at very much lower cost. For a collection of links to Human Resource sites around the Net visit Human Resources On-Line.

Recruitment will, of course, change for ever. Recruitment is all about making connections, of one party finding another and, in essence, this is precisely what the Net is about. Most companies will start by posting job vacancies at their home sites on the Net and this will soon become standard. Hopeful candidates will visit the sites of companies from whom they would like to work and will scan their vacancies. Most companies will provide opportunities for applicants to leave their CVs and this provides a superb low-cost mechanism of finding people who might be right for your organisation. My company now regularly posts vacancies on our Web site and all of the respondents are relatively well qualified because people visiting our site expect to find material about publishing, conferences and communications on the digital society.

The arrival of the Net also brings the threat of disintermediation to recruitment agencies who merely connect a jobseeker with an employer. Like estate agents or High Street insurance brokers, the 'value' provided by the intermediary is relatively low and many of these companies will see an erosion of their business. Specialist recruitment agencies and executive search consultants will not be threatened because in these roles the recruitment professional is actively finding and vetting candidates in a way which cannot be automated. But for middle- and lower-level positions an increasing number of candidates and employers will find each other on the Net.

In future accountants seeking a new job will not ring or visit one of the chains of employment agencies specialising in accounts staff, they will use their PC at home or at work to look at openings offered by individual companies or, more likely, to scan the jobs on offer at one or more of the many recruitment sites springing up on the World-Wide Web.

As with all other aspects of Net marketing, I am sure that super-vertical specialisation will be the key to success here. Accountants will not waste any time scanning media job openings and designers will spend no time at computer-staff sites. Job seekers will search and will find sites where all of the openings in their profession, field or discipline are gathered together *for their geographic location*. This last element is important because geography demands that there will be hundreds of thousands of specialist recruitment sites set-up all over the world. At any one time the majority of people wish to continue to work within reach of their home. The openings for entrepreneurs are phenomenal.

It is easy to see which groups to target first. Start with those who have computers on their desks because of their work and you will be sure that you are tapping a ready market. Computer workers themselves must be first in line and of course the Computer Contractor Home Page came up fairly early.

Many of the sites which came up early were too ambitious to be really useful. Although most were searchable by city and by job type, the result of such a search was usually disappointing because the organisation didn't have the staff on the group to get the vast number of job vacancies in each city, and in each field, into the system. Examples of such sites are The Job Server, which is located in the USA and attempts to connect employers and candidates world-wide, and PeopleBank , which serves both the UK and Australia. This last site invites candidates not only to fill out their CV on-line, it also invites them to take an optional psychological profiling test (the standard 'most/least' choices from four options describing aspects of your character). If you are on-line you can visit these and see how they have developed. Please let me know if I need to modify my critical view.

There is currently a site called Scottish Recruitment which clearly intends to provide local information. When I last looked, this site was general and carried almost every type of job imaginable.

Overall, I think that at the time of writing, on-line recruitment is a sector ripe for exploitation but one which has so far failed to attract investment. The major recruitment agencies such as Price Jamieson, Reed Jobnet and MPL Recruitment have established sites in what I guess are defensive moves, but searching Lycos , YAHOO! , WebCrawler or any of the other main search engines on the World-Wide Web for 'design London job' or 'accountant Cape Town career' or 'journalist New York job' produces nothing. This is a void begging to be filled as all of these workers are in front of a PC every day.

HR and recruitment professionals will find a number of relevant bookmarks on the disk which accompanies this book, but three sites worth exploring for signs of things to come are Career Magazine, a site called Job Hunting on the Net which provides many useful links and the Career Service Professionals Home Page which provides over 200 links which may be of interest.

As a final comment on recruitment on the Net (and on Net marketing in general) I will refer you to a US site called Career Path. This site has been set up by six regional newspapers in the USA and is a perfect example of businesses bringing an old-idea to a new medium. I am sure it seemed logical for the six newspapers to band together to protect their job advertising in this way, but on the Net, only the *specific* works and the first people to apply this law will be those who own the key recruitment sites in each geographic territory.

MONEY GOES DIGITAL

10

> *Money will disappear, crimes related to cash will be reduced, and the nature of crime will change as the flow of assets and money through society comes under computer control.*
>
> Computers and Your Child, Ray Hammond, 1982

Money, and how we will use it on the Net, is one of the most important topics in this book. It has to be considered alongside the role of encryption and the right, or the denial of a right, for businesses and individuals to have absolute privacy from each other, from governments and from security services.

Understanding the degree to which the Net will change business and society, there is intense debate about these issues among the digerati and within the security services. However, few mainstream politicians have yet realised the implications. In the near future they will, and there will then be a massive tussle between those who will seek government regulation of money and privacy and those who believe that the fundamental essence of democracy will be undermined if such were to occur. The outcome will decide the sort of society in which our children will live and the climate in which we will have to run our businesses.

Money has become increasingly abstract over the years and it will shortly exist without any physical reality. The concept was invented 5,000 years ago in the Temples of Sumer in what was then Sumeria (today's Iraq). The first coin was called a shekel, from the Sumerian word 'shay', meaning a bushel of barley, which was its value.

In the early sixteenth century Dutch bankers joyfully discovered the idea of printing paper representations of money (currency) and realised that as people would be unlikely to want to redeem all of their currency at once, they could print more units of paper money than were actually backed up by gold reserves in their vaults. In fact the ratio of printed currency to actual reserves has remained amazingly constant, at between eight and ten to one over the centuries and up to the early 1970s.

From that time until the early 1970s, money — a unit of wealth representation which could be exchanged for a specific value of goods (and, finally, for a set amount of gold) — remained largely unchanged in its relationship to tangible wealth.

Money is, of course, a collective fiction. If the vast majority of us believe that a pound coin or a dollar bill will be accepted as payment by others then it has value. If a minority of us doubt its acceptability its value goes down. If a significant number of us doubt its acceptability the currency collapses. Money is only belief and confidence and, in recent years, it has lost all relationship to reserves that might be considered tangible.

THE IMPORTANCE OF DIGITAL CASH

Digital cash, sometimes referred to as *e-money, e-cash, cyber cash* or *cyber bucks* has already emerged on the Net. It will prove to be all-important.

The use of small strings of encrypted numbers as substitutes for physical cash will make on-line transactions as effortless as parting with a penny in the street. But the development and potential adoption of this seemingly innocent concept has already started to terrify government agencies (if not governments) and bankers alike. Ultimately, it could even threaten national economic suzerainty.

Is this what business people want or need and how are we to balance questions of privacy and anonymity against every business's requirement of an ordered society? Before we look at the dangers, I shall explain why we have to have digital money and digital cash.

In the street most of us are quite prepared to pay small amounts of money for information and services as we go – 50 cents here for a newspaper, 50 pence there to play an arcade game or look through a tourist telescope – and in cyberspace we would be equally prepared to pay if there was any easy method of making 'pocket money' payments. The difference is that in cyberspace the phenomenon of superdistribution coupled with very low delivery costs means that those payments can be five cents or five pence and still allow its publisher or provider to make profits.

As soon as digital cash is widespread we will see newsstands and amusement arcades opening on the Net. I'll be delighted to get my Economist for five pence. I'm sure the teenage boy who lives next door to me will be delighted to play his favourite 3D arcade game for a penny. There will be a million 'tourist telescopes' on the Net available for 0.1 cent/penny showing us everything on Earth and from beyond the Earth.

We can buy and sell today using credit cards over the Net applying encryption techniques to prevent hackers stealing our card number, but this is forcing old analogue representations of credit to work in a new digital medium. It is slow, expensive and clumsy. Transaction costs are expensive – a minimum of 30p/ 45 cents – and the seller's commission is high. The seller also has to wait for payment from the card 'acquirer' and, if the buyer fails to pay the credit card bill in full at the end of the month (like most of us), he is paying extortionate interest on the money used. It's a wasteful, inefficient method and it is not the enabling means for the billions of daily transactions which will happen on the Net in the years to come. What is needed is a new way to make small payments at very low cost. Except for the poorest people in society and for criminals, this is the role to which currency and coinage has already been subjugated in our physical world; most of us make larger payments by direct debit, cheque or credit card and cash is reserved for trivial transactions.

To meet this need in part, credit card companies have developed new 'micro-payments schemes' which will lower the costs of on-line transactions but these are not the same and do not offer the same flexibility as true digital cash. (The first in use was Visa's system at the Sony Station Web site.)

Many of the world's financial institutions and major corporations have realised that there is a very significant opportunity for those whose payment systems become widely adopted on the Net. Consequently, the major credit card companies and banks originally teamed up with technology companies to develop rival alternatives. The battle in this arena promised to be as great as that between Microsoft and Netscape for the Net platform standards. Microsoft teamed up with Visa and these two refused to party with rivals Netscape, Mastercard and IBM. As the printed edition of this book went to press the two credit-card companies announced they were working on a common specification which combined the two approaches to avoid conflicting standards.

If one company or corporate alliance does manage to create a *de facto* standard for non-real-time small payments on the Net (that is, the buyer and seller exchange a promise to pay which is guaranteed by a trusted third party such as Visa or Mastercard) this could be worth billions of dollars a year in micro-commissions. Remember the Penguin's idea for getting rich by collecting every unwanted nickel in Batman. Hopefully we'll have at least two or three alternatives as we do in the physical world.

At the centre of this concept is authentication and trust. An on-line merchant must be able to authenticate that the buyer is who he says he is, the buyer must trust that the merchant will deliver the goods (of an appropriate quality) and both parties have to trust the 'banker' – usually a bank-supported credit card operator who is the 'trusted third party' (the TTP) in the transaction. The TTP provides all these checks. The TTP says that the buyer's credit card account is OK and the person appears to be who he or she says. The fact that the TTP is prepared to allow the seller to take payments on their card provides a good level of reassurance to the buyer and the seller is able to trust the TTP to provide payment.

We will also see Web sites springing up which provide TTP-type identity checking. In an earlier chapter I mentioned the problem of identity authentication in cyberspace and for business to develop on the Net some sort of identity card must be available. I suspect we shall soon find a variety of servers offering to hold information about us which can be checked. When I log into a vendor site the host server will automatically read my platform ID and e-mail address and will ask another server on the Net for verification that I am who I say I am. I may be asked to provide some additional secure information on-line from a small database that has been established previously – in the same way that my voice telephone bank now checks identity.

There will be many other methods of payment used on the Net, just as we have alternative forms in the physical world. One method will be a digital 'cashier's check' or 'banker's draft'. These 'scripts' are drawn on a bank which has put the wealth aside to meet the demand and are thus absolutely guaranteed. They will be signed with unforgettable encrypted digital signatures and, for one-off payments of large sums, they will be an acceptable solution. There is no anonymity in this transaction, all parties concerned know who the others are, but it will be widely used.

Digital versions of traveller's cheques, debit cards and personal cheques will also abound, all using some form of encrypted digital signature, applied by both the issuer and the drawer, to ensure correct identification and to stop digital money being copied and spent twice. Once again, there is no anonymity and the guarantees depend on full and current identification of all parties. The security issues have been solved. Digital signatures are much harder to fake than physical signatures and the security involved in these types of digital money transfer is much greater than the levels of security possible in the real world. This is one factor which makes digital money much cheaper to supply and administrate than physical currency, another is the automation of the administration.

Banks love digital money and they're pushing very hard to make it a reality. Paper currency and coinage is proving increasingly expensive to handle. In the USA it costs about $60 billion a year to move cash around physically. The UK cost is £2 billion. (The difference in the cost is not just due to the difference in the size of the economies. Widespread gun ownership and a far higher crime rate impose a very heavy price for money protection on the US economy.) The handling of cash within the world's banking system accounts for 50 per cent of administration costs. On top of this, paper currency is increasingly vulnerable to fraud as reprographics and printing techniques seep out into the general community following the spread of desktop publishing. Not long ago counterfeiters needed to find a master engraver to make a set of plates to print banknotes. Today, an enthusiastic graphics student with a copy of Adobe Photoshop and a Canon colour copier with a Fiery RIP can do the job (and all-too-frequently does).

There have been pilot digital money trials in the USA, UK, France, Portugal and Hong Kong. All use different systems and have met with varying degrees of public acceptance. But most of them were planned before the first shock from the Net explosion was felt and they have been focused on researching how ordinary people adapt to money on smart cards. The digerati on the networks form a much less representative sample, but it is this group which will drive the move towards the regular use of digital money.

The methods of digital payment I have described above are well tested, quite robust and in use now. As a businessman I would be delighted to both receive and make payments by any of these methods. All parts of the transaction are fully recorded. Like governments, business people like traceability and accountability.

Digital cash, on the other hand, has the potential to be as anonymous as a £10 note or a $20 bill blowing along a deserted street. A transaction made on the Net with digital cash is not a promise by a third party that payment will be made, it is real payment at the point of sale, as real as handing over a dollar note or a pound coin.

If nothing else, this book is an attempt to persuade you that the arrival of the ubiquitous Net is ultra-important, something which will have very far-reaching effects, quite beyond what might be expected from 'a new medium' as the Net is often mis-described. The argument over anonymous digital cash should do it.

Electronic computer networks have already had a significant impact on our economies. The financial world has been fully networked for over 20 years and, as many will know, over 90 per cent of the world's wealth is transmitted from account to account over the closed financial networks as streams of bits. In the largest sense, digital money has been with us for many years and all of the money we have in our accounts (along with our debts) are actually bits on computer hard disks scattered all over the globe.

The greatest effect noticed following the arrival of financial electronic networks has been an enormous increase in the speed of money movements. This was one of the main reasons for installing the networks but it has caused the markets to 'chase' wealth much harder than was ever possible before. This speeding up of the creation and pursuit of wealth is estimated to have increased by a factor of three over the past 20 years. Perhaps it is no accident that the ratio of currency to 'real' deposits (for example, gold) held in the guaranteeing banks such as the Bank of England or the Federal Reserve has increased from eight to one in 1974 to a ratio of over 20 to one in 1994.

The speed with which we can gain information about money also affects the speed of its transfer and value-increase. The financial networks have given investment houses and similar institutions access to instant 'real-time' information about stocks, shares and financial products. Wealthy individuals have also been able to access this information (for a typical charge of £3,500/$5,000 a month plus proprietary hardware) but the arrival of the dedicated financial networks has made it almost impossible for the small, individual investor to compete on equal terms.

The Net is changing this. If you enjoy the gamble of investing you can already gain access to real and almost real-time information from many of the world's stock markets on the World-Wide Web. The American markets insist there is a 15-minute time lag before new prices are posted to sites other than those which pay a large fee for real-time information, but other markets do not impose this restriction.

In a wonderful example of botched management, the London Stock Exchange agreed to license real-time share prices to a new UK firm, Electronic Share Information Ltd which announced its service and started trials. Just as the service was about to go live, somebody within the Stock Exchange realised that it was about to give away the crown jewels. The Exchange announced it was cancelling the deal and ESI cried 'foul.' The press agreed and the Stock Exchange was forced to honour its agreement and provide a real-time prices feed. The long-term effects of these decisions are not yet apparent.

If you enjoy investing, start at a site on the World-Wide Web called Investor in Touch which provides information on over 15,000 firms listed on the world's stock markets. If you want US market prices (with a 15-minute delay) go to USA Today or the disingenuously (or misleadingly) entitled AMEX server – no, it is not operated by American Express. This server is named after the American Stock Exchange who happened to apply for, and be granted, the Internet address amex.com before the charge card company (which is an excellent example of why you must register your company's name as an Internet address NOW, even if you're not yet ready to use it: for details on how to register see the InternNic Web site and Appendix 2).

Many other markets (and related services) have started to put stock prices up on Web servers and you should access Amsterdam, Chicago, Frankfurt, Hong Kong, Johannesburg, London's International Financial Futures, Moscow, Sydney, Warsaw, Zagreb, Asian Business Connection (listings for 12 countries including Korea, Thailand and India), AsiaOne, Philippine Business On-Line , and Asia.

Personal investing is made much, much easier via the Net and if you decide to have a go you might wish to use one of the burgeoning number of on-line brokers who will carry out the transactions for you. The number of accounts now being brokered on-line is approaching one million, according to Forrester Research, and an excellent example is Aufhauser & Company's WealthWEB site. For generally useful financial information see also Money World, Investor's Galleria, Money Web, the Holt Report and the PAWWS Financial Network. Finally, if you are considering investing in US companies, visit the site of the US National Investor Relations Institute, where you will find a wealth of helpful information about US public company law.

DIGITAL MONEY FOR THE REST OF US

When digital money gets into the hands of the general population – or, more particularly, into the hands of the most affluent part of our society – this will again increase the speed of money movements. The speed of money exchange increases the velocity of the economy and increases the amount of money available in society. The gap between wealth reserves and money will increase still further creating a global money supply which is totally abstract. The dangers are obvious but we cannot yet be sure what the impact will be as all methods of billing and payment will change.

Today, most of our regular personal and corporate consumption is paid for in batches at regular intervals – it just isn't economic to collect payment for our electricity or telephone usage every hour. Digital money makes this possible, however, and it will alter our business cost-infrastructure and cash-flows, not just of our utilities and information sources, but almost every type of business. More importantly and far reachingly, it will have a massive impact on credit and money supply. When credit-worthy individuals are able to pay suppliers or money lenders by the hour, the control over our costs and our cash-flows will be far more precise than it is today. Equally, corporations will be able to process accounts much more quickly. In the network economy our typical 30-day corporate requirement for processing accounts and arranging payments will seem antiquated, as will the phrase 'your cheque is in the post'. On its own this increase in transaction speed would cause significant economic change.

All of us in business have noticed that over the last 15 years the pendulum governing profit production has swung away from the old creed of 'more sales, more new business' to 'tighter cost control, better cash control'. This has occurred in part because computers have provided tools to do this with a meaning and precision that was previously impossible. Now, this trend will be further accentuated and a firm's money supply and cash flow will be regulated with micro-precision. In time it will move beyond human ability to control it and software agents will carry out these tasks according to the aims set by the managers. When that happens, those firms with the most sophisticated software agents will have distinct competitive advantage.

Digital money will also give individuals the chance to level the playing-field with the banks and major corporations. Until now, the cost and difficulty of charging interest on money owed, by the month, the week, the hour or the minute has been too great, but simple pieces of software will give us micro-control over our digital cash providing levels of sophistication previously only available to the financial giants. Your software agent will be able to pay your bills precisely when the best discount is available and to choose the currency which will save you the most money at the time. You will be able to seek out the best exchange rates available in the world automatically and as millions start to use digital money on the Net and on smart cards, thousands of clever, imaginative programmers will invent new tools to give individuals previously undreamt-of financial sophistication.

You will realise, of course, that digital money – not just digital cash – and the Net will cut a swathe through our need for today's clearing bank systems with their physical branches and their long out-dated three-day clearance of cheques. It will also spell the end of the institutionalised incompetence and theft which is endemic in the major banks. On-line we will be able to move our accounts, check our payments and get the best advice (perfect information) without leaving our home or office. Whether the existing banking community will be able to move quickly enough to meet the needs of the new Net economy is open to question.

It is hard to know how switched-on the clearing banks are. The following story is provided as illustration.

During the development of this chapter I received a letter from the Chief Executive of one of Britain's best-known direct service telephone-access banks. As you will realise he is much more technically literate than many corporate presidents – something you might expect from a pioneer of telephone transactions. The sentiment and the questions his letter contained provide a good example of how the world's managers are struggling to understand the implications of the network revolution.

He told me that the problem he foresaw with providing an on-line banking service was not the timing, but the method to be employed. He wondered if he should back Microsoft Money, Intuit or whether his bank should write some custom software. He asked (somewhat rhetorically) what attention should be paid to BT's Service on Demand, smart TVs, smart phones and the next generation of PDAs. Then he wondered whether a service should be offered on a private, dial-up, network or via the Internet. He finished his latter by asking 'In short, how do we avoid developing a Betamax and develop the VHS?'

These questions had dead-locked his advisory committee simply because they were too close to the topic. It seemed that he had some difficult choices to make. In response I wrote:

You ask 'how' you should approach an on-line service and you flag the choices to be made in the areas of software, customer access technology and delivery networks. Understandably, you wish to avoid entering a 'technology cul-de-sac'.

The 'right' software is any which allows you to migrate to a replacement with backwards compatibility which remains compatible with earlier systems. Provided the software is proven the decision isn't crucial. Intuit, Microsoft Money or a custom module for Netscape's Navigator would be fine. (Your customers will down-load the client software which allows you to change it when you wish without incurring distribution costs. The export functions from your mainframe package can feed more than one type of server software during any change-over period.)

The 'right' customer access technology for the next few years is the PC. Nothing you develop for that will exclude access by other devices.

Finally, the 'right' delivery network is the Internet using the World-Wide Web protocols as an entry point. All users of proprietary on-line services, e.g. Compuserve or the Microsoft Network, have access to the generic Internet, but not vice versa.

I realise that security is your first, middle and last concern and I am sure that after every precaution has been taken your excellent IT department will still worry about security.

You may, therefore, greet my recommendation regarding the Internet with scepticism. Half-informed opinion has dubbed the Internet 'insecure' but the accusation completely misses the point. The Internet is, of course, without any inherent security whatsoever. The security of your host, and your customers' transactions across the Internet, depends entirely upon the degree of security you apply. Using RSA's (inexpensive) encryption algorithms will provide you with an on-line service with a far greater level of security than your current telephone service. Techniques such as 'transaction ceilings', 'virtual funds' and, of course, absolute secure bridges to the internet, can be employed to further guarantee both your customers' security and the bank's.

It is the demographic profile of regular on-line users which I believe should be of interest to your bank. A large percentage of graduates now leave university after years of regular Internet usage and they expect to remain digitally mobile. It seems very strange to those of us steeped in on-line data communication to have to make a voice call.

Because we are dealing with digital information, not analogue, there is no risk whatsoever of discovering you have invested in a Betamax equivalent. Everything is mobile and therefore hesitation because of technical issues is unnecessary. I urge speed.

Six weeks after I wrote my letter, Netscape and Intuit (the publishers of the 'Quicken' money management application) announced that Quicken was available as a plug-in module for Netscape Navigator, neatly providing a solution. When the bank decides to put their site up on the Web on-line readers will be able to find it here.

DOES BUSINESS NEED PRIVACY?

11

> *Governments are writing laws to prohibit the abuse of information in our new 'information society' but I believe such legislation must prove ineffective and that a lack of information liberty is a price we will have to pay for a better, more ordered society.*
>
> Computers and Your Child, Ray Hammond, 1982

Earlier I made the bold claim that the arrival of digital money and digital cash would threaten the suzerainty of banks and even governments. Once a significant percentage of our population is networked, with the tools to buy, store, manipulate and issue digital money, national economies and currencies will come under severe threat.

If Microsoft decided to issue Microsoft dollars in e-cash – with or without the backing of a US bank – would you feel comfortable keeping a few hundred pounds or dollars in that currency? You probably would, especially if the issuing company discounted those dollars for buying Microsoft products, or linked the value of those dollars to its stock price as well as to a floating rate of exchange against other currencies. What is today's exchange rate between 'Microsoft dollars' and 'Netscape dollars'?

Bill Gates has repeatedly said he doesn't want Microsoft to become a bank, but the company already has more cash reserves than many small banks and, unless the US Government prevents it, either by the threat of legal action or by legislation, I suggest it is inevitable that on the Net some dollar bills will soon be replaced by Bill's dollars.

Britain's leading Internet provider is Unipalm Pipex, a company with significant penetration of the European Internet market. The company was taken over by the American Internet provider UUnet for £50/$75 million in late 1995. The main reason for the deal appears to have been Microsoft's need to find an alternative way of delivering a revamped Microsoft Network based on generic Internet protocols after it became clear that MSN had missed the boat. Microsoft owns 15 per cent of UUnet and the software house bankrolled the Pipex take-over. Soon after the take-over Pipex's chairman, Peter Dawe, announced that his company would be issuing a form of Pipex currency using e-cash technology. This is, of course, deposit taking and would require a licence if conducted in the physical world.

This is only the start of the headaches that are going to pile up for state treasuries and the banks. Perhaps it is a realisation of this that has been behind the on-going jousting between the US Department of Justice and Microsoft. The threat of delay promised by the Department's desire to investigate Microsoft's £1 billion/$1.5 billion acquisition of Intuit, the company behind America's leading home banking and money-management package (which has now teamed with Netscape), apparently led to Microsoft abandoning the deal. But we cannot be sure to what extent Washington decision-makers truly understand the threat to their control of their economy and to what extent they are merely reacting from a mixture of instinct that too much power in one place is wrong and to reaction to the intense lobbying being conducted by Microsoft's vocal competitors.

We can be certain that the digitisation of money coupled with low-cost, high-speed, global, forever-growing, interactive networks will lead to many new forms of economy. If the use of anonymous digital cash and encrypted communication reaches critical mass on the Net, it has the potential to cripple and ultimately destroy the notion of both local and national taxation, it will dismantle corporations and it will fuel a cacophony of black markets, grey markets and sub-economies.

The minting and issuing (and recalling) of currency is central to the concept of nationhood. In the face of overwhelming pressure from its pragmatic European partners, Britain has fought against the federalisation of the EU, holding the British pound before it as a symbol of national sovereignty. Under the Maastricht agreement, all countries in the EU are expected to adopt the Euro (formerly called the Ecu) as the EU's common currency at the very latest by the end of the year 2002.

But I think the Euro may be made irrelevant by the birth of new international currencies on the Net which 'float' against all other currencies or by the widespread adoption of an existing currency such as the US dollar to make it a *de facto* single currency. All of the commerce on the Net will be in these units and they will only be changed into our local currencies when we deposit them in our local banks. Of course, we will have no reason to choose local banks, they may be located anywhere based on any currency standard we choose.

It is also likely that digital currency standards will come from major corporations and although a national currency – for example, the US dollar, the Yen or the Deutschmark – may be a national reference point, the borderless nature and the speed of the Net have the power to make such a base irrelevant.

We already know how rapidly humans adopt new currencies. In times of economic hardship, cigarettes, brandy and silk stockings have all served and it is not hard to foresee a time when there are many corporate dollars at different exchange rates circulating on the Net. Citizens of countries with less stable economies might well embrace AT&T dollars, Marks & Spencer pounds or Mitsubishi yen.

The value of the exchange rate will become the valuation of the corporation, rather than its shareholders' stock price. In time, corporations may issue their currencies in lieu of stock certificates or in lieu of shares themselves. Although ruthless, the currency exchange markets are ultra-responsive and efficient and it is not hard to foresee a time when the same mechanisms are used to value corporate performance.

Large labour unions may also issue currency: they have certainly grown to own banks in the physical world. Members could enjoy using a currency which rises and falls in value reflecting the power and solidarity of the union which issues it.

Less desirably perhaps, ethnic sub-groups in our culture will found entire, untraceable, uncrackable, sub-economies based on para-currencies issued by any group or organisation which inspires trust in that culture – a church, a dominant family or local criminal groups. The reason these may be undesirable is that there would naturally be an inclination to shield transactions in these sub-economies from the gaze of others. Such sub-economies already exist in our physical world in the shanty towns outside some of the world's major cities. These are not candidates for translation to the Net, but relatively well-educated ethnic groups within a host culture are very likely to create such an economic community.

For populations suffering under repressive regimes, exiled political parties may have sufficient power to issue trusted currencies and the subversive power of such a development would undermine a government more effectively than most physical methods. Organised crime with its very specialised and direct ways of loan and currency value enforcement might also generate an environment in which a Mafia currency could be maintained. Currency and money is simply a symbol of trust in the issuer and the knowledge that others will trust and accept it. On occasion, fear can substitute for trust.

As a result, governments will have a difficult time maintaining control in the Network society. As Dr Stephen Mooney of the London School of Economics has said (in a conference on the 'Governance of Cyberspace'):

> *The development of networked information technology threatens to undermine the foundation, power and authority of the nation state. The result will be a continuing fragmentation of the state as economic power is transferred to the cyberstate. Britain will be reduced to little more than a large property management company or theme park while the experts in information technology will form an international free-floating pool of talent generating unprecedented wealth.*

SHOULD E-MONEY BE ANONYMOUS?

Now we come to one of the most important discussions in this book: Should digital cash be truly anonymous or should a court-authorised government agency be able to trace our payments and receipts?

Most business executives would preface any answer with the observation that we do not have complete financial anonymity now – in fact we have very little financial anonymity. Banks, credit card companies, building and savings societies all have records of our deposits, withdrawals and paper and plastic transactions. Business people might justifiably believe that the idea of increasing financial anonymity would lead to economic anarchy (which always leads to political anarchy) and, as such is antithetical to the needs of every business. I can hear many of my business colleagues saying 'Regulate digital cash now' in a year or two's time. But to regulate it, you must restrict the use of encryption and this is something that looks like being impossible. I also suspect that your own needs for encryption will prove to be a powerful opposing force.

Over the next few years your business is likely to become increasingly reliant on Net communications. If you do not use it, you will suffer from a growing competitive disadvantage which could eventually destroy (or at least stultify) your organisation. But, as stated earlier, the Net is inherently insecure. To reach its goals of ubiquity, affordability and self-replication, its protocols are completely open. Any competitor of yours with a knowledgeable hacker on the staff can (and will) intercept your communications, transactions and transmissions. It is a simple task.

You therefore have two choices: the first is to build your own private network, the second is to encrypt your communications. The first option is very expensive and provides very little of the real multiple-reach benefit of the Net. The second is virtually free and the encryption is virtually uncrackable, even by the largest government agency with mountains of super-computers. It's not a difficult choice; you are likely to opt for encryption.

The encryption software freely available on the Net uses a concept called 'public key, private key encryption' which was developed by Whitfield Diffie and Martin Hellman at Stanford and MIT and later by Rivest Shamir and Leonard Adelman at RSA, Inc. This encryption method is considered to be virtually unbreakable and the mathematics on which it depends, predominantly the employment of very large prime numbers, have been published to allow others the chance to try and break it or show a flaw in the methodology. So far, no mathematician has even suggested it is breakable by any sort of practical technique. The methodology was published by RSA, Inc. to whom Diffie and Hellman licensed the technology, but partly because of US export restrictions and partly because of inconsistencies in international patent-filing procedures, the published algorithms and mathematical proofs could not be patented outside of the USA and they entered the public domain. Thus RSA encryption, as it is popularly known, is legally applied in software developed by many individuals and commercial organisations outside of the USA.

The principle behind the concept is ingenious. For millennia, sensitive information has been encrypted using codes or 'keys'. A simple example is a 'book key' in which a message is encoded from its original text into numbers which point to the occurrence of those words in a given book, for example the

Bible. By looking up the page, line and word position references in the book, the recipient can reconstruct the message. Anybody intercepting the message prior to 1941 would have had great trouble identifying which book had been used to create the code and therefore would be unlikely to be able to crack the code.

Until the Second World War such 'single key' codes were virtually uncrackable (although they did have one inherent weakness). Alan Turing, the mathematician and computer philosopher, successfully applied the world's first digital computer at Bletchley Park, England to crack Nazi single key codes during the Second World War. Finally, he and the team for whom he was the intellectual inspiration were able to break codes without having any idea about the key on which the code was based. He went to the USA and taught the Americans how to break Japanese codes and by the end of the war the allies were able to decrypt almost all of the enemy signals they were able to intercept.

From that point onwards, most keys were computer-generated and messages were only broadcast or transmitted when unavoidable. During the height of the Cold War, messengers with briefcases handcuffed to their wrists flew codes all around the world so that messages delivered separately, usually in separate pieces, could be decrypted. The one inherent weakness with single key codes to which I refer above, was that both parties had to know the key. This required that the knowledge of the key had to be shared between at least two people and this was a fundamental and unavoidable insecurity.

The stroke of genius supplied by Diffie and Hellman was to suggest using two keys. In this concept I create two related but different keys, one a 'public' key, the other a 'private' key, using completely random sequences on my computer. The keys are pieces of software which convert plain text messages into apparent garbage. My public key encrypts a message which can only be decrypted by my private key. The public key itself cannot decrypt anything whatsoever.

I give everybody who asks for it my public key (I publish it on my Web site for anybody to take and use) and I give nobody my private key. If you wish to send me a completely private message, you encrypt it using my public key and send it to me. If you wish to make an accusation of a potentially defamatory nature against me, take my public key from my Web site and send the e-mail to me in encrypted form. No matter how potentially damaging the content, I couldn't sue you for libel because absolute encryption has ensured that it was never 'published'. Nobody except me (and that includes you, the original sender) can de-encrypt the message and read it. No matter who intercepts that message, nor how many other people have my public key, they cannot decrypt my message (or copy my digital money). Only my private key can decrypt messages or containers which were encrypted using my public key. Furthermore, I can generate additional pairs of public and private keys as often as I wish and all will be completely different.

At this stage it is right to point out that, in strictly theoretical terms, there is no such thing as completely unbreakable encryption. Given a batch of super computers and enough time, a day, a month, a year – depending on the degree of encryption applied – the encryption will be deciphered. The degree of encryption depends on the numbers of 'bits' used in the generation of the random numbers. The more bits, the longer the string of random data and the more secure the message. But you will understand that a batch of supercomputers is an incredibly expensive resource available to only a few organisations and countries. Applying the millions of dollars necessary for such deciphering (and it can be hundreds of millions of dollars when very long bit strings are used) deciphers only one key. If I've sent my message in two or more parts using different keys, the process has to start over again. This is what is meant by the phrase 'virtually uncrackable.' It just isn't feasible to consider attempting to decipher it except in the gravest of circumstances.

Other factors which make it virtually impossible for RSA-type encryption to be routinely broken (unless there is a major breakthrough in the theory of large prime numbers in pure mathematics) will be that I can double- and triple-encrypt messages. I can hide parts of messages in parts of many other innocent but encrypted items and the sheer volume of encrypted messages now starting to fly on the Net makes it impossible for those who might like to employ routine deciphering even to identify which messages should be tackled and quite unable to cope with the volume.

In outlining this scenario of the future I haven't neglected to consider future learning and development on the part of government deciphering agencies. The reason that I don't suggest such encryption will yield more easily as computing power increases and becomes less expensive is that the same progression will enable users of encryption to lengthen their bit strings. We may be just around the corner from a massive breakthrough in computer design called 'quantum computing'. In this concept a microprocessor is shrunk to atomic size and, at this level, it is able to exist simultaneously in several states, not just the usual 1s and 0s of the binary code. Processing in parallel universities such computers would be fantastically efficient and scientist Peter Shor of AT&T Bell Laboratories has already developed a program which, if it could be run on this theoretical computer, could quickly find the factors of huge prime numbers. But the same computers will be used for encryption and, with ultra-long bit strings available for encryption, mathematics suggests there are not enough particles available in the universe to build the computing power necessary to break the encryption.

The genie is out of the bottle.

A SOCIETY FIT FOR BUSINESS

People buying on the Net with credit cards today already use super-secure encryption. I also encrypt my sensitive e-mail communications using RSA-type encryption. But when you start to use such ultra-secure encryption you are automatically thwarting accountability and traceability. Think of the potential use of such encryption in financial fraud: courts and public investigation agencies are already finding complex financial frauds too difficult to prosecute successfully. Apply impenetrable encryption to every document and the audit trail disappears. What was a difficulty has become an insurmountable obstacle.

One part of the British police force has decided that it will join them if it can't beat them. Much has been written about machines on the Net called 'anonymous remailers'. These are servers set up by libertarians to disguise the origin of electronic mail. If I wish to send an unencrypted message to somebody, but I don't want them to be able to trace its origin, I send it to one of the many remail servers, in Finland, Chile, and so on, and the message is separated from information about its place of origin and the route it has taken over the Net and forwarded to its destination. It is like a Post Office Box on the Web, but anonymity is guaranteed. Concerned about soaring figures for computer theft, the West Mercia police (http://www.demon.co.uk/westmerc/index.html) force is asking informants to send them messages via a remailer that is guaranteeing their anonymity.

How do we balance society's conflicting needs for both accountability and privacy?

If we accept that only the most trivial of our conventional financial transactions are untraceable today, why should we object if that remains the case tomorrow, when so many of those transactions will be done on the Net? The reason is that it is quite time-consuming and expensive to investigate transactions in the physical world. This is our principal protection from abuse. If the IRS, the Inland Revenue or the police wish to investigate us today, it will take them time and money, although in the end, they will be likely to be able to trace most transactions. They have to decide whether a case warrants such expensive investigation. This protects us from frivolous investigation and from investigations for non-essential reasons. Organisations without government or court authorisation find it very difficult to trace transactions in the physical world.

With digital transactions on the Net it is easy to trace all transactions which are not anonymous. The principal fear of those who espouse the need for complete anonymity and untraceability is that at best, our spending and lifestyle patterns will all be recorded through our transactions and we could become sitting ducks for the marketing and direct sales organisations and, at worst, governments will be tempted to use such mighty powers to pursue totalitarianism. One of the most frequently cited examples of an unacceptable use of digital tracking is when an Inland Revenue/IRS organisation will be able to monitor all our financial transactions during a year and automatically deduct what we owe from our electronic accounts. It is not a fantasy, US Revenue officials have already much such a proposal.

But virtually unbreakable encryption software is available to all of us free of charge now. The software is available at many different addresses on the Internet. I suggest you start at Where To Get PGP or search in any of the major search engines for software called 'Pretty Good Privacy' often shorted to 'PGP'. This is based on the RSA public-key, private-key algorithms. (US readers should be warned that they may be committing a criminal offence if they pass this software on to others outside the USA.) If you wish to buy a commercial encryption program based on the RSA algorithms I recommend NetShade which is produced by Atemi Corp., of Champaign, Illinois.

PGP is available at Web sites all over the world and it is completely legal for you to download this and use it (both to and from the USA and elsewhere) except in those few countries such as France which have legislation which specifically forbids its citizens from using encryption. Such legislation is unlikely to be sustainable, but we can certainly expect some major battles over the topic in the years to come.

PGP was written by an American programmer called Phil Zimmerman and is based upon RSA's published cryptographic algorithms which are in the public domain outside of the USA. His decision to write PGP and give it away inside the USA was a political action. He saw governments and major corporations starting to make use of licensed (but unexportable) strong encryption inside the USA and he considered that the balance of power between the state/establishment and ordinary people was about to swing even further away from the democracy and freedom he cherishes. His decision, and the actions of a group of libertarian 'cypherpunks' in San Francisco who distributed it freely over the Net world-wide, could turn out to be one of the most important political acts made in the digital age so far. I cannot identify the medium or long-term consequences of such a move, but whether it turns out to be for good or evil, it cannot be recalled.

The reasons behind these actions have been well explained by another American libertarian, John Perry Barlow, lyricist of the Grateful Dead, Wyoming cattle rancher and founder of the Electronic Frontier Foundation in a foreword he wrote for a book about PGP written by Phil Zimmerman. With his permission I quote the following extract:

> *At present most of us unwittingly leave a highly visible and nearly indelible trail in Cyberspace. Every time we make a modern financial transaction, use the telephone, send an e-mail message, we leave a path of bits from which anyone who's interested and properly equipped can assemble the detailed informational ghosts of our naked selves. If you have something you'd rather hide, don't hide it there.*
>
> *Furthermore, the tools of surveillance are becoming far more sophisticated and conducive to centralization. Massive pattern-recognition engines can be applied to the Net from, say, Washington, DC or Beijing, and specifically tuned to recognize certain kinds of activities. Or even beliefs.*
>
> *Any government that can automatically generate an intimate*

profile of every one of its citizens is a government endowed with a potential for absolute power that will eventually, to use Lord Acton's phrase, corrupt absolutely. Few civil liberties are likely to survive such capacities in the hands of the increasingly panicky authoritarians who run the embattled old bureaucracies of the Meat World.

Any number of citizens armed with PGP and such of its relations as digital cash and anonymous Net remailers can simply vanish from the governmental radar. In many ways, they can effectively resign from the community of the governed and enter a condition in which their actions are ordered by conscience and culture alone.

But what are the choices? Do we allow matters to continue along their present technological trajectory, eventually endowing our government (and practically any marketing organization) with a magnifying window into the least of our lives? Do we allow ourselves to become intimately vulnerable to faceless bureaucracies to whom we will be incredibly well known yet remain faceless ourselves? We have gone too far that way already. But what can prevent a further tumble toward that dark horizon?

Do we try to hide our trails behind laws (favored by Europeans) that would define what might be the appropriate contents for a database? Do we endow government with the ability to define forbidden knowledge? I don't have much enthusiasm for this solution, which sounds to me rather like having a Peeping Tom install one's window blinds, I do not trust government with the ability to regulate information, especially information that contains within it such a long lever of control as those things about yourself you'd rather no one knew.

In the end, it doesn't matter much what they think or I think. The genie of guerrilla cryptography is out of the bottle. No one, not even its maker, can stuff it back in or keep it within what America laughably calls its borders. The genie is all over the Net. It's in your hands as you hold this book. Summon it with a conscience. But be prepared to summon it if you must. [For on-line readers the complete version of John Perry Barlow's introduction is here.]

Zimmerman finished the first version of PGP in 1991 at around the time that the US Senate was considering introducing a bill which would prohibit the use of secure encryption by the people. In response, Zimmerman's hacker colleagues released the software on to the Internet so that it could be distributed to users across America before the new law was passed. But because once something is on the Net it cannot be contained, it rapidly spread all over the world.

The exportation of such technology was already prohibited, despite the fact that it was legally and freely available outside the USA and was, at the time, incorporated in over 200 commercial products sold in 22 countries including Great Britain, France, Germany, Russia, Japan, India, and South Africa. Most European automatic-teller networks use a commercially produced form of RSA-type encryption, although it is a good deal less secure than the freely available PGP.

Zimmerman's distributors knew that strong encryption was already widely available outside of the USA and they offered the, perhaps, rather disingenuous suggestion, that one reason for their distribution of the software was to keep the USA competitive.

In the end the bill banning the use of RSA-type encryption in the USA was not passed, but the technology remained on the list of 'armaments prohibited from export' by the National Security Agency (where it falls into the same category as nuclear weapons).

Two years after Zimmerman's PGP was posted on the Net the government took action against him and threatened proceedings alleging that he enabled the export of a prohibited munition. The case has become a *cause célèbre* in the USA amongst the digerati and I will be updating the situation in the on-line version of this book.

To sum up, I hope you'll now agree that to all intents and purposes unbreakable encryption is now freely available to all, and that one of its most significant powers is when it is applied to money.

ized, digitized forms of cash. Cheques, credit cards, debit cards and smart cards are all beginning to provide the electronic equivalent of paper cash and metal coins. But a large part of the population remains doubtful that electronic transactions are as secure as using notes and coins, and many of us resent the fact that all electronic transactions are tracked, recorded and analysed.

ANONYMOUS   12
DIGITAL CASH

Our economies are now too complex for humans to handle. All Western politics seem to be the politics of expediency and countries are now far too complex for any group of humans to govern properly. Governments lurch from one crisis to another and, if they momentarily relieve the worst effects of the latest catastrophe, they appeal for public approval and another term in office.

Computers and Your Child, Ray Hammond, 1982

The technology to create truly untraceable, anonymous, digital cash already exists. The methodology has been worked out by David Chaum, another liberal American mathematician and cryptologist, who believes passionately that to protect democracy and personal freedom our future forms of cash should be completely beyond any agency's ability to track, trace or identify its movement.

On the Net such cash would be infinitely more anonymous than even physical cash. In the real world large cash transactions cannot be completely anonymous in developed countries and if such currency were to be adopted an oft-repeated fear is that it would be exploited by extortionists, blackmailers, drug dealers, paedophiles and organized criminals. After all, anonymity and absolute privacy are the first requisites of crime.

The idea of digital cash isn't new. We've been used to having small amounts of anonymous digital cash stored on phone cards for years and UK, French and Danish readers have been used to carrying 'debit cards'. Unlike direct-debit cards, where the card is used to authorise a merchant to debit your bank account directly by the agreed amount (and leave a significant trail of spending information for potential use or misuse by marketing people – depending on your view), phone cards contain anonymous cash (or credits) but they can only be spent with the phone companies.

Strangely, US citizens are much less used to forms of digital money than their European counterparts. With the exception of one experiment with the Long Island phone system and commercial pre-payment cards, the take-up of digital money has been wider and faster elsewhere in the world.

True anonymous cash is in the form of 'software units' which may be stored on a computer disk, on a magnetic card or any other machine-readable medium, and which can be exchanged for goods, services or other valuables as readily and untraceably as dollars, pounds or guilders. In fact, true digital cash is completely anonymous and untraceable, especially over the Net. Using such 'coinage,' neither the buyer nor the seller need worry about the other's identity. Providing the computer systems interconnecting can establish, beyond doubt, that the digital cash offered is genuine, that it has not been spent twice or otherwise corrupted, the transaction can, and will, go ahead not merely 'without card-holder present' (as many on-line credit-card transactions are described today) but without any human being involved. In fact, using software agents, we will run our lives by buying and selling things we need, and things from which we profit, without being aware of the individual transactions occurring. This will completely change how we think about wealth, money-making and its role in our lives. Dr. David Chaum and his wife Toby run Digicash bv in Amsterdam. David Chaum started studying how to make digital cash in the late seventies when he was at Berkeley and later as professor of computer studies at Stanford University. He beavered away in his own version of anonymity, filing patent after patent in a field which few considered important, until the Internet and the World-Wide Web exploded and Chaum found himself an international celebrity, the darling of the digerati, and a man whose consultancy is courted by governments and banks.

Chaum's fully anonymous, encrypted digital cash, backed by US dollars first became available as I wrote this chapter and I think its adoption will spread like wildfire throughout the Net. The first bank to offer such currency was the Mark Twain Bank of St Louis, Missouri which started to offer Net users accounts on which they could draw 'ecash' in October 1995. I opened my personal ecash account immediately and I have been logging the growth of sites on the Net which will accept it. Not surprisingly the first 'merchant' which arrived on the Net ready to accept ecash turned out to be Caribbean Casino, a virtual casino at which you can play video poker, amongst other games, using ecash as stake money. More conventional traders then followed. At the last count there were eight and I will be updating this figure on my Web site.

On the Digicash, Web site the company describes the use of ecash as follows:

Opening an account with a bank which offers ecash allows you to make a conventional deposit in an accepted currency and then to draw ecash dollars, pounds, krona or any other currency offered by accessing the bank's Web site, downloading Digicash's software to your computer disk and then making a withdrawal of ecash dollars which are sent to you over the Net to be stored on your hard disk.

The clever part of ecash is that although the bank records your withdrawal, after that your use of the ecash units cannot be traced. Using ecash is like using a virtual ATM (Automatic Teller Machine). When connecting to it over the Internet, you authenticate ownership of your account and request the amount of ecash you want to withdraw, much like in person. But instead of putting paper cash in your wallet, your software stores the digital cash it obtains onto the hard disk of your PC.

When you are asked to make a payment on the net, you confirm the amount, purpose and payee and then your ecash software transfers the correct value in coins from your disk. Sellers, ranging from casual participants in the global Internet bazaar to mega-retailers, deposit the digital coins they receive into their accounts.

Behind the user interface, your computer actually chooses the serial numbers of the electronic coins based on a random seed. Then it hides them in special encryption envelopes, provides them to the virtual ATM for signing, and removes the envelopes from what is returned — leaving the bank's validating digital signature on the serial numbers. This way, when the bank receives from the shop the coins you spend, it cannot recognize them as coming from any particular withdrawal, because they were hidden in envelopes during withdrawal. And thus the bank cannot know when or where you shop or what you buy.

The serial number of each signed coin is unique, allowing the bank to be sure it never accepts the same coin twice. In case you wish to identify the recipient of any of your payments, you can also reveal the serial number and prove that you formed it. And, in case your computer were ever to break down, if you had written down the secret random seed number you chose initially when opening your account, future versions would let you use it to re-create the coins in envelopes and thereby obtain a free re-issue of the signed coins that were lost.

How safe is it?

Security is fundamental to electronic cash. The cryptographic coding protecting every 5 cent ecash payment is the same as that routinely relied upon for authenticating requests to move huge sums between banks and even for national security. But in principle ecash goes beyond such communications security to achieve true multiparty security: no one (buyer, seller, bank) can cheat anyone else, no matter how they might modify their own software; even if two parties collude, they cannot cheat the third.

Replacing paper and coins with ecash would make life much harder for criminals. Because the payer's computer chooses the serial numbers of the coins, he or she can later irrefutably identify blackmarketeers, extortionists, and acceptors of bribes — were they to take ecash. Paper notes, briefcases full of which can be received without leaving any record, allow money

> *laundering and tax evasion today. With ecash, however, all the amounts each person receives are known to their bank. Significant criminal activity could thus be thwarted by completely replacing paper money; moreover, the privacy of ecash would be essential to widespread acceptance of any electronic payment system that in effect becomes mandatory.*

David Chaum's logic is impressive and, if our only concern is our need to protect ourselves from those who might wish to extort our digital cash, his enterprise seems a wonderful idea.

But society, and business, needs more accountability. As much as we all dislike paying taxes, societies couldn't run without them. We have to pay for our communal services and assets, and business relies on a taxed economy of individual accountability to the state to ensure parity. Goods and services provided in an unregulated and untaxed black or grey economy undermine society and its ability (and willingness) to pay for legitimately provided goods and services. This denies legitimate corporations profits and the state its taxes.

Anonymous, untraceable digital cash would allow everyone to hide all or part of their income and expenditure even though an individual has the ability to clearly identify ecash extorted from them. Whilst ecash protects us against the criminals who prey directly upon us, it doesn't protect us from ourselves. Without some attempt at regulation we would all have an easy, effortless and untraceable way to evade our taxes.

For most people who wish to evade taxation, the problem is how to get paid in such a way that it isn't traced and then how to spend the money in a way which can't be traced. I am currently paying tax in the UK. If I write a book for an Australian publisher and I am to be paid $25,000, I can ask the publisher or agent to deposit the sum in my ecash account at the Mark Twain Bank in Missouri. I have now made things extremely difficult for the Inland Revenue.

If I was *really* serious about hiding my money I could encrypt the encrypted cash again and distribute it across the least important pixel of a 20 megabyte image file. It would look like noise and, if anybody dreamt of looking into that chain of pixels, they would find only garbage that would take a supercomputer a couple of years to decrypt. Or I could hide it within a Michael Jackson track stored digitally on my hard disk, a DAT drive or on a CD-ROM. That type of 'noise' wouldn't even be audible, let alone decipherable.

In short, my $25,000 couldn't be traced, but my ecash coins can be spent in the UK or elsewhere with impunity. Nobody can trace them to me, not even the issuing bank. I am the only person who can ever identify them.

It isn't just personal tax evasion which is enabled by anonymous, untraceable e-cash. Consider its impact on the black market and the market for stolen goods, especially those which can be delivered over the Net (pirated music, videos, images, software, books, and so on).

I can buy anything and I am the only person who can prove I bought it. This weapon could be used by *agents provocateurs* acting on behalf of the police, Customs, Revenue or similar agencies, but if anonymous ecash is widely adopted there will be so many small transactions occurring at once that the likelihood of such investigations making any real dent on such criminal or black economies would be very small.

Equally, there are ways of foiling such attempts at detection. If an individual is engaged about serious criminal activity – for example, selling paedophile material or arranging drug deliveries – it is possible to use encryption technology to be sure that the buyer is who he claims to be and avoid detection through infiltration. Pre-configured 'identity guarantee servers' that I mentioned in the section about Trusted Third Parties, could be applied for this purpose.

The technology already exists to make ecash a transferable currency. In its initial trails, an ecash note has to be banked by the person or company receiving it. The bank can then verify that the ecash hasn't been spent twice. If it is spent twice, a rather neat technological twist means that it is only then that traceability becomes important and the bank customer or ecash recipient who attempted to cheat is revealed.

Later versions of ecash could contain technology checking for double spending which allows the ecash to be accepted by one person and then passed on to another as payment. The ecash can remain in circulation and pass through many hands before being returned to its issuing bank for redemption. This would allow simple and effective money laundering to take place and could hide the identity of criminals from their victims.

Criminals, terrorists, violent anarchists, religious extremists are frequently detected through the interception of communication. Successful prosecution often depends on documentary evidence. On the Net it has become impossible to intercept communication and documents are unreadable.

WHAT WE CAN EXPECT

Over the next few years we can expect the debate over regulation of digital cash and encryption on the Internet to enter the mainstream. It will be impossible to rebottle encryption, but I expect there will be attempts to limit our use of anonymous digital cash. As a twentieth-century businessman I support such a move. It will most likely be tackled by legislation which prohibits banks from issuing anonymous digital cash or by restricting the transaction levels which are legal.

But I doubt whether twenty-first-century business people would support the idea, simply because any such attempt is doomed to failure and attempts to police such legislation will prove to be a super-expensive drain on our societies. The weapons in the hands of the people are too potent. Governments must accelerate the already powerful trend to eliminate income tax and raise all of our necessary state revenues through indirect taxation. As our societies have developed, it is logical to tax us on our consumption rather than our earnings.

I (and you) have no alternative but to build our business plans for the new chaos (I cannot bring myself to write 'order'). We must be aware of the terrain ahead and we must use these new weapons for our own survival.

LIFE ON THE NET 13

> By the end of the 1980s record companies will be able to pass their entire catalog of music around the world via the phone service if they choose to.
> The Musician and the Micro, Ray Hammond, 1982

Do you like ambient music, or is your taste closer to jazz-funk? Do you like Jamiroquai, Madonna, Gregorian chants, Blur or Queen? How do you feel about traditional Irish line dancing or Country music? Whatever your choice in music, you will almost certainly find a site on the Net that's just right for you. Some of the sites are so specialised they may cater only for a particular period in a particular type of music, as in 'Led Zeppelin, the 1972 Site' or 'Chet Atkins' 50s Albums'. These are perfect examples of the super-vertical specialisation which is natural to the Net.

At these sites you can read about the artists, the music, the genre, the fans, the concerts, the discography and, at many, you can download the music to your hard disk and play it back at CD-quality on your hi-fi. Some of the sites are official and you buy your music with a credit-card or digital money (take a look at World-Wide Music at 1-800 Music Now); others are illicit and boot-leg and give away (or sell) music to which they have no rights. In the future such sites will contain videos of past concerts and films in which the stars have features.

When I described the potential for the transfer of music over phone lines in 1981 I didn't realise that the power would be wrested away from its creators. I imagined it would be the record companies who would make most use of the technology.

Others thought the same way. In mid-1989 I went to visit Pete Townshend of the Who to consult with him on plans for upgrading the computer systems in his recording studio and he paid me the compliment of recalling *The Musician and the Micro* and its predictions.

As an artist who has felt ripped off by record companies over many years, he saw the imminent delivery of his music over phone or data networks as another way record companies could cheat auditing processes (and avoid paying royalties) rather than being the enabling factor for unauthorised copying. In fact, while I was there he became quite worked up about how to deal with the problems about to emerge. He didn't quite smash his guitar into his amp, but you get the idea.

A few years later, just after Marc Andreessen's first browser had been released for the World-Wide Web, the first Who site came up. But it wasn't presented by the Who's own management company or by any record or publishing company which has had a contract with the band over the years. It was put up by

'Jack', a K12 student at Riverdale High School, Portland, Oregon. Writing about a band which had retired before he was born, Jack stated 'The Who are the greatest band in the world' and although he hadn't put any music on the site when I last looked, there were a selection of down-loadable pictures and the full lyrics to 'Tommy', Pete Townshend's enduring rock opera. There were no copyright acknowledgements or credits on the photographs or on the lyrics. I doubt whether Jack had considered it.

The Who's schoolboy fan has been followed by a myriad of imitators, many of whom provide full digital recordings of their heroes without worrying themselves about rights. (If you're interested, or if you're a lawyer for the band, start here where you'll find links to two Who 'home' pages, dozens of copyright images available for downloading as well as official and bootleg recordings. You'll also find an excellent site called The Who Guitar Music where all of the lyrics and guitar chords to the band's greatest hits are provided. This is a new sort of feedback for Pete Townshend.

Pete's concerns about record labels were, no doubt, well founded but it is the same record companies who will now have to change what they do or cease to exist (with the latter outcome being the more likely). And it is not just the record companies.

From here on in, the digitally mobile will get their music from thousands of jukebox file-servers scattered around the Net. This is the beginning of the end for the record shop, the record company (in its present form) and it will also have some impact on conventional radio stations. The effect on pricing, cross-border sales (when artists frequently sign with different record labels in different territories – on different terms) and the development and popularisation of different music styles will be considerable.

Many music lovers feel uncomfortable paying £12 or $12 for a CD. It feels wrong; things which are information-based and electronically stored have generally gone down in price in real terms over the last decade. Unlike linear books, music is as suited to on-line delivery as it is to physical delivery on a magnetic or optical medium. It's very similar to software.

If digital copies of music are delivered over the Net it does away with the need to press CDs, to quality-check them, to create plastic and print packaging, to warehouse them, to put them into trucks, deliver them to shops and to stock them, audit them and allow for a resellers' margin (which will include a percentage for theft).

So what price should a digital album (let's say 50 minutes of music) be on the Net? If we apply the same percentages as we did to software, a digital album on the Net should cost £1.20 or $2.00.

The Net will also change how a musician or musical act goes about promotion. The singular process of promoting a new recording over the radio airways and via music television stations will come to be far less important. Although the ease of unauthorised copying is a problem still to be solved (or a problem based on concepts that require review and adjustment) the network economy will completely alter a musician's route to an audience.

Recorded music has been distributed on physical media for the whole of the twentieth century and this has shaped the very nature of how music is recorded and marketed. Wax cylinders, acetate, vinyl and plastic have carried music to the shops and we have carried it home.

Over the last 20 years our access to music has been entirely governed by the corporate tastes of half-a-dozen global recording conglomerates and limited to the minute percentage of new music which actually gets played on air and distributed to the shops. I don't mean to suggest that cultural tastes can be manipulated by the record companies, there are far too many over-hyped failures to believe this to be possible, but I know that the physical nature of music distribution has severely limited the range of music we hear and can own. All record companies work on the logistics imperative. How many units can we ship, how much shelf space is there, how long will it take and how fast can we re-stock? There is no point in a music promoter (or 'record plugger' as they used to be called) pushing an album which isn't benefiting from widespread distribution.

This has concentrated power into the hands of those who have been able to distribute and promote effectively. He who controls the trucking network wins. The record industry is one that is entirely dependent on its ability to distribute. In fact, the industry has been so aware of the physical laws governing its existence (some might say paranoid) that it acted collectively to delay the introduction of domestic digital recording systems. You will realise that the introduction of the Compact Disc in 1982 marked the point at which the music industry started to deliver music recorded in digital form. It cannot have escaped your attention that the recordable CD never arrived and the low-cost digital cassette recorder has still to make an affordable entrance. Both technologies have been available for some years but pressure from the recorded music industry – which often has, at the least, strong alliance with the electronics industry (and, sometimes, common ownership) – has prevented their introduction. For the last decade you could have had a 'record' button on your CD player if the music industry had not been convinced that your ability to make digitally perfect reproductions of a favourite piece of music would have damaged sales.

Some technologies have been developed which promise to provide a degree of protection for both record labels and their artists. One novel concept has been developed by a British company called Cyberus which encrypts and compresses digital music before offering it for sale over the Net. The buyer downloads both the music and a piece of decryption software which will work only on one identified computer hard disk. This will allow the purchaser to play the music back from his or her disk, but will not allow any playable copies to be made unless the buyer chooses to lend the decryption software along with the copy.

Such 'half-way houses' will seem very attractive to artists, record labels and the royalty and performing rights collection agencies, some of whom have endorsed the system, but I suspect it is a temporary fix. Cyberspace will be awash with music and I think that micro-payments based on digital cash will provide the method of passing reward back to the creators.

STARS IN CYBERSPACE

So who will be first to test the theory of the new economic model with popular music? Could it be a major artist who chooses not to re-sign with a new label, or to sign only non-exclusive, physical-carrier rights? (Imagine Michael Jackson, George Michael or Luciano Pavarotti testing the market. How many Net users would buy their music in this way? I certainly would.)

But I think it may be a new artist of whom we have not yet heard. I predict that there will soon be artists coming to prominence solely through their presence on the Net. The music itself may be different and the ethos and the image of the act will also be different. Acts which grow and communicate in cyberspace will be unlike any we have seen or heard before. I suspect music will be given away as was the first major piece of Internet software and this will lead to the rapid and instant creation of new stars who will achieve critical mass and global audiences at breathtaking speed. A prime example of this new model at work can be found at SonicNet, a site in Santa Rosa, California devoted to on-line delivery of new music and video from unsigned artists. Prodigy, the proprietary on-line network owned by IBM and Sears (the retailing giant) bought a 20 per cent stake in this site recently and I predict this will be a prototype for the shape of the 'record company of the future'.

There will be many virtual concerts on the Net and many hybrid concerts where there is a physical concert which is also multi-cast on the Net. This technique uses many servers around the world to deliver the same sounds and images. Global hit artists will reach audiences of millions in both real and forwarded time.

We will see file-servers on the Net that become 'hit' sites which are mobbed by on-line fans and we will see sites where hit parades are created. Fans will log-on to hear their favourite type of music and new offerings and will vote on-line for the ones they think are the best. This will produce super-democratic hit parades and, because of the nature of super-vertical markets, there will be as many hit parades as there are categories of music. The sites will rapidly become commercial because 'advertisers', or 'commercial informers', or whatever we should call companies who market on the Web, will be so clearly able to target their markets.

As I write, the first beta version of RealAudio2 software has been made available on the Net (free of charge, of course). RealAudio is a piece of software which is a 'helper application' for the Netscape platform. This enables a server on the Net to pump out FM quality sound as if it were a radio station. Users down-load the software to their own PC or Macintosh, log-on to the site and then listen to either live or pre-recorded 'broadcasts'. I placed that term in quotes because although it appears similar to broadcast (in which sound and pictures are transmitted) it is actually very different. The sites send out no sound until the sound-stream is requested. On-line readers can get a full-listing of RealAudio sites on the Web here.

Now anybody can set up a 'radio station' and we can expect to see hundreds of thousands of them mushrooming across the globe over the next few years. By the nature of the Net the ones which succeed in attracting large or useful audiences will be those which understand the super-vertical nature of the medium and stay firmly within their groove. Radio is a medium which belongs to driving and other activities where the eyes and mind are partly engaged elsewhere and we can be sure we will receive Net-delivered radio in our cars in the very near future.

We can also be sure that most of our traffic information will also come over the Net to our homes and cars. Sites will spring up all around the major conurbations and motorways providing video camera views of busy intersections, city streets and mass-attendance events. There will be inexpensive video cameras perched on the top of every high-rise building feeding independent Web sites. These will provide live pictures and audio on the traffic flow. These sites will be linked to each other so motorists may click forward from Junction 16 to Junction 17 and so on to see how traffic conditions are developing along their route

If I lived near the San Diego Freeway in Los Angeles (the busiest freeway in the USA) or beside London's M25 (the most congested road in the most congested area in Europe) I would be putting that site up *now*. Radio stations like KBIG 104 in the USA or Capital in the UK can pipe their sound-stream on to a server and provide real-time traffic information and pictures directed from their 'flying eyes'. Advertisers will love the added value and there's nothing in the stations' broadcasting licences to stop them *because they are not, technically, broadcasting.*

I wonder if small entrepreneurs will get there first? Local advertising (for a service station or hotel) will provide the revenue and the rest of the content is up to the operator's imagination. We face a future of a myriad information stations, and we will see an explosion of imagination and creativity as operators think up new ideas and themes. (One early example which amused me is The Speed Trap Registry, a site which carries a log of 'inappropriate' police speed traps across the USA. The operators won't publish details on speed traps aimed at catching drunk drivers, nor those set up at accident black spots nor those protecting road repair personnel. Their target is the speed traps set up to increase police revenue.

This type of super-proliferation is also about to take place in the mainstream film, video and TV industries. Forget the prophecies about 500-channel cable TV, interactive TV, digital TV broadcasts and satellite broadcasts. In our networked future, our information and entertainment will not be *beamed at us*; we will go to the server which contains what we want. I'm not relying on my imagination here. TV Net access began at the beginning of 1996 when Viewcall Europe plc started to send fast images over ordinary phone lines to 1,000 households in Glasgow, Scotland. In this pilot project the company provided set-top boxes for televisions, used fractal-compression technology to achieve previously undreamt of speed over phone lines and utilised Netscape technology for serving.

There will be 'I Love Lucy' servers, 'Coronation Street' servers, 'Neighbours' servers, all types of news servers, science servers, 'Mash' servers, 'Clint Eastwood' servers and so on ad infinitum. We won't click from our armchairs or desks to find these. Our software agents will depart with our wishes, negotiate with the server, pay with digital money and return with the items we require. If you want to search for a movie but can't remember its title, or the actors, there is a superb database of movies (film and TV) already on the Net at The Internet Movie Database, which allows you to search with related words. It is now six years old, massive, and constantly growing.

If all of this sounds like hard work for the average couch-potato, we can set the agent to 'browse', and choose to 'hold a channel' with our remote control whenever anything looks interesting.

Inevitably, pornography will be one of the driving forces of 'on-demand' movies and this may be an appropriate point to tackle this thorny issue.

It will be virtually impossible, and commercially undesirable, to stop the massive global trade in pornography now springing up on the Net. It is one of the first industries to make serious money on the Net and for many consumers (as against business users) it will be a prime motivating factor for being connected. The rapidly growing number of 'adult' sites are catering to every predilection and, unlike the anarchic student-posted erotica of the Internet's first decades, such sites are adult-only, membership-based and demand either credit card or digital cash transactions made prior to access being granted.

The reason I consider that any attempt to prohibit the use of the Net by commercial pornographers to be commercially undesirable is that it will be this use which brings in 'ordinary consumers.'

We shouldn't be surprised at this. It was the amount of pornography available on the Internet which first signalled to me that the medium was reaching critical mass. Every important new 'one-to-one' medium has been heavily used for sexual and pornographic purposes as soon as it became practical. Printing, lithography, photography, film and video all went through a period when they were substantially driven by sexual content and these media are still, and will remain, heavily used for this purpose although we no longer think of sexual content as being their *raison d'être*. The video tape sales and rental markets were totally driven by pornography when VCRs were first introduced and many of the consumers who first bought a VCR for that purpose are now part of rental firm Blockbuster's core of customers for mainstream video rentals.

Today's Net can deliver only TV-quality images (as stills, unless you have a very fast connection) with accompanying sounds. But it is the anonymity of Net access which worries anti-pornographers most. The idea that indecent material can be accessed from the privacy of a bedroom sends media and religious fundamentalists into apoplexy.

Should we censor the Net? one might ask. The right question is: *can* we censor the Net? We cannot, and all attempts will fail. However, several pieces of software have been produced which prevent a Net user gaining access to unsuitable sites. These include NetNanny, Cyber Patrol, CyberSitter and Surf-Watch. This type of software should be employed by parents and teachers who wish to prevent children accessing undesirable material either accidentally or deliberately.

As this book is published a new Telecommunications Bill is on its way through the US congress which was due to include a clause prohibiting the transmission of indecent material on the Net. To the horror of civil liberties groups, the wording adopted by the Senate conference committee allows for words as well as images to be included. The entire clause would appear to be in contradiction of the First Amendment and opponents point to the absurdities such a Draconian approach fosters. Fearing further legal challenges, America On-Line adopted a voluntary 'code of decency' as the new bill was being contemplated and found that a breast-cancer discussion group could not function because it needed to use a prohibited word. Updates on this will appear on-line.

For the avoidance of doubt, I consider that the creation of pornography involving children is highly damaging, both to them and to society. Anybody who doubts this needs only to know that research has revealed that almost all female and the majority of male 'actors' and models in pornography were sexually abused as children. People who send such material across the Net (or via any other means) should be brought to justice by every means possible.

THE PRICE OF ENTERTAINMENT

How much should entertainment or audio/visual information cost when it is delivered over the Net? Today it costs a fortune to ship movies and videos to a distribution point near us. Each print of a new three-reel feature film costs £30,000/$45,000 to duplicate for each of the theatres in which the film will play. Hollywood is currently exploring putting in a fibre-optic network to link its cinemas so it can deliver new movies digitally.

This is an expensive undertaking, requiring not just a dedicated network but new projectors, storage facilities, and so on. Each film requires 50 gigabytes of storage. Unless the distributors know they will get a payback in five years, they should stick to the old system. After that movie lovers will have access to Net connections of 45 megabits per second and will pull their movies from the Net in real time – especially the young group which dominates the film-going demographic. Movie houses will continue to exist because of their social role (but I wouldn't buy shares in Blockbuster until I heard about the company's plans for Net delivery).

So how much should films, videos and TV output cost on the Net? The answer is that they will cost very little because of the phenomenon of *super-distribution*. If a film production company can deliver its product to millions of people without any delivery cost, the costs of the entire distribution chain can be discounted.

Such a dramatic change will not happen in the next year or two, but neither will it take 20 years. By the turn of the century there will be many sites delivering movies in this way and we will endure hybrid distribution methods for many years to come. But the financial advantage will be available to all those who use the Net.

SPORT ON THE NET

Sport is a major leisure business and it is already well represented on the Net. Fans were quick to put up unofficial football and soccer sites and nearly every type of sport now uses the World-Wide Web for promotion, entertainment and for sales.

I'm a Wimbledon fan and I was delighted to find that information about the tennis tournament came up as early as 1994. US football clubs and British soccer teams were quick to follow, and the Net now provides an excellent means of checking programmes and making reservations. Real-time audio commentaries from events have already started via Net servers and we can expect live video transmission to follow as bandwidth improves. Because of the Net's super-vertical specialisation it will become viable for minority sports to televise their games to the global Net audiences. Advertising will pay for the relatively low cost of the exercise and as consumers we will be able to switch between watching canoeing in Wales to snow boarding in Vail, Colorado. This will alter the economics of many smaller sports and create global communities of fans who previously had no method of connection.

ONE DAY MY PRINTS WILL COME

Most of us take photographs on holiday. Then, when we have the expensive films expensively developed, we pick a few pictures we like and throw the rest in a drawer where they lie in the dark for years.

Photography, however (like all other forms of information), is rapidly going digital and low-price digital cameras are just beginning to arrive. In the future we will return from our holidays, down-load our digital snaps to our PC (or Net terminal or PC-TV) and view them on the screen. We will select those we want to be printed and send them across the Net to a Web site which will print them at low cost on high quality photographic paper and post them to us within 24 hours. No film cost, no developing cost, just a printing charge.

The photo-processing site will also provide us with sophisticated image editing tools (of the type now found in Adobe Photoshop), and, if we wish, we will be able to edit the images on our own screens whilst connected to the Web site using mini-software applications which the processing site will provide for the purpose. If cousin Charlie was standing in the wrong place in the wedding snaps, we can edit him out and move him elsewhere in the group. We will be able to take the best parts of one picture and marry them together with the best parts of another. We won't need all of the image processing technology on our own machine – all of this will be available on the Net for use only when we need it. When we're pleased with our pictures we can send digital copies to our relatives and friends who can choose whether to have their own prints made.

Much of life will never be the same.

THE OUTLOOK FOR CHARITY, VOLUNTARY AND NOT-FOR-PROFIT ORGANISATIONS

Life off-line forces us to face the world's problems as we pursue our leisure. We can't avoid seeing the homeless on the street and we are surrounded by reminders of how privileged most of us are. Will cyberspace allow us to cut out such awareness?

I believe the charity, voluntary or not-for-profit sector (the terminology changing according to where you live) will actually become a major beneficiary as our society moves towards the Net. Charity and not-for-profit organisations have already started to deliver their message on the World-Wide Web (I've already mentioned some environmental groups and political organisations), but although these sites do solicit donations and membership, they will not really gain the full benefit of the Net economy until various forms of digital money come into use.

I think causes of all types will discover the Net to be their most powerful fund-raising medium ever. By their nature, causes are inherently super-vertical and are thus ideally suited to the architecture of the Net. Someone searching for information about 'coronary heart disease', for example, will almost certainly come across the address of the various charities and not-for-profit groups connected with this disease (providing they have marketed themselves on the Net efficiently). This allows causes and charities to be 'present' for all those concerned about a given topic, but in a passive and non-invasive way ideally suited to the voluntary-sector ethos.

Further, it will become part of corporate social responsibility to provide links from company sites on the Net to the corporations' chosen charities. This is an ultra-efficient way of connecting a corporate community with a supported cause. Last year we put a graphic link to a site containing information about the World Aids Awareness Day on my company's Web site and almost 15 per cent of visitors to our site followed the link.

I expect to see links to favoured causes appear on almost every corporate, organisational and professional site. It costs nothing, it is an effective introduction to the cause or the charity, and it is totally non-intrusive.

But it is the arrival of digital cash which will have the greatest effect on fund-raising. The world is one enormous cry for help. The cities of the developed world are populated by sub-cultures stretching out their palms imploring for assistance. The homeless are not in their state for the lack of shelter. Homelessness is lovelessness, filed under a less accusatory heading. In the developing world, a state described as lovelessness would be considered a luxury. Here the physical needs are so great the individual and society cannot be concerned with psychological well being.

Faced with such need, the majority of citizens in the developed world shut out the horror and salve their consciences by contributing in 'organised ways' through telethons, annual appeals and on special days. The difficulty for most people is that it is very difficult to give a penny. A dollar or 50p is expected as a minimum in a personal meeting with an organisation and larger amounts are usually considered necessary for postal gifts and pledges. We need to be 'seen' to be giving a reasonable amount. Even on the street, we can't bring ourselves to give a penny to a beggar. First, we'd be scared of being abused or worse, second, we know the contribution would be ineffective.

On the Net no such constraints will apply. Using digital cash with a zero or very low overhead for transactions, we can give a penny here, a penny there and, through the power of super-distribution those pennies will turn into millions of pounds or dollars. I don't think I am being fanciful in imagining this will happen. Most middle-class people in Western-style countries have small change as disposable income (some of us are so lazy we even off-load it into jars rather than carry it) and I think the opportunity to donate small sums will be very appealing.

Causes may well try to return value in exchange for any donation above, say, five cents or five pence. Friends of the Earth currently provide a UK guide to pollution. By entering a UK postal code, visitors to their site can see the levels and type of pollution that Friends of the Earth have measured in that particular area. The information available is quite detailed and although it is currently provided free, I would be more than pleased to donate 10 pence in return.

I think this is likely to emerge as one model of the way charities, causes and not-for-profit organisations will collect small donations on-line. Many of the medical research charities are in an excellent position to provide searchable databases on-line. The Red Cross could provide stories, stills, audio and, eventually, video of its work around the world.

We can expect animal causes, children's causes and environmental causes to be particularly popular on-line and everybody will be delighted that this form of personal communication is achieved at zero environmental cost.

Political and social causes will likewise achieve success in reaching their natural constituents because of the selectivity of the Net. Coupled with corporate co-operation, which will become increasingly widespread, the ability to solicit micro-donations, both anonymous and personal, will transform fundraising in the voluntary sector over the next five years.

NET FUTURES   14

The electronic web of computer bulletin boards spread around the globe can be seen as an early underground, a system of communication between the ordinary people which is already working faster and more effectively than organized forms of communication such as television.

The On-Line Handbook, Ray Hammond, 1984

When I first started writing about the future, the subject was considered esoteric and was often confused with pure fantasy and science fiction. Today the speed of technological development is so great it is almost tangible; it can almost be sensed in the street. Accordingly, the technology debate has entered the mainstream and articles and programmes on the future, both factual and fictional, appear regularly in many newspapers, magazines and TV channels.

We have become familiar with concepts such as wearable

computers, walls which publish, doorknobs which know our touch and household appliances which talk to each other and automatically negotiate with suppliers about rates for electricity and other commodities. We are ready for cars which will pay digital tolls with digital cash (anonymous or not) as we pass under road bridges. We will expect to be connected to the Net wherever we are: on a plane, in a car, on a bicycle or in our living rooms. We know that intelligent agents will act as our intermediaries. Most importantly, we have realised that disconnection and privacy will become two of the most treasured qualities of the twenty-first century. But what will happen to business?

In this chapter I am going to attempt to imagine what society will be like for business in the early twenty-first century. I'm not going to guess too far ahead – 2005 will do – but even at this short distance the speed of change makes the number of possible variables enormous. In this projection I am bound to get some aspects horribly wrong, but I hope to get enough right to make the exercise worth while.

Earlier I have been very bullish about the speed at which we will switch to Net communications and the impact it will have on the way we do business. In the past, my predictions about change have always taken longer to materialise than I thought but, when the change has occurred, the effects have been even greater than I imagined. The emergence of the Net as a powerful commercial medium provides an excellent example. I said it would be widespread by the end of the 1980s, but it took a further five years. Although I said the linking of computers would bring about a revolution, I won't pretend that I understood just how profoundly our lives would be affected.

Despite these experiences I still take the view that this particular revolution is likely to happen very quickly: its speed of development is faster than any technological change I have ever seen. I live on the Net – I am on-line for many hours every day – but I have the greatest trouble keeping up. This is why I thought up the idea of providing an on-line version of this book. I needed to make some provision against this information seeming hopelessly dated within a few months.

No sooner do I think of what I fondly imagine to be a new concept than I often find someone has already thought of it – or even implemented it. Electronic cemeteries provide a good example.

I was in a period of deep thought casting about for an idea on the way we will utilise cyberspace which will be unusual and provocative. I realised that when the time comes, our headstones are more likely to be planted in cyberspace than in a country churchyard. I imagined collective Web cemeteries where our loved ones could rent inexpensive space for a permanent memorial or build individual mausoleums on the Net where the prosperous families could demonstrate their earthly wealth on a dedicated server containing biography, video clips from their loved ones and filmed tributes from those who had shared it. It's cheap, pollution free and takes virtually none of the planet's resources. I imagined virtual 'burials' and virtual memorial services. I intend no sacrilege: the sense of intimacy and presence on-line is considerable.

It occurred to me that some nationalities like to advertise their grief – like the Irish with their large 'in memoriam' newspaper classified columns and the Corsicans with their habit of fly-posting a city with pictures on the anniversaries of their former loved ones. I also realised that the concept was a natural extension and corollary of our increasing desire to document our existence. This was brought home to me for the first time a few years ago when I stopped at a bar on Geary Street, San Francisco where I got chatting to a Californian who told me his business was making video documentaries about the lives of rich old people who could pay to leave their story for the benefit of unborn descendants. It is now clear to me that the scrappy photo albums and old letters most of us keep to document our existence will be replaced by information collected on our personal Web sites.

Within a week of imagining a cyberspace remembrance site I found the first Electronic Cemetery on the Web. This was created by Dr Lindsay Marshall, a lecturer in computer science at Newcastle University in England. Over 400 souls, names stored in alphabetical order, are 'remembered' in this 'Garden of PC'. There is a larger than usual percentage of gay and lesbian memorials posted here as Dr Marshall does not censor 'headstone inscriptions' in the way that the Church of England does in the physical world. Another section of the cemetery is reserved for pets. And then I discovered the second – The World-Wide Cemetery...

The speed of development I observe on-line demonstrates that the theory of 'increasing returns' is a reality. The more the Net grows, the more reason it has to grow again. Nicholas Negroponte has suggested that few of us have really understood the meaning of 'exponential' when applied to the topics of technological growth and change. Like many other commentators on the digital society, I've used the term frequently over the years and I understand the mathematical theory, but this doesn't mean I (or anybody else) has known what it actually *feels* like. Negroponte points out that it isn't until the end of an exponential cycle (when very large numbers are doubling) that the real effects can be felt. He says that this is occurring now in the information revolution. I think he's right. The rate of change is now so great it can hardly be tolerated, let alone managed. It isn't a generational thing. I am amazed by the number of young people just starting their careers who voice this view unprompted.

Another reason why I think the growth and adoption of the Net may be even faster than predicted is that it is occurring at a time when, as discussed earlier, there is a complete collapse in telecommunications charges, governments are promoting the Net, unwired territories are leap-frogging old-fashioned technology and PC prices are tumbling.

So, despite my experiences of seeing real change occur much more gradually than I have been prone to forecast, I think this revolution is going to move very quickly indeed and its limiting factor (which may prove significant and divisive), will be our ability to absorb such change, as I intimated in my 1982 quote at the start of chapter 1.

This is one worry which must be included in any backdrop for a scene set in the year 2005. Another is the real threat the Net poses to traditional concepts of property, employment, taxation, money and national sovereignty.

Well, I'm going to gamble that although some of these major issues will be looming very large by the year 2005, our core ability to trade and retain profits will be unaffected. My first draft of the last sentence read 'our core national economies will be intact' but I am not at all sure this will be the case.

There are currently two main schools of extreme opinion about the wider impacts of the Net on society. To my left there is the 'Wired community' which consists of very knowledgeable, libertarian intellectuals who were involved with digital society in general, and the Net in particular, early enough to have understood the issues. Most, but not all of them, are physically located on the West Coast of the USA (although their natural habitat is cyberspace). This group includes names I have introduced before; John Perry Barlow of the Electronic Frontier Foundation, Phil Zimmerman, author of *PGP*, Kevin Kelly, author of *Out of Control* (and executive editor of *Wired* magazine) and David Chaum, creator of anonymous, digital cash.

To paraphrase their view: the Net is uncontrollable. It cannot be managed by state or corporation and it is the first global network joining ordinary people. By its nature it is subversive and it will bring an end to many traditional notions of Western-style economics such as taxation, national currencies and national borders. It means an end to our concepts of intellectual property copyright.

As my quote from 1984 at the head of this chapter indicates, this feeling is not a symptom of nineties disillusionment.

Some of these thinkers (and I think I am also prepared to anthropomorphise in this way) suggest the Net has an early form of distributed intelligence which might be compared to a dim consciousness.

Few of these thinkers are anarchists or are politically motivated to destroy our existing structures. They are all highly ranked intellectuals and their views must be considered very seriously.

To my right there are politicians, regulators and governments who seek to control the Net. Censorship is a favourite topic of right-wing politicians and governments such as those of Singapore and Vietnam have found themselves caught between the desire to have a high-tech infrastructure for their economies and the fear that an uncontrollable ubiquitous network for their own people and to the outside world might prove extremely subversive. The Chinese government appears to believe it can allow the Net into its totalitarian state and control it. This is a serious mistake and may do for China what the denial of computers and networks did for the USSR.

Occupying the middle ground are commentators and technologists who understand the issues but believe that the 'worst-case' scenarios are unlikely. Nicholas Negroponte, in particular, is firmly optimistic. In the closing paragraphs of *Being Digital* (written in 1994) he says:

> *But more than anything, my optimism comes from the empowering nature of being digital. The access, the mobility and the ability to effect change are what will make the future so different from the present. The information superhighway may be mostly hype today, but it is an understatement about tomorrow. It will exist beyond people's wildest predictions. As children appropriate a global information resource, and as they discover that only adults need learners' permits, we are bound to find new hope and dignity in places where very little existed before.*

By 2005 almost every business, organisation, government authority, school and individual professional or entrepreneur will be on the Net and there will be over half a billion users. Its speed and efficiency for users will depend on the type of access businesses and consumers can afford (or choose) to buy. The least expensive form of access (over today's standard copper phone lines) will deliver VCR quality video in real time (this has already been achieved in experimental schemes). Higher bandwidth connections will be capable of delivering several feature films simultaneously, plus, music tracks and sundry information electronically.

BALANCING THE PRACTICAL WITH THE THEORETICAL

It is easy to grasp the idea of connecting the world's computers together over the telephone lines. It is difficult to understand fully how our lives will change as a result of such a simple concept. One reason why it is difficult is that the word computer conjures up a grey box with a screen sitting on an office desk.

This book has business as its focus and I am conscious that it has covered a broad terrain from the practical (how to sell successfully over the Internet) to the theoretical, if not to say philosophical (the impact of anonymous digital cash on national economies). There is an overriding reason for this: I regard business as a highly creative activity, one which demands that protagonists, especially those with serious managerial or proprietorial responsibility, blend a firm grasp of the practical with an appreciation of likely future trends.

Despite all of my worries about the problems facing legacy corporations, and my concern about the apparent collapse in the financial value of information and the approaching instability of our direct-tax economic models, I remain more excited about the prospects for business growth and successful start-ups in the on-line world than I have ever been before. But to plan our businesses for the next century we must have some idea about how life itself will change.

MULTI-USER GAMES

Earlier I have suggested that commercially available pornography will drive consumer take-up of the Net. Hot on its heels will come other forms of entertainment and this will take many new shapes.

I don't enjoy computer games (or, indeed, games such as chess, monopoly or cards) so I am not the person best placed to speculate or imagine how games will develop on the Net. Multi-user games already exist on the Net. These were originally group versions of *Dungeons and Dragons*, one of the early concepts for a computer game, but they have grown up and the players now substitute 'Domain' as a less infantile description.

There are already hundreds of sites prepared to beat you at chess, play cards with you, offer *Trivial Pursuit*-style questions and otherwise provide amusement. I am sure that arcade games of the 'shoot-em-up' variety will spread to the Net and I can imagine 'stalk and kill' games developing across the immensity of cyberspace. Now that I think of it, I am sure we will have *Star Trek*-type games consoles for the Net which we will fly through cyberspace (with all the traditional space/time effects added) to land at distant 'worlds' (servers set up as 3D alien environments). There are already thousands of Star Trek sites on the Net and Paramount Pictures gave up attempting to stop illicit use of images, scripts and clips several years ago. Perhaps servers will spring up offering us 'scripts' for a game in which a journey through cyberspace is plotted by scripted links.

Gambling will be another massive success on the Net. I don't enjoy gambling either, but I was forcefully reminded about its international appeal when I was asked to consult for one of Britain's leading football pools companies. The football pools, a

British-invented form of gaming in which punters have to forecast the outcome of soccer matches each week, is licensed under its own Act of Parliament in the UK. This means that it enjoys certain privileges such as taking bets on-line which are denied to other UK gambling operations such as casinos.

My clients wanted to exploit this freedom in order to attract players from the many countries where the pools isn't available and, before the site was launched, many of our discussions focused on how best to market the site to ensure that players would find it. Should the accent be on football or gambling? The pools enjoys a special place in the hearts of British people and it was decided that a traditional approach would be most appropriate. (On-line readers will find the site here.)

Of course, there are many countries in which gambling is banned and, naturally, there is an enormous hunger for gambling opportunities from these territories. The legal issues of putting a gambling site up on the Net are considerable and, as you might imagine, were the subject of much discussion. Once something is on the Net it is open to all even if it is not intended for all.

There are already a number of virtual casinos on the Net, some of them playing with digital cash and providing the winnings instantly. (If are on-line, you start at Gamblers Corner or a page called Gambling Links.)

THEME PARKS IN CYBERSPACE

I am sure that within the next five years we will find virtual theme parks springing up in cyberspace. Disney will offer them as will

Madam Tussaud's and the other major operators of the physical equivalent. We will take our children to visit them on the Net and, using 3D platforms feeding surround screens or virtual reality helmets, we will enter worlds which spring solely from the creation of the imagineers.

I mentioned the idea of *Star Trek* games in cyberspace earlier: if we pursue this concept we can imagine theme parks which don't exist just at one site. The park could be spread across the Net itself with servers acting as a space station, a star cluster or a Klingon battle-station. The scope of cyberspace is large enough to serve as an immense playground simulating outer space. Equally, hydraulically powered motion seats may well be *the* Christmas present of the year 2004, controlled from the Net site(s) to provide the physical sensations of movement as we experience the ride.

In today's new breed of 'movie ride' such as *Back to the Future* at the Universal Studios theme park in LA and the *Star Quest* in Korea the audience sits on hydraulically controlled 'motion platforms' and experiences movement which corresponds to a special film and computer graphics 'experience'. The extensive filming and programming which goes into the development of these multi-million-dollar rides will be re-purposed to drive VR helmets and 'experience seats' which will allow us to experience incredible powerful 'rides' without leaving home.

We may choose to don pressure-sensitive 'tactility transference' garments which will transfer the sensation of touch (such suits already exist for cybersex activity across the Net). Small fans in our virtual reality helmets will allow us to sample synthesized smells and breezes if we choose.

There will also be on-line games and communities which

combine elements of theme parks and on-line gambling. Perhaps 'treasure' will be strewn around the interior universe of cyberspace for intrepid voyagers to discover.

Standing before conference audiences demonstrating how to make hotel bookings on the Net with a PC and a 28.8bps modem, I sometimes doubt my sanity. Occasionally the gap between what I imagine and today's reality seems too great. But I have to remind myself that the signposts to the future can already be seen.

3D Web platforms are available now from Silicon Graphics and Worlds Inc. and the early 3D environments built on the Net already contain communities with a sense of 'self' as a virtual representation.

I was in Los Angeles in the summer of 1995 and I watched Steven Spielberg show one of the first virtual environments created for the Net. This is what I wrote for *Creative Review* after seeing the demonstration:

ET turned and looked at us. We knew the face. Those huge koala eyes captured the hearts of a generation. Then he waddled off into the sky and met Vanessa, a goldfish, hanging out by a fairy-tale palace in Sky World.

'Where are you?' asked ET.

'By the castle,' said Vanessa sharply, surprised he had to ask.

At that moment, a hotel ballroom in downtown LA erupted. As the applause subsided Steven Spielberg smiled in his shy, embarrassed way and said, 'I mean, which hospital are you in?' The case for virtual worlds on the information superhighway was proven.

Vanessa is a 9-year-old leukaemia patient at the Boston Children's Hospital and her avatar (or virtual character) 'the goldfish' had chosen to rest beside a fairy-tale castle amongst the clouds.

The creative master of Hollywood chooses to find time for charities, especially those which employ high technology. In 1982 he founded the Starlight Foundation to help seriously-ill children and at a private showing held in Los Angeles last month he launched a sister organisation, The Starbright Foundation.

If you consider today's Internet to be a place for maladjusted loners, the on-line environments being created by the new foundation have the potential to change your mind about on-line communication. They are fully rendered and animated 3D 'environments' and navigation is instinctive.

During the conference, Spielberg sat at a Pentium-powered PC to demonstrate 'Starbright World', a cyber environment created across a dedicated network of fibre-optic cables linking six children's hospitals in the USA.

'We are hoping that the absorption of playing in a virtual-reality playspace will help children who are unable to play and travel as healthy children can,' Spielberg told me after the demonstration. 'In the long-term we hope to find out whether immersion in virtual worlds will help to lessen pain. There is some early evidence this may be so and our researchers have found that self-administered pain medication decreases by 50 per cent when the children are playing in Starbright World.'

The audience was delighted by the demonstration which was clearly very real to the three children involved. Spielberg's PC was fitted with a video camera and, using ProShare video conferencing, he was able to switch between a view into Sky

World so that we could see his real patients and they could see him.

The Starbright Foundation has some powerful allies. The four main sponsors (and providers of the technology) are Intel, Sprint, UB Networks and Worlds, Inc. and the foundation has received a multi-million dollar donation from the Heinz Family Philanthropies.

Sky World was created by the programming team at Worlds, Inc. and the initial version includes Cave World, a soothing, nurturing environment, Sky World, a dream-like space, and a dense, dark area called Jungle World.

'It is planned that the pilot programme of six children's hospitals will expand to a nation-wide, multi-user, interactive, point-to-multipoint network with many virtual-reality play-spaces where children can meet and play with other children regardless of their condition, location or capabilities. Work is now going on to develop special joysticks for those with low physical ability and discussions are now under way to expand the network internationally.

(If you'd like to know more about the Starbright Paediatric Network you can contact the Managing Director, Chris Garvey, at *chris@starbright.org*.)

If Steven Speilberg understands VR and the Net to this extent (including hands-on operation during the demo) we can be sure that there will be cyberspace rides on every conceivable theme and topic. Whether *Jurassic Park, Jaws, Back to the Future* or *Star Trek* is first is merely a matter of academic conjecture.

In creating Sky World, the Starbright team has applied an incredibly powerful force for the relief of boredom and pain for many sick children. Most importantly, in providing children with an 'avatar' (a representation of self in cyberspace, formerly called a 'sprite') they have given children a psychic means of escape from their own bodies and state of being. This is a very important development and is a dramatic extension of the type of personality transference frequently seen in sick and disturbed children and adults.

HISTORY NET

Our museums will find their role in society dramatically increased by the Net. From being the repositories of our past they will become (in Nicholas Negroponte's phrase) the 'retrievatories' of our culture and, as such, will be heavily accessed and visited.

This will mean a supremely scarce physical resource will suddenly become available to all as and when needed: curators must be salivating. My Web production company is frequently asked to design and prepare commercial sites for the Web, but when we were recently approached by a major war museum to discuss a concept for a site, my imagination went into hyperdrive. I imagined that in Cyberspace we would one day find a theme-park museum dedicated to illustrating the horrors of physical war and I would like to dream that one day the citizens of cyberspace who took the 'ride' would smile and shake their heads at the stupidity of humans while they were still confined to the physical.

Above all, museums have the most wonderful *content*, and it is this which makes a site wonderful. If you would like to see how some of the museums are squaring up to the exciting challenges of the Net, the following will give you an idea. The

Science Museum, London, Charles Babbage Institute London, Boston Computer Museum, Smithsonian Institution Washington, the Natural History Museum, London, the British Library, UC-Berkeley Museum of Palaeontology (one of the most fêted virtual museums on the Web) and even the Museum of Garden History.

(On-line readers will find a complete list of virtual museums here.)

COMPANIONS ON EARTH

15

Computer scientists are busily creating a new kind of non-biological being and super-intelligent machines will become our companions on earth in the next century.

If we learn how to use artificial intelligence properly (and if we teach artificial intelligence how to respond to us properly) the benefits such servants have to offer are so profound that the over-used word 'revolution' is a totally inadequate description.

The Modern Frankenstein, Ray Hammond, 1986

Welcome to the Network Health Centre. The doctor is always in – and he has time to chat!

On-line communication is going to make a major contribution to the physical and mental health of the world's population. Until now, each country has developed its own, insular approach to caring for its citizens' health and there has been little opportunity to export the valuable resource of highly trained professionals and their diagnostic and therapeutical support systems. This is about to change completely.

The concept of tele-medicine – the notion of health-care providers using on-line communication to share resources, carry out remote diagnosis, remote surgery, and so on – is not new and in recent years articles on the topic have appeared in the world's press with increasing regularity.

What few have realised is that the ubiquity of public-access data networks is going to change the way we all approach our health, both in promoting a preventative approach to personal health and in the way we find information and treatments. The Net is going to replace the 'front line' of public health services (the GPs and the out-patient hospital department) for a significant part of the population and parts of the Network will be made secure and used for remote diagnosis, remote surgery (using human and robot surgeons) and video-conference consultation. The Net is going to change our entire approach to medicine.

Make no mistake, our health is a serious business and all of the countries in the developed world are gasping for a solution to the problems of community health care. We are familiar with the demographics: today 42 per cent of the population in developed countries work and 25 per cent are over 65. Towards the middle of the next century those of working age will make up 32 per cent of the population and those over 65 will represent 40 per cent. Our health-care systems now have armouries of technology – some digital, some not – for prolonging life (but not necessarily the quality of life) and a declining work-force unable to provide the necessary wealth to support our 'legacy population'. Something has to give and this has already shown up in the quality of state-provided care in many countries.

Digital technology and on-line communication are about to revolutionise the way the technologically literate consume health care, while the cultural change which started in California with the 'me generation' in the 1970s will accelerate and further spread around the world. Over the next decade we will be buying health-monitoring devices for our home and offices and using Net resources to analyse the data, provide advice and this will become the new front line to the medical profession.

In essence, the future economic reality of our societies requires that all those who are capable of doing so, must take responsibility for their *own* health. This may seem like a simple and logical proposition to every reader of *Digital Business*, but you are in a (relatively) tiny elite. First, you read books, second you read books about technology and its impact on society. This probably puts you in the top 2 per cent of the world's population. The health revolution will start (or has started) with you! The problem is that the majority of the world's population feels ignorant and helpless about the condition and outlook for their bodies and minds. If they feel unwell, they ask a doctor to fix their bodies, as they would ask mechanics to fix their cars.

Comparatively few people are prepared to take even the simplest preventative measures. As many will know, taking one aspirin a day for those over 40 is the simplest self-prescribed remedy against heart attacks. If all of the over-40s in the developed world took this simple, low-cost preventative, the number of heart attacks would be reduced by 50 per cent. If aspirin – the chemical found inside the bark of the willow tree – was a new proprietary drug discovery, the positive research results which are available would have excited the mass media and the drug would be a world-wide best-seller at £30/$50 a daily dose.

But what has this to do with *Digital Business*? Low-cost 'personal health monitors' and on-line health-care centres are about to join hands and provide a new, massive health-care market with more opportunities for would-be entrepreneurs than you can imagine. At the same time, health-care professionals are about to increase their use of on-line digital technology to extend, amplify and replicate the most valuable resource of all, the doctor. Most importantly of all, our health, both personal and collective, is a prerequisite for all business endeavours.

Let me provide some background to my own interest and involvement in this topic. In 1985 I formed a UK company called Personal Technology Applications Ltd. and over the course of a year I lost a considerable amount of my own money researching what, at that time, turned out to be a futuristic dream. I wanted to build digital Personal Health Assistants (PHAs) which would help to look after us.

I dreamed of a wrist-watch which would double as a guardian, monitoring our health night and day. Early versions of my Health Watch would be passive monitors, checking our pulse and blood pressure, merely providing us with audible warnings if measurements exceeded safe limits. The watches were planned to look like normal analogue or digital designer watches. At that time it was difficult to get accurate blood pressure readings without the use of strong pressure (it still is, although it is now possible) and even reliable pulse readings proved difficult to obtain.

But I pursued my dream. I travelled in the Far East looking for volume manufacturers of custom chips, I looked at the early, clumsy home blood-pressure measuring devices that were finding their way on to the market and I formed a board of directors – medical professionals, technologists, consumer goods manufacturers and financial consultants to advise me about making my dream a reality.

Over a decade ago the technical hurdles turned out to be almost insurmountable – the chips were large, expensive and slow – and much of the technology would have to be custom-made rather than off-the-shelf. The sum I needed to raise for the main start-up rose from an initial projection of £600,000/$900,000 to over £3.3/$5 million as my research continued.

But the main obstacle turned out not to be the technical difficulties nor the increasing capital sum required. Our biggest problem was that of potential liability. If a consumer bought one of our watches and it incorrectly warned him or her of a problem, would the anxiety caused by such a false reading make us liable if the wearer developed a stress-related condition (for example, a heart attack or stroke), the very type of condition we were setting out to relieve?

My business plan called for much more advanced devices to follow. I wanted to develop wrist-watches that were 'ambulatory monitors'. They would record the pattern of pulse, BP and other vital signs over a period of weeks while the wearer went about his or her normal life and this data could be up-loaded to a computer for analysis. The problem for all doctors caring for those with cardio-vascular disease (and some other disorders) is establishing how the patient's system copes with day-to-day life.

Leaving aside the narrow task of observing a heart's performance under differing conditions, such long-term monitoring would provide valuable data about precisely what events, undertakings or activities provoke unacceptable cardiovascular loadings for an individual. Coupled with a built-in chronometer, the patient's life and his or her reaction to it could be clearly demonstrated.

(I also realised that when ambulatory data were collated from many individuals, doctors would have a much better understanding of symptom-free disorders and developmental patterns. Equally, such data would be of enormous value in the development and refinement of drugs and therapies.)

Ambulatory monitors exist today, but they are still expensive and are used in the rarest of circumstances such as diagnosed intermittent heart disorders. I imagined that every few weeks the patient would return to the doctor's surgery where the information would be fed into the surgery computer and the results would be explained by a smiling Dr Kildare reading a tape printout. Wasn't I wrong?

Despite having already written *The On-Line Handbook* I didn't realise to what extent ubiquitous global computer networks were going to remove the need for the patient and doctor to be together in real-time: this convenience will greatly enhance the productivity of medical professionals (just as packet-switching increases the efficiency of networks) although the vital role of human interactivity between patient and doctor will be endangered. Often, a 'cure' to a disorder has a lot more to do with this interaction than the near-placebo treatments prescribed during the consultation.

I dreamed that the Health Watch would develop to become an interventionist agent. Initially, diabetics might wear a watch which monitored insulin levels (difficult but possible without non-invasive technology) and which could either prompt the user to supply insulin manually or would intervene and inject a microjet of gas powered compressed insulin directly into the body.

We wanted to go further: we wanted a watch that would inject adrenalin when the wearer had a heart attack and automatically telephone for an ambulance via a built-in cellular telephone messager which would stay on the air until the wearer was located. This would have been coupled with an audible alarm.

We wanted to build black boxes which would sit on your sideboard. In the morning you would come down, rest your hand on top of the box and say 'Good morning. How am I?'

Of course, parts of these devices have come on to the market through the industry and vision of others more determined than me. Pop into any *Sharper Image* or *Leading Edge* and you will find a whole range of electronic health aids (including some just starting to offer short-term data storage for comparative analysis) but, as I seem to be saying constantly throughout this book, ready yourself for dramatic developments.

In my 1980s scenario, patient, technology and doctor came together physically to process the information. The Net removes this requirement and this single development will fuel the growth of the on-line medical industry.

There are already many 'health resources' on the Internet. These range from medical dictionaries to mutual self-help groups such as Web sites for sufferers of almost every condition. These sites are all passive, but their role in improving medicine and, more importantly, persuading us to take responsibility for our own health, is enormous. Until the Internet existed only dedicated on-line professionals (and enthusiastic amateurs like myself) were able to access the riches of 'MedLine' – the largest medical database in the world. On-line, point-to-point information of the highest quality has been available for decades and for years I have been kept busy searching out the latest information on treatments and research on behalf of family and friends with various medical concerns. I commented on this in *The On-Line Handbook* in 1984 as follows:

> *If your doctor tells you that you have sarcoidosis, you can now return home and, if you're brave enough, tap Medline to find out what research has been done on the disease and who are the world's experts; in many cases, the abstracts of information contained in the file will give you an instant insight into your condition. On-line information is transferring power away from those who have guarded it so jealously in the past.*

Now, the Internet has allowed thousands of self-help groups to flourish globally. This is especially useful for rare disorders and it has the effect of levelling and equalising international knowledge to the highest common factor (an interesting juxtaposition to the idea of consumer goods pricing being reduced to the lowest commonly available by software agent-assisted purchase).

As I write, there are designated web sites from American Academy of Ophthalmology Eye Care FAQs to Midwifery, Pregnancy and Birth-Related.

INFORMATION IS PATIENT POWER

In the near future, we will be able to find and choose our doctors, dentists and other professionals by shopping for information on the Net in a way which is impossible today.

A Web service called Medsearch helps US patients find doctors who fit certain criteria, and there is great public demand for this sort of information. If demand exists, fleet-footed entrepreneurs will rush to meet it. (One service which strikes me as particularly ripe for transition is the 'quality-dentist guaranteed' advertisement which runs constantly in the US. The service provides telephone advice about dental professionals and attempts to sell the services of those registered. It would work very well on the Web.)

But passive advice is only the beginning. Most would accept that non-invasive monitors (the ambulatory wrist monitor for those with heart murmurs, for example) are a relatively benign application of technology. Couple these to a Web site which will analyse the data, store it in archive and forward to a physician and something much more powerful is emerging.

Increase the use of technology to include ambulatory data collection of blood pressure, liver performance, respiratory performance, and so on, and you suddenly have sufficient information to make preventative medicine a meaningful possibility.

So what will a Web Health Centre do? Apart from providing information on health topics, Web Health Centres will accept patients who agree to take full personal liability for their use of the centre. They will dispense advice and provide 'guess diagnoses' – all with the caveat that such responses require confirmation.

You own doctor will soon have a Web site where you will make appointments and dump your personal body data for analysis. You will receive e-mails from the surgery confirming appointments, arranging visits and providing advice. But all this is merely the application of current thinking to a new paradigm. It misses the point.

What will happen is that the Net will be populated by 'consultant sites' where specialist conditions will be discussed and treated. If you have sarcoidosis, you will go to www.sarcoidosis.org and here you will find specialist knowledge and specialist treatment. The global nature of the Internet and its low cost suggest considerable pressure for such sites to spring up quickly. The first users may well be medical professionals themselves who will consult specialist sites on your behalf, but for those ready (and able) to take responsibility for their own health, direct interaction with such sites will quickly follow.

For the human consultants the benefits are irresistible. Human medicine relies on comparative data for diagnosis and prognosis. 'Give me more information about how this condition has presented and developed in others and I will prognosticate about you,' say the doctors. The Net will gather this faster than any other medium.

OUR HEALTH RECORDS ON THE NET

If we are taken seriously ill when we are away from home, the treating physician has to work in the dark. He or she needs the information contained in our medical records and the telephone, fax and modem have all assisted in bridging this communications gap in recent decades. Now I think the Net will provide a permanent solution.

If I had a serious medical condition and I wanted to ensure

my records were always available, I would post the relevant information on my Web site and I would either carry a card or wear a tag which provided my Net address and the password to gain access to those pages.

I am sure that entrepreneurs will set such sites up on a commercial basis and we may see many 'medical information centres' popping up. I would hope that hospitals would start to exchange information in this way using closed Intranet versions of Web technology. All health care services are short of cash, but this low-cost approach is something that can be developed piecemeal as and when budget is available. In many countries (including the UK) medical information is still held in physical rather than digital form and thus most of its potential is lost. The greatest task facing health services is in becoming digital in their daily lives.

REMOTE SURGERY

The first successful experiments in remote surgery on a living human patient took place in October 1995 in San Francisco. In this example, a surgeon in one room controlled robot arms to carry out surgery on a super-contagious patient in another.

In the future, surgery centres will exist solely as Net 'anterooms' and surgeons will carry out surgery all over the world without leaving their own facility. Paramedics will provide patient care and on-the-spot security during routine operations.

The breakthrough in micro-robotics which occurred at the beginning of 1996 has provided us with 'steam' engines so small that they cannot be seen by the human eye. Despite their diminutive size, such engines are already capable of turning a gear 1,000 times larger than the drive wheel and we can expect these engines to assist in micro-surgery and to migrate into our bodies in the coming decades. This development is so new that it will be some time before all of the implications become apparent.

The Net (in its future high-bandwidth form) will provide surgeons with normal and microscopic video views of their patients, touch and feel feedback and a secure 'non-interruptable' link between the operation room and the surgeon. This will allow surgeons to carry out a far higher number of routine operations and will dramatically increase their efficiency.

NON-JUDGMENTAL MACHINES

The Net and machine intelligence in general appear to be a powerful aid to accurate diagnosis and machine diagnosis is often described as 'superior' to human diagnosis. In some situations this may well be because the human patient is more prepared to discuss ailments and weaknesses with machines than with apparently censorious humans. This characteristic of man-machine interaction was first observed in a Glasgow study in the early 1980s. Alcoholics visiting a rehabilitation centre were presented with menu-driven computers which asked them about their drinking habits. Almost universally the patients told the machine interviewers that they drank between 50 and 100 per cent more alcohol than they told a parallel team of human interviewers.

The 'non-judgmental' aspect of machine intelligence is already being exploited by insurance companies on the Net who are finding considerable success at selling life and health policies from sites where humans can take their time in completing requests for quotations and are able to do so in a 'non-pressure' environment and without a judgmental human being present.

The concept of 'non-judgment' has long been an important weapon in the psychotherapist's armoury and this discipline is going to find itself extended by the Net.

PSYCHOTHERAPY SITES ON THE WEB

We all want somebody to talk to. We want somebody to listen. Sometimes, we don't much care who that is and research has shown we are more than prepared to talk to machines; especially when they mimic human response.

This was first demonstrated accidentally by Professor Joseph Weizenbaum at MIT in 1964–66 with his ELIZA experiment. Intending to demystify computers for incoming students, he wrote a short natural-language processing program to demonstrate that computers can only regurgitate what humans have fed into them. He wrote ELIZA (named after the Pygmalion character whose speech is improved with education) to mimic a Rogerian psychotherapist which could respond to human statements only by echoing back a question containing the subject (or an associated word) of the human statement or by encouraging the subject to continue. In those days the students had to type their questions in on teletext terminals and read the responses on ticker-tape paper.

In his important and still-relevant 1976 book Computer Power & Human Reason, Joseph Weizenbaum explains how his students instantly anthropomorphised the program and treated it like a human psychotherapist. The program was copied and spread to every campus in the USA and professional psychiatrists published papers speculating on when ELIZA would be able to take over their role. Weizenbaum was appalled at the power of humans to delude themselves. As a humanist he sees human and machine destiny as entirely separate. The final straw was when his secretary (who had watched him creating the ELIZA program during the summer holiday) asked if she could 'talk to Eliza'. After a few exchanges she asked Weizenbaum if he would leave the room so she could talk privately to ELIZA.

In his book, Professor Weizenbaum reproduces a typical exchange between one of his students and the ELIZA program. The computer's responses are printed in capital letters.

Men are all alike.
IN WHAT WAY?
They're always bugging us about something or other.
CAN YOU THINK OF A SPECIFIC EXAMPLE?
Well, my boyfriend made me come here.
YOUR BOYFRIEND MADE YOU COME HERE.
He says I'm depressed much of the time.
I AM SORRY TO HEAR YOU ARE DEPRESSED.

It's true. I am unhappy.
DO YOU THINK COMING HERE WILL HELP YOU NOT TO BE UNHAPPY?
I need some help, that much seems certain.
WHAT WOULD IT MEAN TO YOU IF YOU GOT SOME HELP?
Perhaps I could learn to get along with my mother.
TELL ME MORE ABOUT YOUR FAMILY.
My mother takes care of me.
WHO ELSE IN YOUR FAMILY TAKES CARE OF YOU?
My father.
YOUR FATHER?
You are like my father in some ways.
WHAT RESEMBLANCE DO YOU SEE?
You are not very aggressive but I think you don't want me to notice that.
WHAT MAKES YOU THINK I AM NOT VERY AGGRESSIVE?
You don't argue with me.
WHY DO YOU THINK I DON'T ARGUE WITH YOU?
You are afraid of me.
DOES IT PLEASE YOU TO BELIEVE I AM AFRAID OF YOU?
My father is afraid of everybody.
WHAT ELSE COMES TO MIND WHEN YOU THINK OF YOUR FATHER?
Bullies.
DOES THAT HAVE ANYTHING TO DO WITH THE FACT THAT YOUR BOYFRIEND MADE YOU COME HERE?

The result of this experiment devastated Weizenbaum and he became a cuckoo in the computer-science nest, constantly arguing that our societies do not understand the de-humanising dangers of handing over more and more control to machine intelligence. He argued that because a computer can do something it doesn't mean that it should be allowed to.

(If you would like to meet ELIZA yourself, she is waiting for you on the Net here.)

In the short term, we will visit sites on the Net for therapeutic purposes. The trend has started. The Samaritans started to provide counselling by e-mail in 1994 and they reported a considerable take-up by those who wished to communicate their worries. Psychotherapists know that many people suffering real or psychologically induced worry and depression will first turn to the pages of an anonymous self-help book before seeking human help. As a result, being non-judgmental is central to a volunteer Samaritan's training.

There will be many psychotherapy 'groups' which meet regularly on the Net, some of them guided by professionals, some of them not. There are many disadvantages about non-real meetings, but there seem to be as many advantages, not least the fact that people who are likely to join them are often those who are least likely to visit a local town hall for a meeting in a physical world. It is often said that once a person has gathered the courage to face his or her peers in the real world and admit to having problems, the battle to learn to live with them is well advanced.

Early but strong and vital manifestations of this interesting and encouraging use of the Net may be found in on-line discussion groups such as alt.suicide.holiday and alt.support.depression and these form a Network of independent support mechanisms which are global and outside of national or cultural boundaries. They are highly populated, used responsibly and, as far as I can ascertain through 'lurking' in the background of some discussion groups, are likely to provide great comfort.

There is an old saying among Net users that 'on-line, nobody knows you're a dog', and the inherent anonymity of today's Net communication does allow individuals to shield their identity and gender if they so wish. I am not qualified to comment on how effective such co-counselling is on the Net, but I am keen to see greater access to companionship and group support.

In the future many of these groups will be led by professionals and I think it likely that many psychotherapists who practise in the real world will choose to have private or group sessions in cyberspace. As Net technology develops and live audio- and live video-conferencing become everyday, such sessions will come to resemble physical meetings more closely. I understand that it is an absolute necessity for a patient to discuss and confront difficulties in the physical presence of another human (in order to externalise them in the real world) but I suspect a great deal of preliminary work can be done on the Net and a great deal of general support can be provided.

The issue of mental health will become the largest sector of medical care in the years to come. In the USA spending on mental health care approaches £33/$50 billion annually – the same as is spent on treating coronary heart disease – while in the UK it is believed that at any one time 5 per cent of the population is suffering from severe depression. Net counselling will have an important role to play as an early self-help mechanism for those who, at one time or another, need to know they are not alone.

In the longer-term future I expect to see automated 'therapy' sites on the Net. These will be the distant descendants of Joseph Weizenbaum's ELIZA and will mimic human responses surprisingly well. When they fail, and when they reveal themselves to be merely the products of human trickery, their human 'customers' will indulge them and make allowances. This is inherent in our relationship with machines and unlike Joseph Weizenbaum I think intelligent machines have a central part to play in our evolutionary destiny.

We will develop multiple cyberspace 'personas' for ourselves and these avatars will be our 'representatives' in many human transactions and, especially, in cyber communities. Patients approaching on-line therapy sessions (individual and group) will choose and shape the extension of themselves that venture out on to the Networks dependent on how they feel at that time. People with sexual identity problems and people with serious psycho-sexual disorders such as attachment damage, will find comfort and succour from the intimate yet distanced contact available on the Net.

Many readers are likely to sympathise with Joseph Weizenbaum's revulsion at an idea which seems so dehumanising, but I think on-line contact and communities will be a supplement, not a replacement for normal social interaction. Of course there are inadequate individuals who are more comfortable with machines than they are with humans and such developments will provide great comfort for this group, but I think the overall increase in connection and interaction increases one's sense of others rather than diminishing it.

In the 1940s Alan Turing proposed a method of testing machines to decide at which point we will acknowledge they possess a level of intelligence we might grace with the description 'human'. Now called the 'Turing Test', this suggests that if a human enters into a free-ranging conversation with another human (via keyboards at remote sites) and, at some point, a machine takes over one of the correspondent's roles, if the remaining human is unable to detect that it is a machine which is conversing, then the machine deserves to be awarded the accolade of having intelligence 'equivalent to the human's'. I would estimate that the arrival of machines with such 'apparently human intelligence' will occur during the second quarter of the twenty-first century. The Net will be a central part of their being.

Futurologists (like science fiction film-makers) achieve dramatic effect by plucking ideas from the future and presenting them in the context of today. We never arrive at the future in that state. Over the next 30 years we will come to understand fully and appreciate what ubiquitous machine intelligence and data networking mean. It means that it will be everywhere and we will only notice it when it is not there: as when the air conditioning or the central heating fails.

We will start to talk to machines regularly in the next five years and they will talk back, all in fairly natural language. When we do eventually arrive at a machine, or a collection of networked machines, which can pass the Turing Test, we will be unlikely to notice or to care. Our dialogue with machines will be constant and it will be amusing to imagine that such ideas once inspired awe.

Back in 1986 I dubbed such machines our 'first companions on earth' but I clung to a mental model of this intelligence being held in a single container. Despite my years of experience on-line, I hadn't understood that the processing power will be distributed and that it is the Network which will hold the intelligence. Our new companions are waiting for us now, on the Net.

The concept of a 'computer', a piece of 'software' or a Network will blur and these elements will fuse together to present us with a global intelligence mechanism for conducting both our business and personal lives.

Our offices and homes will be run by personal 'servers' who screen and manage the incredible flood of information enveloping the globe. We will come to redefine and re-understand the nature of information to arrive at a point where we accept that all physical existence is actually information: a new superstore building informs us of its presence, the solidity of its owners, the 'class' of customer it expects to attract and its likely requirement of our time and money. The information in its bricks supports the roof and the information in the roof keeps the store dry.

We are all, and everything is, information, as Stephen Hawking has so clearly demonstrated. From now on, information will be created, sought, found, delivered, sifted, sold and resold on the Net. Connection is all. It is our future.

APPENDIX 1: WHAT IS THE INTERNET?

> *The reason why international data communication is so cheap is that many users can share the same telephone line. The telephone authorities use computers to control the flow of data as it is sent at high-speed along lines in 'packets' which are individually identified. Thus many users can be sharing a line across the Atlantic or Pacific and not know that their parcels of information are between parcels 'addressed' to other users.*
>
> The Writer & the Word-Processor, Ray Hammond, 1984

> *Almost every developed country has established 'data networks,' dedicated lines and transmission channels which are intended solely for computer communication. In the past these have been used by big business, government and universities, but now ordinary personal computer users are making increasing use of these links to gather on-line information and to send electronic mail.*
>
> The On-Line Handbook, Ray Hammond, 1984

he Internet is a generic term, a collective noun, for over 50,000 different data networks which exist in most countries around the world. The networks are in independent ownership and nobody owns 'the Internet'. It is a concept rather than a piece of property. Information passes between the different networks using a common communications protocol which irons out all incompatibility issues (you can use any type of computer you like on the Internet).

Think of 'the Internet' as a nervous system in which information leaps from branch to branch. Each branch (or network) inspects a piece of information, deduces its destination and speeds it on its way. Along the routes are millions of post-boxes (your computer might be one) and millions of 'publishing' computers waiting for you to call on them for information. (I use the word 'publishing' in its broadest sense. Computer sites selling jeans or books by mail order are 'publishing' their information on the Internet.)

These networks are owned and maintained by thousands of different organisations – telecommunications companies, governments, research institutes, universities, and so on – and each owner allows data from other networks to travel over its lines at such low cost that it is virtually free. This is made possible by the way the data is packaged (explained below) and by the introduction of new automated switching techniques.

It is a subtle but important point that many of these data networks are actually sharing cables, networks and satellites used for normal voice, data, radio and TV telecommunications. If I wished to set up my own high-capacity Internet link between the USA and Europe, for example, with the intention of selling Internet access to thousands of business and domestic users I would be unlikely to have to pay for a special cable with my name on to be laid under the ocean. I would merely contract to rent a specific amount of 'bandwidth' (data capacity) from one of the many companies including AT&T, MCI, British Telecom and Cable & Wireless who have cables with spare capacity available which they can sell. They mark that 'pipeline' as being for data traffic which uses the Internet language (or protocol) and it is connected to routing devices which, in turn, connect that data stream to more network paths using the same protocol. My 'network' is actually a 'virtual network' using the same cables and lines used for phone calls, the financial networks and private corporate networks.

Many Internet network operators were formerly funded from government or educational funds – in the USA the National Science Foundation, for example – but most are now switching over to making their income from charging users small monthly amounts for access to the network (often via re-sellers of Internet access known as 'Internet providers').

Have the last few paragraphs left you puzzled? I would be surprised if they had not. For all of us, the idea of a communications medium without ownership, without control, without borders, without an 'on-off switch' is very strange. Any one government could theoretically pull the plug on the Internet, but whether that would stop data travelling across networks in their country conforming to Internet protocols is very doubtful. Policing data is practically impossible.

I said that it helps to think of the Internet as a nervous system. What is strange is that it appears to have 'evolved' without concerted effort or global agreements. This is not to disparage the very hard work done by the academics and engineers who spent years and billions of dollars building up the Internet backbones in the USA and persuading international friends to adopt similar protocol standards, but the outcome has exceeded any of their expectations: a network in cooperative ownership whose growth is driven by demand. It is, in fact, a product of the digital age occupying no territory, demanding no agreements, outside of all controls, yet already changing the world.

The lack of controls is a serious issue for everybody in business, but the main difficulty in controlling a network made up of so many independent networks is that there cannot be any global consensus about who should administer such controls. I suspect control will be devolved and this distribution of responsibility may reach as far down as individual users.

While on the subject of the networks which constitute the Internet, you may have read scare stories which claim that this fledgling, uncontrolled, anarchic network is in severe danger of collapsing under its own weight. The opposite is true. Our planet is swathed in redundant copper and 'dark fibre' (laid but unused fibre-optic cable) and how much capacity is made available for Internet traffic is simply a matter of economics. On top of this, 13,000 miles of new fibre are laid each day in the USA alone. To complete the picture I shall add that an alliance between Novell and Utilicorp in the USA and Norweb, a small power utility in the UK, has announced technology that allows it to provide network services over ordinary power lines right into every home. The speed available with these technologies is sufficient for them to send 15 videos simultaneously over the line into your home. The foundations for the information super-highway are already laid.

As Internet traffic grows, so the diameter of the 'pipes' made available will increase. You may often find Internet access slow (see below), but this is usually through the parsimony or technical difficulties of your Internet provider rather than any inherent incapacity of the Internet circuits themselves. Often, Internet access providers aren't too mean to buy additional capacity, they just can't keep up with the explosive growth of their customer base.

The Internet has grown out of data networks laid down by the US government in the late 1960s and which were developed to connect the computers in defence establishments, government departments and universities. In the 1970s the networks were extended and enlarged and the government specified that the network should be able to survive a nuclear attack. Out of this design imperative came the architecture which makes today's Internet so open and resilient.

The key to the Internet's efficiency and resilience was the design decision to use a technology called 'packet switching'. In this concept the information sent out of your computer is chopped up into small packages (packets) which are individually addressed to the same destination. These packets zip out over the networks at close to the speed of light and routers (the computers which control traffic on the networks) read the addresses and send them on their way independently of each other. When they are received at the destination computer the packets are reassembled into one message (or picture, piece of music, video, and so on) at such high speed that the operation is virtually unnoticed by the human user.

The big advantage to this design, and the key to understanding how the Internet works, is that many packets from many computers for many different destinations *can share the same lines simultaneously*. Thus, hundreds of computers can be communicating within the network space that a single voice telephone call would occupy. This makes it far, far less expensive for computers to communicate around the world than humans.

The second benefit of the packets concept is that the fragmented information can find its own way to its destination. As an addressed packet of information arrives at a routing device, the router reads the address and sends the data forward by whichever route is the best available. As the Pentagon demanded, this design means that the networks can still function if chunks are eliminated. As you read this, trillions of data packets are traversing the globe with the network sentinels selecting the most appropriate path. If we could suddenly sever every trans-Atlantic network link, data would still flow over the network between the USA and Europe because it would find its way across the Pacific and Asia. There would be delays; not because of the distance involved — this means nothing, on a clear line a packet of data can circumnavigate the globe in a split second — but because a backlog of packets waiting to be directed would build up at each routing computer along the way.

Finally, unrestricted public access to the Internet is one of the unanticipated benefits which has followed the ending of the cold war. Although the US military had already shifted a lot of its sensitive communications off the Internet before the Berlin Wall came down in 1989, the 1993 decision by the US Government to allow commercial use within the protocol domain (which is really how the Internet should be thought of) started the Internet explosion.

THE WORLD-WIDE WEB

Just as 'the Internet' is not a specific piece of wire running round the planet, the World-Wide Web is not a separate network, nor 'a section' of the Internet. The phrase 'the World-Wide Web' makes the concept sound as if it is a different network. It actually describes those computers on the Internet which publish information in a graphic form which is most-easily viewed through a window-type 'browser' or 'client' situated on the user's computer. The technical terminology for this type of approach is called 'client-server.' I shall explain.

In 1984, when I wrote *The On-Line Handbook*, all computers on the Internet and the other data networks communicated in what is known as a 'peer-to-peer' fashion. I would dial a particular number for a given computer and, once granted access, I would interrogate that computer over the network by answering the 'prompts' I saw on its screen. These prompts would ask me what terms I wanted to search in a database and return the answers. I could up-load and down-load files but if I wanted to access another computer I would have to disconnect and dial the new number.

On the World-Wide Web this model is stood on its head. I connect to the Internet by telephoning my local Internet access provider and bring my piece of 'client' software, my browser, to my screen. This gives me a 'window' on the screen through which I can look at any of the millions of 'server' computers which are publishing using the World-Wide Web formats. I type in the location of the first 'site' I wish to visit and, almost instantly, I am looking at the opening or 'home' page of that particular computer. It is delivered to my 'client' software by the 'server' at the site. On this page information is laid out in a graphical form. I may see a colour logo, a photograph and some opening text. A 'button' on the screen may invite me to click to hear some music or watch a video. Almost certainly, some of the pictures and text will be 'active,' that is, something will happen when I click on them.

This brings us to the core concept of 'hyper-links.' The essence of the World-Wide Web protocol is 'point and click.' To achieve this the designers of the protocol allowed text and objects to become pointers and link to other objects. These links may be to another file within the computer being visited, or the links may contain the address of a computer on the other side of the world. Text which contains a hyper-link to further information is usually underlined to indicate that a link exists (as are so many of the words in this book, indicating that they contain links in the on-line version) and a picture or graphic will usually tell the 'visitor' that it has a hyper-link contained within it (although not always; sometimes site designers build unannounced links into graphics to increase the subtlety of the site).

A single mouse click on the hyper-linked item and the browser is taken directly to the information required, whether inside the same server or an address of a server on the other side of the world. This concept has fostered the concept of 'surfing' the Internet because so many users hop from site to site, clicking on the links just to see where they might be taken. A visit to a virtual art gallery on the Web might be followed by a visit to a live transmission of a House Music party on another continent. I know one enthusiast who was so enthralled he spent the night glued to his computer, jumping from video camera to video camera stationed around the world to watch the sun rise over each successive continent.

HAVE YOU HEARD THAT THE INTERNET IS TOO SLOW?

The Internet and the World-Wide Web can sometimes be slow to use, especially when accessed via a standard telephone line and an inexpensive modem. But such difficulties and a certain tedium which might irritate the impatient, should not stop us realising the potential. All important new technologies develop from humble beginnings. In the late 1970s and early 1980s, friends and relations would appear at my house to 'look at Ray's computer'.

'What can it do?' these fascinated novices would ask. I would puzzle for a moment and, dependent on their age or interests, would show them a game, a word-processing document or a spreadsheet.

At first they would gaze at the green 11-inch monitor with great attention, but as the minutes passed I was always aware of their increasing disappointment. Even if they persevered I had to explain why it took so long to load a program from an audio cassette and then deal with their incomprehension when, quite frequently, it failed to run.

At its most extreme form their disappointment would manifest itself as 'well, let me know when computers can do the housework', while my more thoughtful visitors would mutter about getting a machine so they could 'experiment' for themselves.

In essence, the technology was not yet sufficiently advanced 'for the rest of us'. Only computer geeks would tolerate such poor performance. But without being a nerd or interested in technology for its own sake, I was fascinated by the potential as much as by the reality. So it has been, and to a certain extent still is, with the Internet.

Over the last few years I have sat many friends down beside me to show them the Internet. Before the explosion of the World-Wide Web this was usually a reasonably efficient and impressive thing to do, but in recent years, the situation has come to resemble my early days of microcomputing – especially if I logged on at the wrong time of day.

The Internet providers who have sprung up around the globe have been swamped with a demand which has constantly outstripped supply and many of the communications bottlenecks have been inside their own connection systems. It is also fair to say that the most popular Web sites, such as the main search engines at YAHOO!, Lycos and WebCrawler have all struggled to cope with exponentially growing demand and have found that as soon as they up-grade to more powerful server computer systems and ever larger data pipelines to the Internet, demand has risen so quickly that they have to up-grade all over again.

If your experience of the Internet so far has been limited to dial-up access from home or office over ordinary phone lines, you may be forgiven for thinking that my vision of a networked future is pure hyperbole. Certainly public access to the Internet has been a tedious and hit-and-miss business. But this doesn't give us the excuse (one clutched at by many technophobes) to ignore it.

When someone complains to me that a computer or a network is no good for solving a particular problem because 'It isn't fast enough' or 'There isn't enough storage', I respond, 'Well, there's no problem then.' We can always be sure that computers will go faster and have more storage.

I remember meeting printers in 1988 and telling them that their expensive, purpose-built workstations for producing large colour files would be replaced with Macintosh PCs. They found the idea ludicrous – how could a Mac handle an 80 megabyte file? But someone with even a rudimentary understanding of theoretical computing would not have argued with me. The signs were there to be seen years earlier:

> *One exciting development which is just on the horizon is digital picture composition. Computerized newspapers have been using computer-generated pictures for some time, but the falling costs of microprocessors and the introduction of inexpensive memories mean that this facility is about to become available to the individual.*
> *The Writer and the Word-Processor.* Ray Hammond, 1984.

Today there are very few workstations left in pre-press preparation for printing and Macintoshes had 90 per cent of the world's colour files for printing.

Tomorrow's network will be permanent, or at the very least it will feel as though it is. Your desktop machine will be permanently connected to a high bandwidth phone line and, whenever you are using your machine, you will be connected to some part of the global network. This will be very low cost and will alter the way we use computers. There will be new distributed applications and resources of a type we cannot yet imagine: when the vast global network is permanent, high-speed operations and procedures will be possible of which nobody has yet dreamed. There was no concept of a spreadsheet before there was a personal computer.

But if *today's* Internet is slow, who's going to build the 'information superhighway' that we need before networks become really useful? Such worries and questions are irrelevant. It is now clear that the necessary technical performance will arrive through a form of 'driven evolution' as the world's software, computing and telecommunications companies race to wire the planet.

APPENDIX 2: FREQUENTLY ASKED QUESTIONS ABOUT BUSINESS ON THE INTERNET

All of the information now stored in these huge databases has been available before, but for the first time we have a way of accessing information, of finding precisely what we want from the vast sea of information in which we have been swimming for years.

Until very recently we have had no way of finding what we need. Yesterday's newspapers weren't much good for anything other than wrapping up fish and chips.

Now that we can index these papers into a computer system which can retrieve information in seconds, every word that has been printed on every subject under the sun has taken on a new value: we can find it when we want it.

The On-Line Handbook. Ray Hammond, 1984.

I'm writing this book in quiet spells between bouts of frantic activity as my company presents conferences, seminars and exhibitions on Internet-related topics in the UK and mainland Europe. I'm also commuting to the USA almost every month to speak on the same topic. Our events include such topics as 'Retailing on the Internet', 'Advertising, Selling and Sponsorship on the Internet', 'Insurance, Banking and Financial Services on the Internet', 'Commercial Opportunities on the Internet', 'Publishing On-Line' and 'Doing Business on the Internet'. We are often sold out and have to turn delegates away.

During these events our speakers present case-histories from large and small organisations which have pioneered Net commerce and the question and answer sessions which follow each presentation reveal the enormous hunger of the business community to understand the nature of the new medium and the type of opportunities it presents.

Cyberspace veterans get used to novices asking the same questions (as early personal computer pioneers did) and the most common solution found on the Internet is to supply a list of answers to 'Frequently Asked Questions' (FAQs) and ask newcomers to read this before asking their own questions.

It is therefore appropriate to try to provide some brief answers to some of the most common FAQs which have arisen during and after my conferences. These provide a useful checklist of the immediate issues.

FAQ 1: Are people actually parting with money for goods while at Web sites?

Answer: They are, but only when sites sell and market themselves in a way appropriate to the Web. There are now many well-established businesses making profits trading solely on the Web.

FAQ 2: Is it safe to take credit card payments over the Internet and do customers feel confident of the idea?

Answer: There is as much nonsense talked about this as there is about the Net as a medium dedicated to pornography. It is completely safe to send credit-card information over the Internet if secure encryption is used, for example at a Netscape secure site. Customers are increasingly ready to trust this and, according to a mid-1995 survey by Global Concepts of Atlanta, 72 per cent of shoppers on the World-Wide Web would currently prefer to buy using credit cards although 65 per cent said they would like to use digital cash. The lack of privacy about purchases on the Net was cited as a major worry by 60 per cent. (Details of the latest survey can be found on-line here.)

The issues to be aware of are where the liability rests in the case of a disputed transaction or disputed delivery. The arrival of digital money over the next few years will be the real spur to network commerce and this will change the economic nature of Web commerce.

FAQ 3: It appears that in the Internet culture information has to be free. I have information I wish to sell. How can I persuade people to pay for it?

Answer: There is a lot of 'free' information and entertainment on the Web and this is paid for by advertisers – in the way that terrestrial TV and radio gain revenue. This appears to be a well-established model on the Internet, but it is not the only one, merely the first. Publishers offering highly specialised information, indepth information and reference works can and should charge for it through on-line registration and credit card debit (today). Digital money will again alter the economics of information publishing and provide publishers with the ability to make small charges (micro transactions) for information.

FAQ 4: When I put my company, organisation or product up on the World-Wide Web, how will the millions of Internet users know I'm there?

Answer: Cyberspace marketing is now a profession in its own right and Web publicists (like Chen Jian, above) are able to offer an increasingly sophisticated range of services. The most important skill is in understanding how the various search mechanisms work on the Net. They all take different approaches and they must be approached differently. In addition to ensuring your site is properly represented in the search engines, you must market your site to other compatible sites in the Net community.

The key to successful Net marketing is understanding the nature of the medium and how it works. I have tried to provide this information in this book, but it is no substitute for experience. Unless you are very familiar with the Net it is more cost-efficient to hire a professional company to carry out cyberspace marketing for you.

One tip is to make use of a Web site which automates part of the search-engine posting process. Called Submit It, this site carries out postings on your behalf to search engines including YAHOO, Infoseek, Lycos, and WebCrawler.

FAQ 5: I only have local distribution rights to products I wish to sell on the Internet. If users all over the world have access to a site on the World-Wide Web, how can I limit my site to local users?

Answer: By requiring users to register before granting entry. This will require visitors to confirm they live within a certain geographic area. Although you won't be able to stop other visitors gaining access through deception (at least, not without significant levels of security), you will have discharged your obligations to limit distribution to a given area.

FAQ 6: Should I put up my own server or should I rent space on a commercial server? What are the costs?

Answer: This depends entirely on what you wish to achieve. If you merely wish to present a 'shop window' you can rent space and publish on the Web for only a few hundred pounds/dollars a year. If you wish to start a transaction-based business, or if your site is likely to generate heavy traffic – thousands of visitors per day – you will probably need your own server and your own leased line connection. These costs are likely to be above £50,000/$80,000 annually.

FAQ 7: How can I, or others, audit the popularity and the use my Web site gets?

Answer: Most of the audit ratings organisations – Nielson, ABC, and so on – now offer an auditing service for Web sites. In addition there are many new cyber companies offering techniques and services which go beyond the type of audits carried out in earlier media. (See chapter 8.)

FAQ 8: How can I register my company, organisation or product name on the Internet? How can I then protect it?

Answer: The registration of 'domain names', as they are called, is handled by the InterNic Society and costs about £60/$100. As yet, there is no mechanism for protecting a name, but this is changing.

It is *vital* that you get a registration for your company or organisation's name as soon as possible.

Bill Gates was reportedly furious to discover that Steve Jenkins, a 24-year-old student from Utah had successfully registered windows95.com and McDonalds was not pleased to discover that a *Wired* journalist had taken mcdonalds.com. It is still like the Wild West and InterNic must surely have cleaned up their act by the time you read this.

But whatever has happened, apply for your registration now because if you are called 'Turkey Design' (for example) you will have no chance of using 'Turkey' as the main name in your address if someone has beaten you to it.

FAQ 9: When I put a site up on the World-Wide Web which country's laws must I observe?
Answer: The short answer is 'all', which is close to impossible. Jurisdiction is one of the biggest problems for publishers on global networks and there will be no easy solution (see chapter 10).

FAQ 10: How can I protect the copyright of material I publish on the Web when any visitor can instantly copy it and, if they choose, republish it?
Answer: This is another area of major difficulty. Some argue that our concepts of copyright and the ownership of intellectual property will be forced to change as more information becomes digital. There will none the less be some technical solutions and some practical measures which will help (see chapter 10).

APPENDIX 3: THE DEMOGRAPHICS OF TODAY'S NET USERS

You're fed up with computer games. You find it easier to keep track of the household bills on the back of an envelope. And programming is a tedious bore. When all is said and done, WHAT CAN YOU REALLY DO WITH A PERSONAL COMPUTER?

The answer, quite simply, is that you can go on-line and meet the world.

The On-Line Handbook, Ray Hammond, 1984

THE COMMERCENET/NIELSEN INTERNET DEMOGRAPHICS SURVEY

Executive Summary
Released: October 30, 1995

Preface

The Internet revolution is sweeping the globe with such swiftness that companies are desperately trying to understand what is occurring, what it all means, where it is going, and how to leverage this new opportunity. Countless organizations are exploring how they can best use the Internet, in particular the World-Wide Web (WWW), for business applications such as marketing, supply chain management, public relations, customer support, product sales, and electronic data interchange.

Internet-based commerce has limitless possibilities, but it has left companies with many more questions than answers. For example,

- What are the legal ramifications of conducting business on-line?
- How will my company's marketing programs be impacted by a presence on the Internet?
- When will purchasing on the Internet be as easy as paying with a credit card at my local department store?

To guide the evolution of Internet commerce and to help businesses understand the opportunities, sound information is of critical importance. Understanding the demographics, attitudes and interests of Internet users – and how they differ from those of non-users – is essential to move the industry forward. The CommerceNet/Nielsen Internet Demographics Survey directly addresses this need by:

- Identifying Users of interactive services (i.e., the Internet and commercial on-line services) as well as their demographic profile.
- Defining Usage, including how much time is spent with various services, where people are accessing services, and how access is provided.
- Examining the Utility of assessing interactive services via WWW site or on-line surveys.

This research is a key milestone in the measurement of the Internet and WWW usage. For the first time, users of the Internet, the World-Wide Web, and the on-line services have been scientifically surveyed about their interactive usage, interests, and on-line activities. Albert Einstein once said, 'The whole of science is nothing more than a refinement of everyday thinking.'

By conducting this survey and broadly distributing its results, CommerceNet and Nielsen Media Research are redefining and clarifying individuals', businesses', and organizations' understanding of the use and possibilities of the Internet. The result is benchmark research that provides nationally projectable information that will serve as both a means to plan Internet business activities and a baseline against which to compare future studies.

1. Introduction

The CommerceNet consortium was formed to address all issues related to Internet-based electronic commerce. A non-profit organisation of over 130 electronics, computer, financial service, and information service companies, CommerceNet is working to accelerate the use of the Internet for business applications.

As part of its efforts, CommerceNet is examining the large number of questions that have to be answered before the Internet is generally accepted by individuals, companies, and organizations as a key means for conducting business. Answering the question of 'Who are the users of the Internet and what are they doing on it?' is what CommerceNet, in partnership with Nielsen Media Research, chose to tackle when it initiated this Internet Demographics Survey.

1.1 Why an Internet Demographics Survey?

The lack of information about Internet user demographics is a major obstacle prohibiting the Internet from moving from trial activities to mainstream business applications. CommerceNet and Nielsen are working together to eliminate this hurdle – first by conducting an Internet study that will accurately profile Internet users, and then by making the survey results readily available to the industry as a whole.

While the CommerceNet/Nielsen Internet Demographics Study is not the first one ever conducted, it is the first Internet survey whose results represent the population as a whole. Academics and market research companies have previously completed a number of Internet studies. While these studies have proven valuable in promoting Internet-based commerce, they have been inherently biased, limited in scope, or both. For instance, numerous surveys have relied on the Internet itself to obtain baseline data. This introduces bias, because only people on the Internet who find the questionnaire can complete it, and only those who want to fill out the survey provide the requested information. Other Internet surveys have used more traditional market research techniques (such as telephone-based surveys using a random digital dial methodology) attempting to remove these biases. These surveys to date, however, have only focused on Internet users – excluding commercial on-line users and people who aren't connected to either the Internet or an on-line service. In addition, these research programs have typically been proprietary which limited the release of survey results and disclosure of the accompanying methodology to the companies sponsoring the study.

1.2 The Study's Impact on Business

Because this Internet Demographics Survey is the most rigorous Internet study completed to date, it is expected to have a significant impact on how companies conduct business on the Internet. The results seem to indicate that – while a number of Internet obstacles need to be eliminated and various questions require answers – the Internet business applications are limitless. For example, the survey has shown:

- There is widespread access to the Internet within the US and Canada
- The Internet user is an extremely attractive target (educated, professional, and upscale)
- An Internet marketplace has already emerged (e.g., more than 2.5 million people have purchased products and services over the WWW)

The study's results will certainly change companies' perspective on the opportunity that the Internet provides, and many businesses will likely use these results as the foundation for their next Internet business planning cycle.

1.3 Availability of the Results

To promote widespread knowledge of this medium, CommerceNet and Nielsen are pleased to make this study – both the Executive Summary and the Final Report – available to the industry as a whole. The Executive Summary is being distributed for free via the Internet on CommerceNet's (www.commerce.net) and Nielsen Media Research's (www.nielsenmedia.com) WWW servers. The Final Report is available for purchase from CommerceNet (phone: 415–617–8790; e-mail: survey@commerce.net) and Nielsen Media Research (phone: 813–738–3125; e-mail: interactive@nielsenmedia.com).

2. Survey Design

To ensure the validity of the information gathered and make the results reflect the population of the US and Canada, Nielsen applied a rigorous methodology in conducting the CommerceNet/Nielsen Internet Demographics Survey. The following sections review the research methodology and questionnaire design.

2.1 Survey Methodology

The CommerceNet/Nielsen Internet Demographics Survey addresses three types of users in the US and Canada: Internet users, on-line service users and non-users. The baseline questionnaire was made up of more than 40 multiple-part questions, and the actual survey involved a gross sample of approximately 280,000 telephone calls and yielded more than 4,200 completed telephone-based interviews.

It was of utmost importance to make the results reflect the population of the US and Canada so that the results could be projected to the population as a whole. Accordingly, Nielsen employed a rigorous scientific methodology to conduct this research. For example:

- Nielsen used an unrestricted random digit dial (RDD) sample frame for this study; that is, they employed a list of all telephone numbers among exchanges that operate within the US and Canada.
- Researchers stratified the sample frame by geography to provide a proportionate geographic distribution of telephone numbers.
- Nielsen selected a systematic sample of telephone numbers with each telephone number in the frame having an equal probability of selection.
- Interviews were conducted with a randomly-selected member (who was 16 years of age or older) of a randomly-selected household.
- The data was weighted to reflect household differences – for instance, to adjust for households with more than one phone number which have a higher probability of being selected.
- Up to eight attempts over three days were made to contact each selected person.
- Data was collected from August 3, 1995 to September 3, 1995.

The study was designed to net approximately 1000 completed interviews for each of the three types of users, or cells. Because of the overlap between the Internet and on-line services today, the definition of each type of user was defined by a combination of access and usage. The precise definition of each cell was:

- Cell 1: People who have direct access to the Internet and have used it in the last three months. They may or may not have an on-line service account.
- Cell 2: People who have access to an on-line service and no direct Internet access.
- Cell 3: People who have no recent Internet access in the last three months and no on-line service.

In addition, the Internet user portion of the questionnaire was placed on a WWW site during roughly the same time period. Over 32,000 responses were collected in four weeks. The purpose of the Internet-based study was purely to measure the bias of on-line surveys. (Results from the Internet-based questionnaire are clearly labelled.)

2.2 Questionnaire Design

The questionnaire included more than 40 multiple-part questions. Questions were focused on each of the three cells: Internet user, on-line service user, and non-user. Based on their initial answers, a respondent would be asked a portion of the 40 questions.

The interview started with questions to select a random person in the home 16 years or older. If the selected member of the household was temporarily living elsewhere, such as a college dormitory, the interviewer asked for the phone number to contact them at the temporary residence.

The first detailed questions of the survey involved the Internet, starting with locations of access, speed of access, and monthly fees paid. It then branched to questions that focused on the respondent's most-recent use of the Internet. Prior to these questions, the respondent was clearly asked if his or her most-recent use was within the previous 24 hours or prior to that.

The interviewer asked several questions about the interviewee's most recent usage such as location of access (home, work, or school), duration of session, and activities used on the Internet. The questionnaire then transitioned to a series of general Internet questions based on the overall experience. Respondents were asked to describe their overall level of usage of various Internet services such as: their frequency of use of e-mail, the features they would most like to see, the location of most-frequent use (home, work or school), and the purpose they most frequently used the Internet for (e.g., personal, business, academic), among other questions.

If they indicated that they used the World-Wide Web, the respondents were asked a series of WWW questions such as the last sites they visited, the methods they use to navigate the WWW and find information, their willingness to pay for various services, their skill level, and their general purchasing behavior. People who indicated that they used the WWW for business were asked a number of business-specific questions – for instance, their typical business use, their occupation, and the size of their company.

The respondents who fell into Cell 2 who exclusively used on-line services were asked the same questions but tailored to their use of the on-line service only. People in Cell 2 who used the Internet were asked about both their Internet use and their on-line service use, separate from the Internet.

Respondents who were categorised into Cell 3 (non-users) were asked if they had heard of the Internet, the WWW, and various on-line services, in both unaided and aided questions. They were asked about their intentions to subscribe to either the Internet or on-line services in the near future.

All respondents were asked about ownership of PCs,

modems, faxes, CD-ROMS, intent to purchase computers, and access to computers outside the home. In addition, all respondents were asked demographic questions such as education, age, income, occupation, and whether or not there were children in the home.

3. Results

3.1 Survey Highlights

The results of the CommerceNet/Nielsen Internet Demographics Survey provide the most definitive answers to date about the Internet. Some of the key findings are:

- 17% (37 million) of total persons aged 16 and above in the US and Canada have access to the Internet.
- 11% (24 million) of total persons aged 16 and above in the US and Canada have used the Internet in the past three months.
- Approximately 8% (18 million) of total persons aged 16 and above in the US and Canada have used the WWW in the past three months.
- Internet users average 5 hours and 28 minutes per week on the Internet.
- Total Internet usage in the US and Canada is equivalent to the total playback of rented video tapes
- Males represent 66% of Internet users and account for 77% of Internet usage.
- On average, WWW users are upscale (25% have income over $80K), professional (50% are professional or managerial), and educated (64% have at least college degrees).
- Approximately 14% (2.5 million) of WWW users have purchased products or services over the Internet.

3.2 Survey Details

Analysis of the Internet Demographics data uncovered numerous results relevant to the promotion and acceleration of Internet-based electronic commerce. This section discusses some of the key results of the survey.

3.2.1 INTERNET ACCESS AND USAGE

Regarding Internet access and usage, the CommerceNet/Nielsen study found that:

- 17% of the total population of the US and Canada 16 years of age or older report that they have access to the Internet.
- 11% have used the Internet in the past three months. (Throughout this summary we will refer to these individuals as users.)

The 17% incidence indicates that approximately 37 million people (16 years of age or older) in the US and Canada have access to the Internet. The 11% incidence yields a current base of Internet users (16 and older) of approximately 24 million. This demonstrates that there is an additional peripheral market of 13 million persons with access (37 million minus 24 million) who can potentially be reached with an Internet delivered service.

3.2.2 ACCESS LOCATIONS

The study found that, while home Internet connections are important, locations other than home were significant sources of access. 62% of the users said that they had access at home. Interestingly, the research showed that 54% of the users had an Internet connection at work and 30% had access at school (as the sample consisted of persons 16 years and older, at school is synonymous with college in most instances).

These percentages translate to 6.7% of total persons 16 and older in US and Canada having access to the Internet at home and 5.8% and 3.2% at work and school, respectively. On average, Internet users had 1.4 different types of access locations.

Note that at school does not necessarily mean that the service is provided by the school. Family members who were away from home at college were included in the sample frame and eligible for selection. The 'at school' totals also include individual subscriptions in the student's own quarters. Similarly, roommates of on-line subscribers could consider themselves as having access.

3.2.3 LOCATIONS OF INTERNET AND ON-LINE USAGE

Respondents who had used the Internet in the past three months were asked when they had last used it. Those who had used the Internet within the past 24 hours were then asked to identify the access location.

- 66% indicated that they had last used the Internet at work.
- 44% had most recently accessed it from home.
- 8% of the respondents had most recently used the Internet at school.

Persons who used the Internet in the last 24 hours used an average of 1.2 access locations.

A comparison of 'location of access' (previous section) versus 'location of use' (this section) shows a disproportionate degree of usage occurring at work. That is, even though a higher percentage of people have access in the home, people use the Internet more frequently and for greater durations at work than at home. (Note that the survey period was in August when presumably most students would be out of class and therefore not using the Internet in the same manner they would during the normal school year.)

Respondents who had used the Internet in the past three months but not within the past 24 hours demonstrated a similar pattern. When adjusted for multiple locations, work still accounts for a disproportionate amount of the total sessions.

The measure of location of use within the last 24 hours for on-line services again points out the importance of the work environment. The results show that use of on-line services is more frequent and for greater duration at work than at either home or school.

Those respondents who indicated using an on-line service, but not within the last 24 hours, demonstrated a 'location of last session' pattern that more closely resembled the distribution of their potential location of access. While the more frequent users of on-line services use them most often at work, the less frequent users indicate a more consistent usage across locations.

3.2.4 HOURS OF USAGE

Overall usage of both the Internet and on-line services was significant. On average, all persons 16+ in US and Canada who have used the Internet in the past three months used it for 5 hours and 28 minutes per week. For on-line services, the average person with on-line service access (who had ever used it) used their service for an average of 2 hours and 29 minutes per week. To provide a common base for a more direct comparison, the average minutes per week among all persons (in US and Canada, ages 16+) was calculated. The average for the Internet was 35 minutes per week per person in the US and Canada and 24 minutes per week per person for on-line services. In total, the Internet is receiving 46% more usage than on-line services.

To obtain a better understanding of Internet usage, these results were compared to the viewing of rented videotapes. While on the surface appearing small, the 35 minutes per week per person 16+ of Internet usage is similar to the time spent in total viewing rented videotapes.

3.2.5 DURATION OF USAGE

While persons 16+ with a direct Internet connection made up only 44% of those with access, they accounted for 60% of persons using the Internet in the past three months and 73% of those who used it in the past 24 hours. The differences in usage between the Internet and on-line services may be much more a function of having the meter running on on-line services than it is content or other issues. (Note that, in this survey, direct Internet access is a connection through an Internet service provider or via an employer's direct access to the Internet; indirect access is a entry to the Internet via commercial on-line services.)

3.2.6 GENDER DIFFERENCES

Users of both the Internet and on-line services are primarily male. Males comprise 66% of users of the Internet. In addition, males tend to use the Internet with both greater frequency and duration than females, accounting for approximately 77% of the total usage. Males comprise 59% of the users of on-line services and are responsible for 63% of the total usage. There is less of a gender skew on on-line services than there currently is with the Internet.

3.2.7 USES OF THE INTERNET

While many people think of the Internet as simply E-mail, its applications go far beyond that (see tables). For those persons using the Internet in the past 24 hours, accessing the WWW exceeded E-mail in use. The percent of Internet users in the past three months who indicated frequent use of Internet applications other than E-mail was also considerable.

Uses of the Internet: Percent of Persons 16+ in US and Canada Using the Internet in the Past 24 hours Who Used it to . . .

- Access the WWW   72%
- Send E-mail   65%
- Download software   31%
- Participate in an interactive discussion   21%
- Partake in a non-interactive discussion   36%
- Use another computer   31%
- Utilize real-time audio or video   19%

Uses of the Internet: Percent of Persons 16+ in US and Canada Using the Internet Over 24 hours Ago Who Used it to . . .

- Access the WWW   44%
- Send E-mail   48%
- Download software   19%
- Participate in an interactive discussion   21%
- Partake in a non-interactive discussion   43%
- Use another computer   21%
- Utilize real-time audio or video   17%

3.2.8 WWW USAGE AND DEMOGRAPHICS

Of those individuals 16 years of age or older in US and Canada who have used the Internet within the last three months, 76% have at some time used the World-Wide Web (WWW). This is equivalent to more than 8% of total persons 16+ in the US and Canada having used the WWW.

WWW users are clearly upscale compared with the population as a whole. For example:

- 25% of WWW users earn household income of more than $80,000 whereas only 10% of the total US and Canadian population has that level of income.
- 50% of WWW users consider themselves to be in professional or managerial occupations. In contrast, 27% of the total US and Canadian population categorize themselves to have such positions.
- 64% of WWW users have at least college degrees while the US and Canadian national level is 29%.

Ever Use the WWW to . . .

- Search for information on products/services   55%
- Search for information on companies/organizations   60%
- Search for other information   73%
- Purchase products or services   14%
- Browse or Explore   90%

Ever Use On-line Services to . . .

- Search for information on products/services   50%
- Search for information on companies/organizations   42%
- Search for other information   61%
- Purchase products or services   18%
- Browse or Explore   74%

WWW users were more likely to use the WWW to search for information than their on-line counterparts (see tables above). 55% of the WWW users indicated that they had used the WWW to search for information on products/services. 60% had used the WWW to search for information on companies or organizations. The equivalent numbers for on-line services were lower; this may have been due to a substantial population of the on-line market which utilize their on-line service primarily for E-mail and chat.

3.2.9 BUSINESS USES OF THE WWW
Percent of WWW Users Who Have Used it for Business Purposes Who Have Used it For . . .

- Collaborating with others   54%
- Publishing information   33%
- Gathering information   77%
- Researching competitors   46%
- Selling products or services   13%
- Purchasing products or services   23%
- Providing customer service and support   38%
- Communicating internally   44%
- Providing vendor support and communications   50%

Approximately half of all persons 16+ in the US and Canada who had used the WWW have done so for business purposes. Key business applications are: gathering information, researching competitors, collaborating with others, communicating internally, and providing customer/vendor support.

3.2.10 INTERNET-BASED SURVEY VS. PHONE-BASED STUDY

An additional goal of the CommerceNet/Nielsen Internet Demographics Study was to test the validity of results collected via Internet-based questionnaires. CommerceNet and Nielsen hypothesized that there would be a fundamental difference in the results of a survey conducted on-line versus results collected via telephoning a nationally-representative sample. They also speculated that the results from the Internet-based questionnaire would be skewed by heavy users. The **following graphs** demonstrate a few key comparisons of the results from the two surveys (WWW site-based questionnaire versus telephoning a random national sample) that support their hypotheses.

As the results clearly indicate, studies based on data collected from the Internet cannot be used to project to the population as a whole. These examples show that projections from WWW site surveys differ from the results of surveys of the broader users. The WWW site studies, for instance, would overstate Internet usage, overestimate the skill level of the Internet users, and downplay the size of the female market for Internet services. The use of such inaccurate information could result in miscalculations in businesses' current use of the Internet and ongoing Internet plans. This is not to say that these WWW-based surveys have no value. It is, however, extremely important to understand the limitations of information gathered from WWW site questionnaires.

4. Conclusion

The lack of information about Internet user demographics is a major obstacle prohibiting the Internet from moving from trial

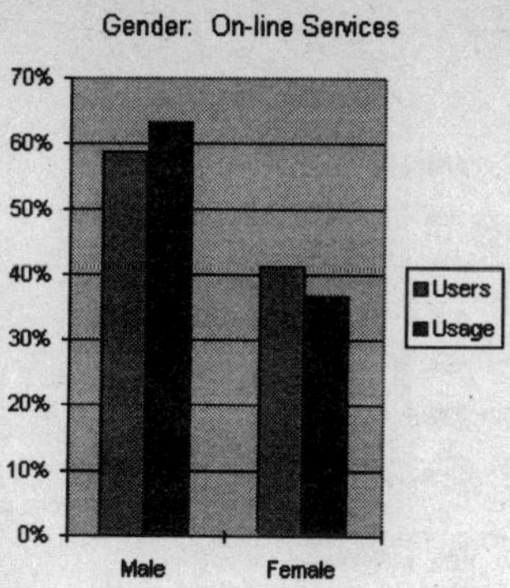
Gender: On-line Services
70%
60%
50%
40%
30%
20%
10%
0%
Male
Female
Users
Usage

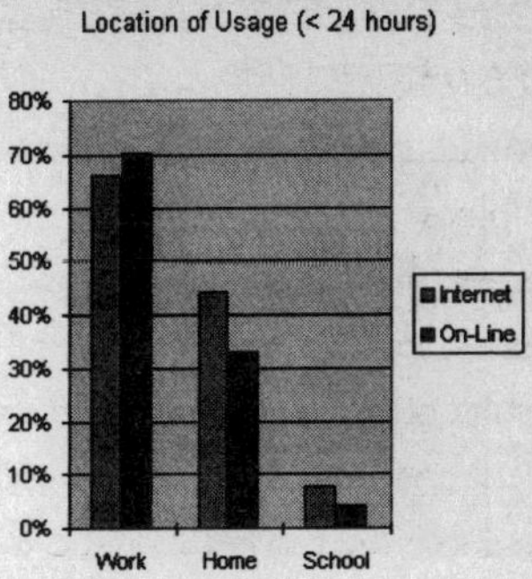
Location of Usage (< 24 hours)
80%
70%
60%
50%
40%
30%
20%
10%
0%
Work
Home
School
Internet
On-Line

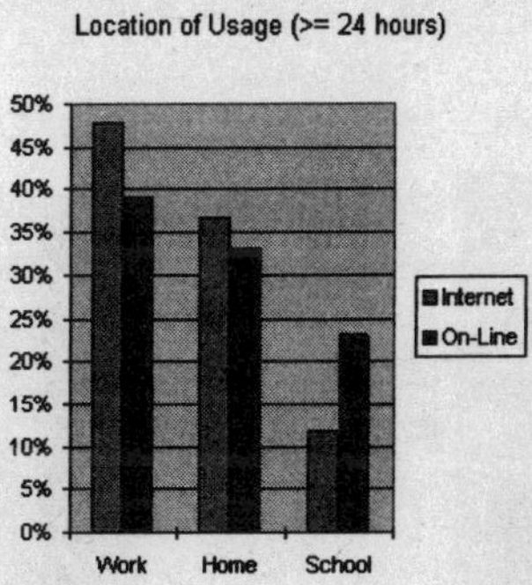
Location of Usage (>= 24 hours)
50%
45%
40%
35%
30%
25%
20%
15%
10%
5%
0%
Work
Home
School
Internet
On-Line

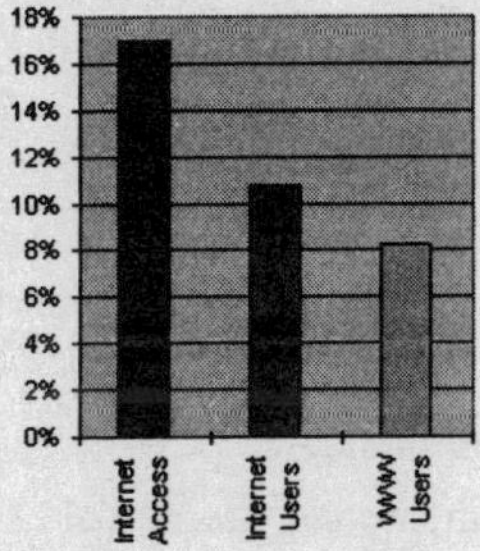
18%
16%
14%
12%
10%
8%
6%
4%
2%
0%
Internet Access
Internet Users
WWW Users

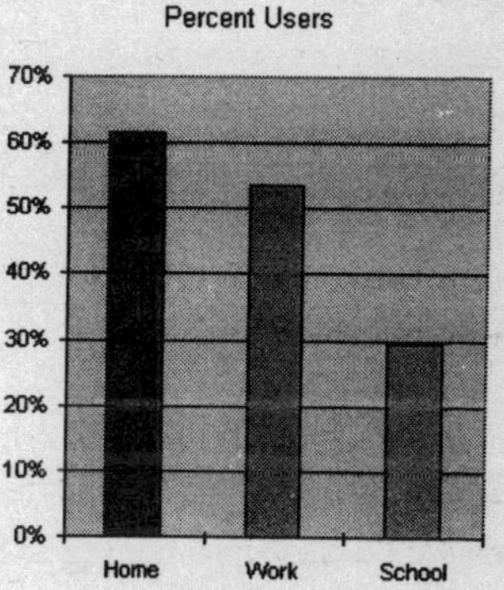
Percent Users
70%
60%
50%
40%
30%
20%
10%
0%
Home
Work
School

Frequency of Use

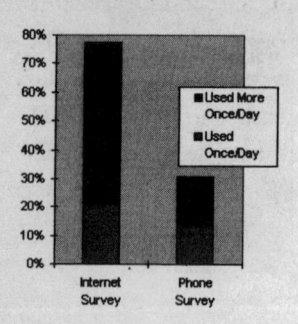

Gender Differences

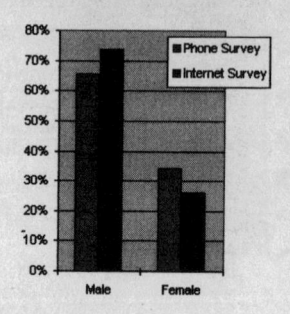

Gender: Internet

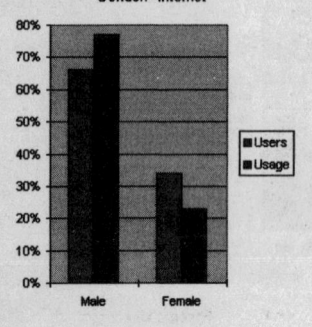

Percent of Total Population with Access

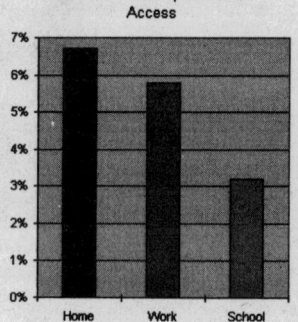

activities to mainstream business applications. CommerceNet and Nielsen are working together to eliminate this hurdle by conducting the CommerceNet/Nielsen Internet Demographics Survey. This research is a key milestone in the measurement of the Internet and WWW usage. For the first time, users of the Internet, the World-Wide Web, and the on-line services have been scientifically surveyed about their interactive usage, interests, and on-line activities.

Because this Internet Demographics Survey is the most rigorous Internet study completed to date, it is expected to have a significant impact on how companies conduct business on the Internet. The results seem to indicate that – while a number of Internet obstacles need to be eliminated and various questions require answers – the Internet business applications are limitless. Some of the key conclusions from the study are:

- There is a sizable base of Internet Users in the US and Canada
- 24 million Internet users (16 years of age or older)
- 18 million WWW users (16 years of age or older)
- WWW users are a key target for business applications
- They are upscale, professional, and well educated
- Approximately 2.5 million people have made purchases using the WWW
- The Internet is heavily skewed male in terms of both usage and users
- Access through work is an important factor for both the Internet and on-line services
- Total Internet usage exceeds on-line services and is approximately equivalent to playback of rented videotapes
- The use of the Internet differs from that of commercial on-line services

- Internet-based surveys do not represent the population as a whole.

To promote widespread knowledge of the Internet, CommerceNet and Nielsen are making this study – both this Executive Summary and the Final Report – available to the industry as a whole. This Executive Summary illustrates a number of high-level key findings that resulted from the study. In contrast, the Final Report consists of over 150 pages of tables that provide many detailed results, including cross-tabulations of each survey question against approximately 30 user characteristics.

The results from the CommerceNet/Nielsen study will certainly change companies' perspective on the opportunity that the Internet provides. CommerceNet and Nielsen anticipate that many businesses will likely use this Executive Summary and the survey's Final Report as the foundation for their next Internet business planning cycle.

Appendix A – Notes on the Interpretation of the Results

The following details are miscellaneous notes regarding the interpretation of the survey results.

1. The Internet poses some very difficult issues for anyone attempting to conduct projectable research on how it is being used. One of the challenges stems from the fact that the Internet is not restricted to use at any one particular location – it may be used at home, work, school, a friend's house, or anywhere a PC might travel. Although household projections are possible, they do not provide for a complete measure of usage. As a result, it is preferable to measure persons.

2. It is important to differentiate between subscriptions, access, and users. The key factors to keep in mind are as follows:

1. There may well be multiple people associated with each paid subscription. Households which subscribe to either on-line services or other Internet access providers tend to contain more household members than the average household. Consequently, persons in these households will generally represent a greater percentage of total persons than they do of total households.

2. Access is self defined. There are many people who do not presently use the Internet but feel that they have access. Some people are provided access as a primary user by their employers and still do not use it. Others may feel that they have access to the Internet through another family member; for example, the spouse of a person with access to the Internet at work may still request that the other person retrieve information from the Internet when needed. In this fashion, they can still be said to have access despite never using the Internet themselves nor perhaps even having a computer in their home. To ignore this large peripheral market would be to miss out on a true opportunity.

3. Usage was defined in this survey as using the Internet for something other than e-mail in the last three months.

Copyright © 1995 CommerceNet Consortium/
Nielsen Media Research

AFTERWORD

Three years ago I started work on a book called *Why Bill Gates Must Not Succeed*. A year later I put my half-written manuscript aside because it seemed as though everything was changing and it was by no means certain that Microsoft would succeed in dominating the information technology industry. Instead I went to work on the first draft of *Digital Business*.

Back in 1994, with the launch of Windows 95 supposedly imminent, it seemed as if we were heading towards a dangerous monopoly. I was concerned that a true point-and-click interface for IBM-compatible PCs built on a proper 32-bit operating system would wipe out the Apple Macintosh operating system and thus remove any semblance of competition that existed in personal computing. But then the Internet explosion occurred, millions were energised by it, and Microsoft started to look dangerously like a company that had lost the plot.

Netscape Communications burst into cyberspace like an information supernova and the entire anti-Microsoft camp (basically all those competing computer and software companies who hoped to have an independent future) aligned themselves behind the wizards of the World-Wide Web and, for a year or so, seemed as if they could alter the computing landscape.

Larry Ellison talked up the Network Computer, Netscape threatened to make desktop operating systems irrelevant and Silicon Graphics decided to produce low-end machines to compete for the graphics desktop alongside Apple.

But then Bill Gates did something astonishing. He turned the mighty Microsoft through 180 degrees and became the first market-leader of one technology generation to successfully restake his claim to lead the next. Before him, each successive wave of technology wiped out the existing market leaders and replaced them with completely new companies. This isn't to suggest that Netscape has failed or that the Network Computer won't find a market (it is now securing significant orders from Fujitsu and Boeing amongst others). I merely acknowledge that through an expensive and probably painful effort, Microsoft has reasserted its leadership of the computing industry and that in Chapter 1, I was wrong to suggest he had left it too late.

I have therefore decided to go back to work on my book, although in recognition of his success, I am thinking of changing the title to 'Why Bill Gates Must Be Stopped!'

But this is an 'afterword', and as well as commentating on Microsoft's achievements it allows me the opportunity to update my view of what has been happening in on-line commerce. By definition, a book must be a snapshot of a particular moment in time. Even a book which seeks to peer into the future can only represent the view of the moment when the type passed from the author's hands to the publisher.

I hope *Digital Business* has changed that to some extent. Since the first hardback edition of this book was published a year ago, the companion Web site has been periodically updated with news and views which supplement the comments contained in the printed version. The site has also proved my theory that the only thing which stands between an author and his readers is a communication barrier. I have been delighted to receive thousands of e-mails from readers of the hardback edition and I hope you will also send me your thoughts, comments and criticisms.

What has happened? Well, Netscape's share of the browser market is now around 70 per cent and Microsoft has 30 per cent. This is also the ratio in the more important market for server software although the figures will have changed again by the time you read this.

The press has recently been full of 'failure stories' about the Internet as a business medium and I am increasingly asked how money can be made. As I predicted, the most dramatic failures have been the old ideas which were translated onto the Web. Argos, the catalogue shopping company, left the Barclay Square shopping mall in the middle of 1996 complaining that after a year's effort it had sold only 22 items, the most expensive of which was a £25.95 'Wallace and Gromit' alarm clock. This won't surprise you because it is obvious that the super-vertical nature of the Net makes a nonsense of offering a linear print collection of goods such as the Argos collection.

I was wrong to be so critical of the Condé Nast UK site in Chapter 4. Although the company has now abandoned the proprietary software approach I disliked, heroic efforts have been made and Nicholas Coleridge, the ebullient Managing Director of the UK company, recently stood up in a conference of chief executives I was addressing and told us that his company had now made profits of over £100,000 from the site. The *Financial Times* has also improved its site dramatically, and the *Wall Street Journal* has developed the finest newspaper site I have ever seen. Dow Jones, the parent company of the Journal, was brave enough to make the site 'subscription only' (after offering free access for some months) and it now has over 40,000 paying subscribers at $149 each.

The real success stories have come from the USA, of course, as have the biggest tales of disaster. As we might imagine, it has been new companies with new types of offering which have made real headway. Amazon.com, the bookstore mentioned in the main text, has proved to be a huge success – so much so that it is now threatened by the largest US bookstore chains such as Borders who are readying their own 'virtual bookshops' for the Net.

Another massive success has been on-line auction companies. Onsale.com started selling used computer equipment from its Palo Alto base in May 1995 and today it is turning over $12 million a month, offering two global auctions of computer equipment a week, and is being imitated by a dozen others.

American Airlines copied the Cathay Pacific move of offering a few seats on selected routes for sale by auction on the Net, and both airlines have found such success with the approach that the experiments have been extended to permanent auction sites. American Airlines has reported that its yield from seats sold by auction on the Net has been higher than it achieves when seats are sold through the normal retail channels. This discussion of the travel industry leads us back to Microsoft again.

Microsoft has stated that it will spend $400 million over the next two years to develop and market Expedia (www.expedia.com). The site already offers information and on-line booking facilities for 30,000 hotels world-wide. On its own, this is a stunning facility which is free to users. Visitors can search for hotels by type, price and map location, downloading details and street maps for print-out.

Expedia has completed commission deals with most of the

world's major airlines and has a direct link to Worldspan, one of the 'big four' central airline reservation systems. This allows visitors to the site to check all airline schedules and book airline tickets direct using a credit card.

In the UK the service has partnered with A.T. Mays, one large travel agency which has taken the threat of disintermediation very seriously. Tickets will be dispatched to UK travellers by A.T. Mays and, in addition to offering access to the world's scheduled airlines and seats, the British company is making its own wholesale collection of 700,000 discounted air fares (formerly called 'bucket shop' seats) available to British Expedia users. If you can't find a good fare at a particular time, the site offers an e-mail service which will notify you when cheap fares on your selected route become available.

Microsoft will be adding a 'travel button' to the browser interface which will replace the desktop in Windows 97, and Expedia has partnered with American Express to provide management services for corporate travel. As the site gathers momentum we can expect to see Expedia packages being presented and, five years from now, we may well be booking our Microsoft package holiday on the Web unless Richard Branson and VirginNet get there first.

A director of any travel business should quake to learn that a new competitor with a development and marketing budget of $400 million is arriving in their market, but when this arrival is coupled with an entirely new type of infrastructure and a completely different cost base, the state of alert should pass through amber to red.

I am also pleased to report that the British supermarket chain Tesco is in the middle of a very serious on-line shopping trial in the spirit of my 'LowestLocal' business game which appeared in Chapter 5. The store started the pilot scheme in the Ealing, Osterly and Chiswick areas of West London in October 1996, and friends who live in the area have reported reliable deliveries of excellent quality. All of them have seized on the service with glee, even though the company charges a £5 premium for the home delivery. I also note with some pleasure that both Tesco and Sainsburys have now decided to become banks and have thus brought a very quick fulfilment of my predictions about new 'corporate banks' in Chapter 10.

Perhaps the most important development which will kickstart Internet commerce has been a deal agreed between Microsoft and Digicash. This deal was done but not announced at the time of writing, but I understand that e-cash technology is to be an integral part of every Microsoft Merchant server. Since the first edition of this book was published Mastercard has bought Mondex, the smart card and electronic cash company, and Visa is readying its own micro-payments technology. Some of these systems are being piloted around the world (although none in the UK) and we remain on-course for small value transactions to enter the mainstream of Net commerce in late 1997. As I have said over and over again, I am sure that it will be the ability to 'spend a penny' which will really fuel the growth of Net business.

All of this activity, and the sense of expectation which surrounds the rise of the 'networked society' as we approach the millennium, has produced many academic responses around the world. One of the most exciting has been the announcement of the Advanced Computing Environments Laboratory (ACElab), a £15 million research and development facility which is to be built on the new annexe campus of the University of Nottingham in the UK. The lab, which already boasts a 180-degree Silicon Graphics-driven 'Reality Centre', was founded by Professor David Brailsford (who kindly reviewed the original manuscript of this book before publication), and I have been honoured to join the team to help direct research into new digital environments and to create ties between the lab and the business world.

As a final note, it is appropriate to note that the number of Internet users around the world has risen to over 90 million. I remain confident that this figure will rise to around 400 million by the year 2000AD. As I am writing this Afterword, new research was published which showed a shift in the balance of Internet usage around the world. The USA is no longer the most 'Net-centric' country and the UK has lost its lead in Europe. The figures in January 1997 were as follows:

Percentage of households with access to the Internet

Japan	18.4
USA	16
Germany	11.7
Hong Kong	11.7
Taiwan	10.3
UK	9.5
Australia	8.9
Singapore	7
France	6.5
South Korea	6.3
Italy	5.8

Source IDC/Link January 1997

Finally, on the day this Afterword was due to be completed, representatives of 68 countries concluded a deal at the World Trade Centre in Geneva to liberalise the world's telecommunications market. Under the agreement, 90 per cent of the world's telecommunications will be opened to competition. The price of international calls – voice, data, radio and satellite transmission – will drop by 80 per cent in the years to come. Welcome to the on-line world.

Ray Hammond
February 1997

INDEX

Accountability 185
Advertising industry 130
Advertising via the Net 84, 127–35
Andreessen, Marc 10, 23–4, 25, 50, 55
Anonymity 168–88
Apple Computers 22–3, 26, 58
AT&T 36, 38, 41

Banker's drafts 152
Banks
  clearing 159–62
  Net providers as 43, 163–5, 182
Bell Telephone Co. 36
Bookmarks 14, 107, 145
Books 106–8
Bookselling 75–7, 113
Branding 84, 135
British Telecom 36, 38
Browsers 10, 24, 249

Cars 99
Cashiers cheques 152
Cemeteries, virtual 209–10
Censorship 199–200, 210, 212
Charities 137–8, 204–6, 219
Clancy, Tom 108
Clothes shopping, virtual 33
Coin-handling 153
Condé Nast 66–7, 70

Conferences 33–4, 140
Copyright 110–7, 122, 259
Credit cards 51, 74, 150, 257
Criminals 108, 167, 186–7
Currencies on the Net 164–7
Currency/reserves ratio 148, 155
Cyber bucks <u>see</u> Digital cash
Cyber cash <u>see</u> Digital cash
Cyberspace
  definition 20
  'claim-staking' in 21

Data networks 37, 40
Debit cards 152, 181
Demographics <u>see</u> Net, users
Desktop computers 56–9
Desktop publishing 61–3
Digital Business
  on-line version 14–15, 106, 209
  quoting from 118–19
  updating of 15, 106–7, 119–20
  Web site for 14, 123
Digital cash 73, 84, 137, 149–50, 154, 194, 205–6, 216
  anonymity of 168–89
  control of 157–9
  trials of 153–4
Digital copying 108, 117
'Digital fingerprinting' 117
Disadvantaged, access to Net 89–90

'Disinformediation' see Distribution
Distribution, elimination of middle levels 47, 91, 101, 143
see also 'Super-distribution'

E-cash see Digital cash
E-money see Digital cash
Economies of scale 73, 79, 87
Electronic Telegraph 68–9, 131
Email 16, 139
Employment agencies 91, 143–4
Encryption 117, 139, 141, 150, 161, 168–79, 183–4, 194
Environmental/ecological benefits 32, 83–4
Estate agents 91–5, 143
European Union 38–9, 117

Feedback via Internet 108–9, 120
Fiction 107–8
Films 115–7, 197–8, 201
Financial electronic networks 154–5
Financial information, access to 155–7
Fund-raising 137–8
Future scenarios 9, 72, 207–222

Gambling 73, 182, 215–6
Games 215
Gates, Bill 42–6, 164, 260
Groupware 140–1

Hackers 16
Hearst family 21, 22, 46, 116
Hobbies 103–4
Hotels 98–100
Human resource management 142–3
Hyperlinks 14, 15, 250

IBM 141, 151
Import tariffs 78
Information
 cost of 214
 location of 123
 ownership of 122–3
 'perfect' 18, 85–90, 159
 representation of 29–35
 selling via Internet 257–8

Information superhighway 7, 38, 45, 213
Insurance brokers 91, 144
Internal networks see Private networks
Internet 7, 45
 auditing use of 259
 connections to 15–16, 38, 116, 213
 description of 243–54
 name registering 259–60
 payments on 256–7
 publishing on 63–70
 security of 16
 software delivery via 47
 speed of 15–16, 251–4
 telephony packages 38
 testing of software on 56
 training for 16
 user behaviour 11, 139
 see also Net, Networks, World-Wide Web
Internet Society, The 20
Investing, personal 155–7

James, Peter 107–8
Java language 57–9

Legal compliance 75, 260
Libraries 123–5
Location of organisations 17
London Stock Exchange 155–6
Lotus Notes 141

Marketing 18, 65, 195–6
 to Net searchers 72, 94, 119, 258
Medicine 223–240
Memorials 209–10
Micro-payments 123, 137, 149–51, 194, 205–6
Microsoft 6, 42–3, 44, 47, 53–4, 55, 151, 163–5
Money 147–162
Museums 221–2
Music 189–96

Navigator 14, 23, 51, 54–5, 56
Negroponte, Nicholas 20, 35, 123, 125, 210, 213

Net 7, 32, 35, 41
  computers on 25
  control of 45, 167, 212
  definition 7, 19
  financial information on 155–7
  payment systems on 151
  permanence of 8
  revenue 19–20
  statistics of use 19, 132–5
  users 20, 74, 131, 133–4, 261–83
  see also Internet, Networks, World-Wide Web
Netscape 6, 10–11, 22, 26, 52–3, 54, 56, 151
Networks 7
  'concealed communication' on 53–4
  control of 43
  currencies 164
  development of 98
  growth of 210–11
  importance of 9
  private 139–42
  see also Internet, Net, World-Wide Web
Niche markets 18, 65

Object-oriented programming 58
Olé language 58–9
OpenDoc 58–9

Packaging 74, 83
Paper-based books 108
Paper currency 153
'Perfect' information 18, 85–90, 159
Personal cheques 152
Photography 202–3
Physiotherapy 218–21
Pirating 114–16, 190
Platforms 10, 24, 25, 67
Political parties 137, 167
Pornography 73, 198–9
Pretty Good Privacy (PGP) 175–9
Price differences 76–7, 87
Privacy 147–8, 163–79
Private networks 16, 139–142
Private publishing 112, 141
Psychotherapy 235–40

'Public key, private key' encryption 169–79
Publishing 30, 61–70, 76, 112–3, 141

Radio, virtual 196
Reading 110–1
Record companies 190–4
Recruitment 17, 136–7, 143–6
Registering Internet names 259–60
Restaurants 98
Retailing 30–2, 71–90
Royalties 109, 190
RSA 161, 169

Searching the Net 18, 64, 72, 85, 88–9, 94, 119, 128, 158, 258
Security 52, 139, 153, 161
Security services 147
Self-help groups 229–30
Self-modelling, virtual 24, 34, 218–21, 240
Selling on the Net 17, 127–135
Servers 51, 259
Service sectors 95–104
Shareware 49–50
Shelley, Mary 103–4
Shopping malls 77–8
Smart-Food Coop 31, 79
Smells 217
Social interaction
  at conferences 33–4
  in shops 32
  at work 17
Software, choosing 159–62
Software delivery 47
Software testing 55–6
Specialisation see 'Super-vertical specialisation'
Speed of money movements 155, 157
Spielberg, Steven 218–20
Sport 202
'Super-distribution' 119, 150, 201
'Super-vertical specialisation' 65, 67, 73, 79, 101–2, 144, 189
Supermarkets 30–2, 79–85, 87

Taste 24
Taxation 73, 175, 185–7, 188, 214

Telecommunications
   costs 35–41
   deregulation of 36–39
   growth 21, 36–41
   security of 38
Television 197–8
Terrorists 108
Testing of software 55–6
Theme parks 216–7
Touch 24, 217
Traffic information 196–7
Tourism and travel 96–103
Travellers' cheques 152

Unions 166
USSR, collapse of 40

Venture capital 22, 70
Viruses 16
Voluntary organisations 204–6

Windows 95 43, 53–4, 55
Wines 73–5
Wireless, for telecomms networks 41
World-Wide Web 9, 30, 31, 249–51
   see also Internet, Net, Networks